Policing and the Law

❖

Policing and the Law

❖

JEFFERY T. WALKER
Editor
University of Arkansas at Little Rock

M. L. DANTZKER
Series Editor

Upper Saddle River, New Jersey 07458

Library of Congress Cataloging-in-Publication Data
Policing and victims / Jeffery T. Walker, editor.
    p. cm. — (Prentice Hall's policing and . . . series)
    Includes bibliographical references (p.).
    ISBN 0-13-028435-1 (alk. paper)
    1. Police—United States. 2. Criminal investigation—United States. 3. Law enforcement—
United States. I. Title.
    KF5399 .W35 2002
    345.73'052—dc21

        2001036443

Publisher: Jeff Johnston
Executive Editor: Kim Davies
Production Editor: Russell Jones, Pine Tree Composition
Production Liaison: Barbara Marttine Cappuccio
Director of Production Manufacturing and: Bruce Johnson
Managing Editor: Mary Carnis
Manufacturing Manager: Cathleen Petersen
Creative Director: Cheryl Asherman
Cover Design Coordinator: Miguel Ortiz
Cover Designer: Marianne Frasco
Cover Image: David Hiller/PhotoDisc
Marketing Manager: Ramona Sherman
Assistant Editor: Sarah Holle
Editorial Assistant: Korrine Dorsey
Composition: Pine Tree Composition, Inc.
Printing and Binding: Phoenix Book Tech

Pearson Education LTD
Pearson Education Australia PTY, Limited
Pearson Education Singapore, Pte. Ltd
Pearson Education North Asia Ltd
Pearson Education Canada, Ltd.
Pearson Educación de Mexico, S.A. de C.V.
Pearson Education -- Japan
Pearson Education Malaysia, Pte. Ltd

10 9 8 7 6 5 4 3 2 1
ISBN 0-13-028435-1

Dedication

In writing a book, the people who often bear the brunt of the author's time restrictions, and often his or her frustrations, are family members. It is no different in my household, where the statement "You are writing another book!" means that my wife has figured out that I slipped another book deal in with the last conference attendance. For that reason, I want to dedicate this book to my lovely wife, Diane Walker, in partial return for all that she has to put up with while I am working on a project such as this.

Contents

❖

Preface

There is no question that the law is intimately linked with policing. Although activity studies tell us that much of what the police do involves service to the public, what defines the police is their ability to enforce the law (and to use force is necessary to do so). Beyond using the law as a tool in police work, the police also receive a great deal of oversight from the law. Practically everything that police officers do is potentially subject to judicial review. From the probable cause needed to make an arrest to entrance exams that do not racially discriminate, the professional lives of police officers are mired in the law.

This text grew out of the acknowledgement that a more detailed and broader statement of the law in relation to policing needed to be made. There are many excellent resources that address the operational aspects of policing (search and seizure, use of force, etc.) as they related to the law. There are fewer resources that address the administrative and personnel issues related to policing. There are no sources, however, that address both of these issues in more than a summary form. Futhermore, there are no sources that go in-depth into some particular areas of policing as they relate to the law, such as police use of canines or privacy rights of police officers. After hearing the pleas of police officers in training sessions I have conducted, and after numerous discussions with other faculty and trainers, I decided it was time to put together a book that crossed the boundaries of operational and administrative legal issues, and that provided some in-depth analyses of areas where guidance for police officers was lacking. This book is the result.

This book contains eleven chapters of material that is vital to police officers. This book should appeal to both the officer on the street who needs some additional information about operational issues such as when lockers of students can be searched or how long a person may be detained while a narcotics sniffing dog is summoned, and the administrator who must make decisions about hiring that are not discriminatory and must occasionally investigate his or her own officers for misconduct. All but a few of the authors of chapters in this text have been police officers and supervisors, and have made the transition to training and education. Most of the authors have experienced first hand the subject they are writing about, and understand the frustrations of not knowing what the law says in particular areas. And all of the authors feel strongly about what they are writing and want to make sure that police officers and potential police officers get the proper information in a format that can be understood and applied.

This book is broken into two major divisions – operational aspects and the law, and administrative aspects and the law. While the book does not give equal attention to each of the divisions, each contains chapters that address, in-depth, topics that police officers deal with on practically a daily basis.

The first six chapters address legal issues of police operations. Beginning with chapter one, Walker provides an overview of Supreme Court decisions that are most important to all police officers: those related to the Fourth, Fifth, and Sixth Amendments. This establishes a foundation for the rest of the operational chapters, as well as addressing many legal issues that are not covered elsewhere in the book. In chapter two, Hemmens provides a more in-depth examination of Supreme Court decisions related to Fourth Amendment issues. He then makes application of these issues in addressing the war on drugs; specifically through no knock searches and through traffic stops by police officers. Golden and VanHouten extend Hemmens' discussion by examining court decisions related to a more specific aspect of traffic stops: roadblocks and check points. This discussion is also accompanied by a examination of the automobile exception to the Fourth Amendment requirement of obtaining a warrant prior to a search and seizure. In chapter four, Stevens addresses the dynamics of arrest and liability lawsuits against the police. Specifically, Stevens addresses the question of whether potential and actual civil lawsuits against police have dampened police officers' willingness to make arrests in certain situations. In chapter five, Golden and Walker return to Fourth Amendment issues with an in-depth discussion of the use of canines in search and seizure. This chapter provides a legal foundation for police officers using narcotics sniffing dogs that has not been adequately provided in other sources. In the final chapter of the operational division, Taylor and Morgan examine the legal issues of police investigations concerning computers and the Internet. Although this chapter may have less direct application to many police officers, it demonstrates that the legal nature of the law is ever changing, and that police officers must strive to maintain awareness of changes in the law and how it may affect their activities.

Chapter seven begins the division focusing on the administrative aspects of legal issues in policing. Buerger introduces this section with a discussion of how police officers and police agencies typically react to changes in the legal environment. In this chapter, Buerger proposes that the police typically have one of four responses to changes in the legal environment: two illegitimate (avoidance and monkey-wrenching) and two legitimate (distinguishing and lobbying). In chapter eight, Bloss takes up some of the legal issues that are involved in the privacy rights of police officers. Since police officers are seen as public officials, there is often the perception that they have fewer rights than private citizens. Bloss addresses these issues as they relate to employer authority to regulate police employee conduct, searches and seizures involving police officers in the workplace, drug testing of police officers, medical fitness issues (including AIDS), and employer regulation of police employee sexual conduct. In chapter nine, Gaines and Schram address in-depth the legal issues surrounding affirmative action and police selection. This chapter includes practical application of Title VII of the 1964 Civil Rights Act and the 1991 Civil Rights Act, as wells as a discussion of affirmative action as it relates to physical agility testing and written selection tests. In the next chapter, Pascarella addresses the related issue of age limitations and discrimination of police officers. Pascarella's research found that involvement of the EEOC in a lawsuit against a police agency was a important predictor in the success of the suit; as was the specific policy issue in question or the provisions of the law challenged.

In the final chapter, Dantzker summarizes the themes presented in the book and addresses legal issues that may become important to police officers. This chapter reinforces the importance of the relationship between the police and the law, and shows how many of the themes of this book are interrelated.

The goal of this text is to provide students, officers, and supervisors with information that they need, in sufficient detail that it is useful in practical application, and written in a manner that is easily understood and applied. Using respected scholars in the field who have a background in policing provides a level of expertise that should show through in the discussions in each chapter. The bottom line is that police officers must work within the law, in terms of both how they carry out their duties, and how their duties are controlled by the law. The understanding provided by this book should give students, police officers, and police supervisors the material they need to carry out their duties while understanding and complying with the law.

Jeffery T. Walker
Editor

Contributors' Biographical Information

❖

William P. Bloss is an Associate Professor of Criminal Justice at The Citadel, The Military College of South Carolina, and Curriculum Coordinator for the South Carolina Police Corps. He received his Ph.D. in criminal justice from Sam Houston State University; and prior to entering academia was a police officer, academy instructor, and regional academy director. Bloss works as a consultant to various police departments in training, needs assessment, and promotional programming. He has authored several articles, book chapters, and other publications on police ethics, employee privacy rights, police liability, and police training, as well as being the current Editor of the *South Carolina Police Corps News*, the official publication of the South Carolina Police Corps.

Michael Buerger is an Associate Professor of Criminal Justice at Bowling Green State University (Ohio). Since starting his career as a municipal police officer in New Hampshire, he has alternated between academia and police practice. He has been the on-site project manager for federally-funded research on problem-solving and proactive Hot Spots patrol in Minneapolis, and a Visiting Fellow at the National Institute of Justice. He was a member of the Urban Institute's site evaluation team in the National Evaluation of the "Cops On The Street" Initiative of the 1994 Crime Bill, and most recently was Research Director for the Jersey City, New Jersey, Police Department. His primary research interest is police organizational change, focusing on the role shift inherent in community- and problem-oriented policing, and its impact on recruitment, training, and management issues. He is wanted in six states, not wanted in seventeen others, and Known To The Police in the remainder.

Larry Gaines currently is a Professor and Chair of the Criminal Justice Department at California State University at San Bernardino. He received his Ph.D. in criminal justice from Sam Houston State University. He has police experience with the Kentucky State

Police and the Lexington, Kentucky Police Department. Additionally, he served as the Executive Director of the Kentucky Association of Chiefs of Police for 14 years. Gaines is also a past president of the Academy of Criminal Justice Sciences. His research centers around policing and drugs. In addition to numerous articles, he has co-authored a number of books in the field: Police Supervision, *Police Operations, Police Administration, Managing the Police Organization, Community Policing: A Contemporary Perspective, Policing Perspectives: An Anthology, Policing in America,* and *Drugs, Crime, and Justice.* His current research agenda centers around the evaluation of police tactics in reducing problems and fitting within the community policing paradigm.

James W. Golden is an Associate Professor in the Department of criminal justice at the University of Arkansas at Little Rock. He holds a Bachelor of Science in Radio Television (1974), a Bachelor of Arts in Criminology (1981), and Master of Public Administration (1985) from Arkansas State University. He holds a Doctor of Philosophy in Criminal Justice from Sam Houston State University (1994). Prior to assuming his present position, he was the Senior Research Coordinator at the Criminal Justice Institute at the University of Arkansas at Little Rock. He spent eight years as a patrol officer, traffic accident investigator, and criminal investigator with the Jonesboro, Arkansas, Police Department. He has served as a consultant and trainer for the Police Foundation and the COPS office. He is currently working as a member of a team exploring crime and poverty in the Mississippi River Delta in Arkansas.

Craig Hemmens is an Assistant Professor in the Department of Criminal Justice Administration at Boise State University. He holds a J.D. from North Carolina Central University School of Law and a Ph.D. in criminal justice from Sam Houston State University. He has written two books and more than eighty articles on a variety of criminal justice topics. He is currently completing a textbook on criminal procedure, to be published by Allyn and Bacon in 2003.

Deanne Morgan is a graduate student at the University of North Texas, pursuing a Master of Science degree in Criminal Justice. She received a bachelor's degree in Biological Science from the University of Guelph (Canada) and a second bachelor's degree in Emergency Administration and Planning from the University of North Texas in 2000. Her areas of interests include the technical and policy difficulties and implications encountered in computer and Internet crime. In addition to conducting several computer crime investigations, she has also worked as a loss prevention investigator in Dallas, Texas. Her plans include continued graduate study in a doctoral program in Information Science at the University of North Texas, concentrating in Information Security and Law.

Joseph E. Pascarella is a New York City Police Lieutenant and an Adjunct Professor of Sociology at Queens College, City University of New York. His research interests include police personnel hiring requirements, standards and measurements of police performance, and the role of the police in the contemporary social order. He recently published an article in *Justice Research and Policy* that tested the relationship between police salaries and community housing characteristics.

Pamela J. Schram received her Ph.D. from Michigan State. She is now an Assistant Professor at California State University, San Bernardino. Her research interests include women in the criminal justice system, particularly women in prison and general issues in corrections. She is also involved in research on juveniles with a particular interest on programs to divert at-risk youth.

Dennis J. Stevens received his Ph.D. at Loyola University of Chicago in 1991 and is an Associate Professor of Criminal Justice, College of Public & Community Service at the University of Massachusetts, Boston. He has taught, counseled, and lectured police officers at police academies and stations such as the North Carolina Justice Academy. He has also taught and led many group encounters among male and female felons at maximum custody penitentiaries. Currently, through Boston University, Stevens instructs felons at high custody prisons in Massachusetts, and has conducted profile assessments of sexual offenders. He has published over 60 articles on subjects that include criminology, corrections, and the police. His current books include *A Case Study of Community Policing* (2001) and *Communities and Community Policing,* as editor (2002), both with Prentice Hall. Stevens is writing a text on Community Policing with Allyn Bacon and expects publication in 2003. Previous books include *Inside the Mind of the Serial Rapist* (Austin Winfield) and a corrections reader for Coursewise.

Robert W. Taylor is currently Professor and Chair of the Department of Criminal Justice at the University of North Texas. Taylor has taught at four major universities and served as a sworn police officer and major crimes detective in Portland, Oregon for over six years. He has authored or co-authored over seventy-five articles, books, and manuscripts focusing on police administration, international and domestic terrorism, drug trafficking, computer fraud, and criminal justice policy. Taylor has been the recipient of over $1 million in external grants and is an active consultant to various U.S. and international criminal justice agencies. He is an active member of the Academy of Criminal Justice Sciences, where he currently serves as the Chair of the Police Section. Taylor is a graduate of Michigan State University (Master of Science-1973) and Portland State University (Doctor of Philosophy-1981).

Amy VanHouten is a graduate assistant at the University of Arkansas at Little Rock. She holds a Bachelor of Science in Education (1999) from the University of Arkansas at Little Rock. She has contributed to articles on a variety of criminal justice topics including sexual offenders and targets, use of deadly force by police officers, and drug treatment programs used in prisons. Her current research includes examining the poverty and crime correlation in the Mississippi River Delta in Arkansas.

Jeffery T. Walker is a Professor of Criminal Justice in the Department of Criminal Justice at the University of Arkansas at Little Rock, where he has taught since 1990. Walker also serves as the Research Director for the Arkansas Statistical Analysis Center, which directs research and data gathering in criminal justice in Arkansas. He has served as President of both the Arkansas Criminal Justice Association and the Southwestern Association of Criminal Justice. He currently serves as the Secretary of ACJS. Editorial experience includes service as Editor of the *Journal of Criminal Justice Education,* Editor of *Critical Criminology,* and as Editor of *ACJS Today.* His two primary areas of research are criminology and law enforcement. In addition, he has researched and written on computers in criminal justice, distance education, legal issues concerning the police, and gang behavior. Previous publications include articles in the *Journal of Quantitative Criminology, Journal of Criminal Justice Education, Journal of Gang Research* and the books *Leading Cases in Law Enforcement* and *Statistics in Criminal Justice: Analysis and Interpretation.*

Policing and the Law

1

Laws of the State and the State of the Law

The Relationship Between Police and Law

Jeffery T. Walker

INTRODUCTION

For almost the first one hundred years of the history of the United States, the law set few parameters on policing. This resulted in numerous problems, including the police corruption that was rampant in the early 1900s (shakedowns, extortion, or officers committing crimes themselves), the practice of coercing persons into making (sometimes false) confessions that was unchecked until the mid-1900s, and the ability of police officers to use deadly force on practically anyone seeking to escape that was not changed until 1985. Although the legal system seemed reluctant to control itself, over time, laws were changed in many areas related to policing that changed the way police officers performed their duties.

Near the end of the nineteenth century, states and the federal government began to more closely examine police conduct as it applied to rights guaranteed by the Constitution. In *Boyd v. United States* (1886), the Supreme Court held that the forced disclosure of papers amounting to evidence of a crime violated the Fourth Amendment, and therefore the evidence could not be used in court. This ruling established the exclusionary rule, which made the fruits of police misconduct inadmissible in court, rather than the more common practice at that time of requiring a separate trial on the evidence or misconduct.

Following *Boyd*, there was a slow but progressive movement by the courts and lawmakers to incorporate the Bill of Rights to the states and to make it applicable to federal police agencies. This chapter briefly outlines those efforts, especially as they apply to Supreme Court decisions. The decisions of the Supreme Court were chosen to establish the state of the law because many of the legal restrictions and freedoms placed on the police came from the Supreme Court; and in many cases the Court has overturned state or other laws governing police behavior. Several of the issues included in this chapter will be addressed in more detail in the chapters that follow.

PROBABLE CAUSE

The foundation of the relationship between policing and the law falls within probable cause. The relationship between probable cause and searches and seizures is obvious, but probable cause is also necessary for almost all other interactions with the police, from investigative stops to use of deadly force. Probable cause is also closely linked to alleged police misconduct, such as racial profiling of drivers of stopped vehicles.

Probable cause is a very elusive concept, the definition of which is often debated in court cases. Although courts (even the Supreme Court) have defined probable cause in different ways, an accepted definition comes from *Brinegar v. United States* (1949). This definition provides that probable cause exists when "the facts and circumstances within the officers' knowledge and of which they had reasonably trustworthy information are sufficient in themselves to warrant a man of reasonable caution in the belief that an offense has been or is being committed."

Even with this definition, it is obvious that probable cause is a subjective measure that varies from one police officer to the next and one judge to the next. The strongest case for probable cause is having a search or arrest warrant. Failing that, officers are required to be able to articulate the "reasonably trustworthy information" available to them that supports "the belief that an offense has been or is being committed." Although there are many cases that determine the present parameters of probable cause, three are briefly discussed here to show some of the important points in this key element of policing and how they have developed.

In *Draper v. United States* (1959), an officer received information from an informant that Draper had gone to Chicago to bring three ounces of heroin back to Denver by train on either the morning of September 8 or 9. The informant also gave a detailed description of Draper, and the clothes he would be wearing, and said that he habitually walked really fast. Based on this information, police officers set up surveillance of all trains coming from Chicago. The morning of the eighth produced no one fitting the informant's description. The next morning, officers observed an individual matching the exact description the informant had supplied get off a train from Chicago and begin to walk quickly toward the exit. They overtook the suspect and arrested him. Heroin and a syringe were seized in a search incident to the arrest. The informant died before the trial and was unable to testify.

The issue in this case was whether information provided by an informant, which was subsequently corroborated by an officer, could provide probable cause for an arrest. The Court held that this information could be used to establish probable cause when verified by the officer. This case is important because, prior to it, officers could only use information they personally generated. This case allows officers to also use information from other sources in establishing probable cause—as long as they can verify the veracity of the information before going further.

Following *Draper*, there were several cases outlining the requirements for establishing probable cause based on information not generated by police officers. Specifically, *Aguilar v. Texas* (1964), and *Spinelli v. United States* (1969) established a two-pronged test that both the informant and the information had to be verified for the information to be valid. That standard was changed in *Illinois v. Gates* (1983).

In *Gates,* Illinois police received an anonymous letter stating that Gates and his wife were engaged in selling drugs, that the wife would drive her car to Florida on May 3 to be loaded with drugs, that Gates would fly down and drive the car back, that the trunk would be loaded with drugs, and that Gates had more than $100,000 worth of drugs in his basement. Acting on the tip, a police officer obtained Gates's address and learned that he had made reservations for a May 5 flight to Florida. Arrangements for surveillance of the flight were made with the DEA. The surveillance disclosed that Gates took the flight, stayed overnight in a hotel room registered in his wife's name, and left the following morning with a woman in a car bearing an Illinois license plate, heading north. A search warrant for Gates's house and automobile was obtained on the basis of the officer's affidavit and a copy of the anonymous letter. When Gates arrived home, the police were waiting. A search of the house and car revealed marijuana.

The issue in this case was whether the anonymous tip, which was later corroborated by the officers, was sufficient to establish probable cause even though there was no identified informant. The Court held that the two-pronged test established under *Aguilar* and *Spinelli* was to be abandoned in favor of a "totality of the circumstances" approach. This means that in determining whether an officer has probable cause for taking action, courts will look at all the information available to the officer. The application of this standard of establishing probable cause is evident in many actions of police officers. One such application is discussed below—investigative stops.

In *United States v. Sokolow* (1989), Sokolow purchased two round-trip tickets under an assumed name. He paid for the tickets from a roll of $20 bills that appeared to contain about $4,000. He appeared nervous during the transaction. Neither he nor his companion checked their luggage. Based on these facts, which fit a "drug courier profile," officers stopped the couple and took them to the DEA office at the airport where a drug dog examined their luggage. The examination indicated the presence of narcotics in one of Sokolow's bags. Sokolow was arrested and a search warrant obtained for the bag. No narcotics were found in the bag, but documents indicating involvement in drug trafficking were discovered. Upon a second search with the drug dog, narcotics were detected in another of Sokolow's bags. Sokolow was released until a search warrant could be obtained the next morning. A search of the bag revealed 1,063 grams of cocaine.

The issue in this case was whether pre-established guidelines that represented a "drug courier profile" were sufficient to meet the standard of totality of the circumstances when verified by police officers. The Supreme Court held that the circumstances of this case were sufficient to establish probable cause under totality of the circumstances. This is important in police work because of the current controversy surrounding racial profiling. While stopping people because of their race is clearly discriminatory, the totality of circumstances standard for establishing probable cause is sufficient to allow officers to make investigative stops if there is sufficient evidence that a crime is being or has been committed.

THE EXCLUSIONARY RULE

Closely related to the issue of probable cause is the exclusionary rule. As stated above, the exclusionary rule was created in an effort to control misconduct by the police. Subsequent to *Boyd*, the exclusionary rule was applied to federal police actions in *Weeks v. United States* (1914). This case held that evidence illegally obtained by federal officers was not admissible in court. It was almost fifty years later, however, before the exclusionary rule was applied to state and local police officers.

In *Mapp v. Ohio* (1961), police officers went to Mapp's residence on information that a wanted person was hiding out in her home. The officers knocked on the door and demanded entrance, but Mapp, telephoning her attorney, refused to admit them without a warrant. The officers again sought entry three hours later after the arrival of more police. When Mapp did not respond, the officers broke open the door. Mapp's attorney arrived but was denied access to his client. A search of the house produced a trunk that contained obscene materials. The materials were admitted into evidence at the trial. The Supreme Court held in this case that state and local police agencies could not circumvent the protections of the Fourth Amendment and have the evidence admitted into court. Although this did not end Fourth Amendment issues, it did establish that the exclusionary rule would be applicable to searches and seizures of all police officers.

Once it was determined that evidence obtained illegally could not be admitted at trial, courts had to deal with the issue of how such illegality could affect the rest of an investigation. This issue, called "fruit of the poisonous tree," was addressed in *Wong Sun v. United States* (1963). In this case, the Supreme Court held that statements made or evidence obtained as a result of an unlawful search or arrest is not admissible in court. Furthermore, any evidence obtained as a result of the misconduct is also not admissible. The Court conceded, however, that a suspect's subsequent act of free will breaks the chain of illegality and makes any evidence collected after that admissible. This case was also important in that it subjected statements to the exclusionary rule (a standard not commonly applied to confessions and admissions; see below).

Tainted evidence may also be admissible in court if officers can prove that the evidence would have been discovered anyway. In *Nix v. Williams* (1984), police interrogated Williams illegally [see *Brewer v. Williams* (1977) below]. As a result of this decision, Williams was given a new trial. His confession was not admitted at the new trial, but the prosecutor presented evidence that the police had determined that the body of the child was located between the site of abduction and the place where Williams's car was found. In fact, search teams were less than two miles away from where the body was found, and were headed toward the body site. The trial court ruled that the state had proved that if Williams had not led the police to the body, it would have been found by the searchers anyway. This ruling came to be known as the "inevitable discovery" exception to the exclusionary rule. In this case, no *Miranda* warnings were given to Williams prior to his confession, so the confession was excluded during trial. Because the Court concluded that the body would have been discovered anyway as a result of the continued search, it held that the evidence could be admitted.

There are many other issues that fall under the exclusionary rule. Most of them are applications of the rule, however, in cases involving Fourth Amendment issues of search and seizure. These will be discussed below.

FOURTH AMENDMENT ISSUES

Fourth Amendment issues make up the bulk of court decisions involving police actions. This is because of the variety of situations governed by the Fourth Amendment. Those that will be discussed here include searches in general, searches with consent, plain view searches, vehicle searches, the crossover between searches and seizures—stop and frisk, searches after an arrest, arrests, and other types of seizures.

Searches in General

There are many different categories of searches. These include searches with consent, plain view searches, and vehicle searches, which will be discussed below. There are also cases involving searches that do not fit into predefined categories. Some of these cases are discussed in this section. Some of these issues are also covered in more detail in the chapters dealing with the use of canines in policing (Chapter 6) and the progression of Supreme Court cases concerning search and seizure (Chapter 7).

One of the more interesting cases concerning searches is *Maryland v. Garrison* (1987). In this case, police officers obtained a warrant to search "the premises known as 2036 Park Avenue third floor apartment," for drugs belonging to a person named McWebb. The police believed that there was only one apartment at the location; in fact, there were two apartments on the third floor, one belonging to McWebb and one belonging to Garrison. Before the officers became aware that they were in Garrison's apartment instead of McWebb's, they discovered contraband that provided the basis for Garrison's conviction on drug charges.

One of the elements of a valid search warrant is that it must specifically describe the "places to be searched and the things to be seized." The warrant in this case was overbroad (it only described one upstairs apartment when in fact there were two). The Supreme Court held, however, that this mistake by the officers was reasonable, and therefore the search was valid. Furthermore, the evidence seized in the mistaken search was also admissible in court.

Another issue for police officers is the requirement to knock and announce their presence and intentions before executing a search warrant. This issue has reached the Supreme Court in several cases. The first case is *Wilson v. Arkansas* (1995), in which the Court held that the Fourth Amendment requires officers to knock and announce before entering a dwelling unless there are exigent circumstances. The Supreme Court strengthened this ruling in *Richards v. Wisconsin* (1997), when it held that the state could not create those exigent circumstances by allowing a blanket exception to the knock and announce rule when executing felony drug warrants. Instead, the Court held that exceptions to this rule must be decided by a judge on a case-by-case basis. The Court did side with police, however, in *United States v. Ramirez* (1988), when it held that the fact that officers must destroy property (breaking a window or door) does not require a higher standard than the no-knock requirement outlined in *Wilson*.

There are other cases addressing important legal aspects for police. For example, in *California v. Greenwood* (1988), the Supreme Court authorized the search and seizure of trash left for collection in an area accessible to the public. Also, the Court held in *Minnesota v. Carter* (1998) that persons who are overnight guests in a home may claim a separate Fourth Amendment protection from the owner, but persons who are invited guests of the owner for a short time do not have the same protection [*Minnesota v. Olson* (1989)].

Somewhat of a crossover between searches and seizures is the provision that people may be detained at the place of the search while the search takes place. In *Michigan v. Summers* (1981), while officers were executing a warrant to search a house for narcotics, they encountered Summers descending the front steps of the house. They requested his assistance in gaining entry to the house. He replied that he did not have keys to the front door but would ring someone over the intercom. Another occupant of the house answered the door but refused to admit the police. The officers gained entry to the house by forcing the door open. Officers detained Summers and eight others in the house while the premises were searched. When narcotics were found in the house, the police determined that Summers was, in fact, the owner of the house and arrested him. During a search of Summers incident to the arrest, officers discovered heroin in his coat pocket. The Supreme Court held in this case that a warrant to search carries with it the limited authority to detain any occupants while the search is conducted.

Searches with Consent

One of the more frequently used exceptions to the warrant requirement of the Fourth Amendment is consent to search. Valid consent under the law is based on two things: that the person is authorized to give consent, and that the consent is given voluntarily and intelligently, meaning that the person understands what he or she is doing. There is no requirement that the consent be written, but silence or failure to object does not indicate a valid consent.

The first requirement of valid consent to search is that the person is authorized to give consent. Consent may be given by a wife or husband to search their home [*People v. Cosme* (1979)]. Consent may be given by a roommate, but only for the areas of the home that are common to both [*United States v. Matlock* (1974)]. The driver of a vehicle may give consent even if he or she is not the owner of the vehicle [*United States v. Morales* (1988)]. High school administrators may also give consent to search within the building [*New Jersey v. TLO* (1985)]. Finally, officers can assume consent from a person who appears on the face to have valid authority to give consent [*Illinois v. Rodriquez* (1990)]. This case will be discussed in more detail.

In *Rodriquez*, after being summoned to a house, the police were met by Gail Fischer, who showed signs of a severe beating. She informed the officers that she had been assaulted by Rodriguez earlier that day in an apartment on South California Street. Fischer and the police subsequently drove to Rodriguez's apartment because she stated that Rodriguez would be asleep and she could let them into the apartment with her key so they could arrest him. Several times, she referred to the apartment as "our" apartment and said that she had clothes and furniture there, but she did not specifically state that she was currently living there. Upon entry, without a warrant but with a key and permission provided by Fischer, police observed in plain view drug paraphernalia and containers filled with cocaine. The officers seized this and more paraphernalia found in the apartment where Rodriguez was sleeping and arrested him. The court ruled in this case that the determination of consent to enter must be judged against the facts available to the officer at the time of the entry. If the officers had reasonable belief that the consenting party had authority over the premises, then the consent and the search were valid.

There are also persons who cannot give consent to search. These include landlords [*Stoner v. California* (1964)], owners of homes where an overnight guest is staying [*Minnesota v. Olson* (1989)], college or university administrators [*Piazzola v. Watkins* (1971)], and hotel clerks [*Stoner v. California* (1964)]. It should be noted, however, that hotel clerks can provide access with a key for valid arrests or searches without making the activities inadmissible.

Voluntariness, as with other aspects of searches, is based on the totality of the circumstances. This standard was decided in *Schneckloth v. Bustamonte* (1973). The Supreme Court held in this case that while the suspect's knowledge of the right to refuse consent is one element of valid consent, such knowledge is not a prerequisite.

On the other hand, officers cannot gain consent by claiming to have a valid search warrant when none exists. In *Bumper v. North Carolina* (1968), during a rape investigation, but before his arrest, officers went to Bumper's home where he lived with his grandmother. When the officer announced that he had a warrant to search the house, the grandmother responded, "Go ahead," and opened the door. The officers found a rifle in the kitchen, which was seized and entered as evidence. The Supreme Court held that the search was inadmissible because the consent was not valid. This was because the consent was only based on the belief that the officers possessed a search warrant. The Court also held in this case that a search conducted with a warrant could not later be justified based on consent if it was determined that the warrant was invalid.

Plain View Searches

Police officers also heavily rely on plain view searches, especially when conducting vehicle stops. The plain view doctrine states that items within the sight of an officer may be seized as long as the officer is legally in the place from where the contraband is viewed and the material is immediately recognizable as subject to seizure.

In addition to allowing plain view of officers, the courts have placed very little limitation on how this is undertaken. For example, in *California v. Ciraolo* (1986), after receiving a tip that Ciraolo was growing marijuana in his backyard, police went to his residence to investigate. Realizing that the area in question could not be viewed from ground level, officers used a private plane and flew over the home at an altitude prescribed by law. They identified marijuana plants growing in Ciraolo's yard. Based on this information and an aerial photograph of the area, officers obtained a search warrant for the premises. A search was made that found numerous marijuana plants, and Ciraolo was convicted of marijuana possession.

The second requirement of plain view is that an officer must be able to immediately recognize the object to be seized as contraband. In *Arizona v. Hicks* (1987), officers went to Hicks's apartment as a result of a bullet fired through the floor, injuring a man below. In Hicks's apartment, they discovered three weapons and a stocking-cap mask. An officer noticed several pieces of stereo equipment that seemed to be out of place in the ill-appointed apartment. Based on this suspicion, he read and recorded the serial numbers of the equipment, moving some of the pieces in the process. A call to police headquarters verified that the equipment was stolen. A search warrant was then obtained and the equipment seized.

The Supreme Court held in this case that probable cause to believe that items being searched are evidence of criminal activity is required for a plain view search; and that the officer's action of moving the stereo to obtain the serial numbers to be checked against records of stolen items constituted an illegal search. The reason the Court gave is that the officer was in the apartment investigating shots fired, not stolen equipment. The legal reason for the officer to be in the apartment, therefore, did not allow him to move the stereo equipment.

Although material must be "immediately recognizable" as subject to seizure, more certainty by the officer is not required. In *Texas v. Brown* (1983), an officer stopped Brown's vehicle at a driver's license checkpoint. The officer asked Brown for his driver's license and shined his flashlight into the automobile. When Brown withdrew his hand from his pocket, the officer observed a party balloon fall from Brown's hand onto the seat. Based on his experience, the officer knew that such balloons frequently contained narcotics. Brown then reached across and opened the glove compartment. The officer shifted his position to get a better view of the glove compartment and observed several small plastic vials, a quantity of a white powdery substance, and an open package of party balloons. The officer picked up the balloon, which had a white powdery substance in the tied-off portion, and showed it to another officer, who also recognized the balloon as one possibly containing narcotics. The officers placed Brown under arrest. A search of Brown's vehicle incident to the arrest revealed marijuana. The Supreme Court held in that "certain knowledge" of the illegality of materials is not necessary to fall under the plain view exception, so the officer's actions were reasonable. The Court also held that officers may use a flashlight to aid them in their search without breaking the boundaries allowed in plain view searches.

Vehicle Searches

Vehicle searches represent one of the longest and most complicated lines of search and seizure cases. This is primarily because of the many different situations that can occur in the stop of a vehicle.

The seminal case governing vehicle searches is *Carroll v. United States* (1925). In this case, officers observed the automobile of Carroll and gave chase but failed to apprehend Carroll. When Carroll was later apprehended, he and his companion were ordered out of the car. No liquor was visible in the front seat of the automobile. Officers then opened the rumble seat and looked under the cushions, again finding no liquor. One of the officers then struck the "lazyback" of the seat, tore open the seat cushion, and discovered sixty-eight bottles of gin and whiskey. Carroll was arrested and convicted of transporting liquor.

The issue in this case was whether the officers could search the vehicle without a search warrant but with probable cause that it contained evidence of a crime. The Supreme Court held that the risk of the vehicle being moved or the evidence destroyed or removed justified a warrantless search as long as there was probable cause to believe that the vehicle contained items subject to seizure. This case was extended in *Chambers v. Maroney* (1969) to allow officers to search a vehicle after it had been impounded if the circumstances would have allowed a search at the place of contact with the vehicle.

One place where officers are prevented from stopping and searching a vehicle is where there is no probable cause for the stop. In *Delaware v. Prouse* (1979), without observing traffic or equipment violations or suspicious activity, a police officer stopped

Prouse's vehicle to check the driver's license and registration. Upon approaching the vehicle, the officer smelled marijuana. He then seized a quantity of marijuana in plain view on the floor of the vehicle. The Supreme Court held in this case that stopping a vehicle and detaining the driver simply to check the license and registration are unreasonable under the Fourth Amendment. The only way a stop of a vehicle is legal is through probable cause that some law has been or is being broken.

Like other searches and seizures, vehicle searches are based on the standard of totality of the circumstances. This was established in *United States v. Cortez* (1981). In this case, officers determined, based on an extensive investigation, that the transportation of illegal aliens was occurring in a particular area. Based on these deductions, they set up surveillance. Of the fifteen to twenty vehicles that passed the officers during their surveillance, only two matched the type they were looking for. As one truck passed, the officers got a partial license plate number. When the same vehicle passed them again, they pursued and stopped it. In the back of the truck were six illegal immigrants. The Supreme Court held in this case that the totality of circumstances is to be used in determining probable cause to make an investigative stop. The Court also held, however, that officers must have "a particularized, objective basis for suspecting that the individual stopped is engaged in criminal activity." The officers in this case met that standard.

Once a vehicle is stopped, there are several situations where police are authorized to search different parts of the vehicle and its contents. Most of these situations relate to whether an arrest of the occupants is made and the amount of probable cause the officers can articulate.

First, after a valid stop, officers may make a limited search of the passenger compartment looking for weapons. In *Michigan v. Long* (1983), officers observed an automobile swerve into a ditch and they stopped to investigate. They were met at the rear of the car by Long, who "appeared to be under the influence of something" and did not respond to a request to produce his license. After a second request to see his registration, Long began walking toward the open door of the vehicle. The officers followed him and noticed a large hunting knife on the floorboard of the vehicle. They then stopped Long and frisked him. No weapons were found. One of the officers shined his flashlight into the car and discovered marijuana. The Supreme Court held in this case that officers can make a search of the passenger compartment of a vehicle if they have a reasonable belief that the suspect is dangerous and might gain immediate access to a weapon. This search is limited, however, to places where a weapon might be placed or hidden. If, however, the officer finds other contraband during this protective sweep, then he or she may seize the contraband under the plain view doctrine.

Once a vehicle has been impounded, there are certain guidelines that govern inventory searches. First, police can only conduct inventory searches pursuant to departmental policy [*Florida v. Wells,* (1989)]. If the department does not have a policy governing inventory searches, officers only have the same probable cause that they had on first contact with the vehicle to support a search, which is typically much more limited than inventory searches. On the other hand, if the department has a policy for inventorying vehicles, then officers have wide discretion to do so within the policy.

In *Colorado v. Bertine* (1987), Bertine was arrested for driving under the influence of alcohol. After he was taken into custody, and prior to the arrival of a tow truck to impound the van, another officer inventoried the van in accordance with departmental procedures. During the inventory search, the officer opened a backpack and found various containers of drugs. The Supreme Court held in this case that inventory searches without a warrant are permissible. Furthermore, containers in the vehicle may be opened even if there is no probable cause that they contained contraband.

In *California v. Acevedo* (1991), a case allowing the greatest latitude to police officers making vehicle stops, the Supreme Court addressed the issue of whether police are required to get a warrant to search a container in a vehicle if there is no probable cause to search the vehicle. In this case, a police officer received a telephone call from a DEA agent who stated that he had intercepted a package containing marijuana that was to have been delivered to J. R. Daza. The agent arranged to have the package sent to the police officer, who verified the contents as marijuana and took it to the Federal Express office for a controlled delivery. A man claiming to be Daza picked up the package and took it to an apartment. A short time later, Daza left the apartment and dropped the box and the paper that had contained the marijuana into a trash bin. At that point, one police officer left the scene of the apartment to obtain a search warrant. A short time later, other officers observed another man leave the apartment carrying a knapsack that appeared to be half full. The officers stopped the man as he was driving off, searched the knapsack, and found 1½ pounds of marijuana. Later, Acevedo arrived at the apartment, stayed about ten minutes, and left carrying a brown paper bag that appeared to be the size of the one that contained the marijuana packages. Acevedo placed the bag in the trunk of his car and started to drive away. At that time, the police stopped him, opened the trunk and the bag, and found marijuana. The Court held that probable cause that a container holds seizable evidence can justify a warrantless search of the container, even if there is not probable cause to search the vehicle.

One case where a restriction was placed on the police was *Knowles v. Iowa* (1998). In this case, Knowles was stopped for speeding and issued a citation (although the officer had the authority to arrest him). The officer then conducted a full search of Knowles's car, where he found marijuana. At trial, the officer conceded that he had neither consent nor probable cause for the search, and that he relied on state law that permitted "searches incident to citation." The Supreme Court held in this case that while it is permissible to search a vehicle pursuant to an arrest, it is not permissible to search a vehicle pursuant to issuing a traffic citation absent consent or specific probable cause.

Other decisions important to vehicle stops include *California v. Carney* (1985), which held that motor homes used on public highways are automobiles for the purposes of the Fourth Amendment, so the same search and seizure rules apply. In addition, the Supreme Court held in *Wyoming v. Houghton* (1999) that when officers have probable cause to search a vehicle, they may also inspect the belongings of passengers that would be capable of concealing the object of the search.

Based on these cases and others, police officers may do the following pursuant to a valid stop of a vehicle:

1. Search the entire vehicle, open the trunk, and open any containers found in the vehicle that might reasonably contain the items for which the officer is searching, *United States v. Ross* (1982).
2. Search a container in the vehicle if there is probable cause to believe that it contains items subject to seizure, even if there is not probable cause to search the car itself, *California v. Acevedo* (1991).

3. Search the passenger compartment of the vehicle and its contents incident to a lawful arrest, *New York v. Belton* (1981).
4. Make a warrantless search of the vehicle even if there is time to obtain a warrant, *Pennsylvania v. Labron* (1996).
5. If there is probable cause to search the vehicle, officers may also inspect the belongings of passengers in the vehicle as long as the belongings are capable of holding the object of the search, *Wyoming v. Houghton* (1999).
6. Officers are not required to tell motorists that they are free to go before obtaining consent to search the vehicle, *Ohio v. Robinette* (1996).

In recent years, the Supreme Court has supported most efforts by the police to increase their ability to make stops of vehicles (see Chapter 2). This has led to some problems, however, in terms of police officers being accused of racial profiling and making stops for less than probable cause. This area will continue to be a source of court cases requiring officers and others to remain abreast of changes issued by the courts.

Stop and Frisk

Stop and frisk is a fairly well defined area of law for police officers. The concept of stop and frisk was introduced in the case of *Terry v. Ohio* (1968). The Supreme Court held in that case that the police have the authority under the Fourth Amendment to detain a person for questioning even without probable cause to believe that the person has committed a crime. The only thing required for this stop is that the officer be able to articulate a reasonable suspicion that criminal activity may be taking place. An officer may then frisk the person for weapons if the officer reasonably suspects that he or she is in danger. None of these actions constitutes an arrest.

Four years later, the Court extended the *Terry* decision, stating that a stop and frisk is authorized based on information provided by an informant [*Adams v. Williams* (1972)]. Stop and frisk was further extended in *United States v. Hensley* (1985) to allow police officers to stop persons who are the subject of a wanted flyer.

The Court took up the issue of the length of time that it is reasonable to detain a person during a *Terry* stop in *United States v. Sharpe* (1985). In this case, a DEA agent was patrolling in an area suspected of drug trafficking when he observed Sharpe's car driving in tandem with an apparently overloaded truck. After following the two vehicles for 20 miles, the agent radioed for a marked car to assist him in making an investigatory stop. The two officers followed the vehicles several more miles at speeds in excess of the speed limit. The DEA agent stopped the car driven by Sharpe, but the officer was forced to chase the truck, which he stopped a half-mile later. The DEA agent radioed for additional uniformed officers to detain Sharpe while the situation was investigated. These officers arrived ten minutes later. The DEA agent arrived at the location of the truck approximately fifteen minutes after it had been stopped. The agent's requests to search the truck were denied, but after he smelled marijuana, he took the keys from the ignition, opened the back of the truck, and found marijuana. The driver was then placed under arrest, and the officers returned to arrest Sharpe approximately twenty minutes after his car had been stopped.

The Supreme Court held in this case that the twenty minutes taken by the officers was not unreasonable. The Court stated that there was no specific time limit to be established in a *Terry* stop, and that the time taken is dependent upon the actions necessary to carry out the stop. Furthermore, the Court stated that judges should defer to police officers concerning how much time it takes to carry out a stop; but officers must be able to justify the amount of time taken.

In *Minnesota v. Dickerson* (1993), the Supreme Court took up the issue of what actions are authorized by officers in *Terry* stops. In this case, two police officers observed Dickerson leaving an apartment building that one of the officers knew was a crack house. Dickerson began walking toward the police, but, upon making eye contact with them, walked in the opposite direction and into an alley. Because of his evasive actions, police decided to stop Dickerson and investigate further. They pulled into the alley and ordered Dickerson to stop and submit to a pat-down search. The search revealed no weapons, but the officer found a small lump in Dickerson's pocket, which he said he examined with his fingers and determined that it felt like a lump of cocaine in cellophane. The officer reached into the pocket and retrieved a small plastic bag of crack cocaine. The Court held in this case that any *Terry* pat-down must be "limited to that which is necessary for the discovery of weapons which might be used to harm the officer or others nearby."

Searches After an Arrest

The final area of searches involves those that occur after a person is taken into custody. As a general rule, officers may search the person and the area immediately surrounding the person for contraband following a legal arrest.

The case that established police authority to search following an arrest was *Chimel v. California* (1969). The Supreme Court held in this case that when an arrest is made, it is reasonable to search the person arrested for weapons and for evidence. In addition, officers may search "the area into which an arrestee might reach in order to grab a weapon or evidentiary item." The authorization to search the body of a person following an arrest, even when there is no suspicion of a weapon, was granted by the Court in *United States v. Robinson* (1973). The Court further held that there is no time limit to when a search following an arrest could occur. In *United States v. Edwards* (1974), the clothes of an arrestee were searched after he was taken into custody. The Court held that a search that would have been valid at the time of the arrest may be conducted at a later time (after being placed in custody), even if a substantial period of time has elapsed.

The Court limited the area that could be searched following an arrest in *Vale v. Louisiana* (1970). In this case, Vale was arrested on the front steps of his house. The officers then searched the house without a search warrant. The Court held that for a search to take place inside a house, the arrest must also take place inside the house.

Arrests

The principal issue in the law of arrest pertains to when an arrest occurs. The Supreme Court cases in this section show that an arrest occurs when a person is taken into custody against his or her will for the purposes of criminal prosecution [*Dunaway v. New York* (1979)]. When this occurs, however, is often a matter of legal contention.

The Court held that the test to determine when a seizure occurs is whether a reasonable person would conclude that he or she is not free to leave. In *Michigan v. Chesternut*

(1988), Chesternut began to run after observing the approach of a police car. Officers followed him to "see where he was going." As the officers drove alongside Chesternut, they observed him pull a number of packets from his pocket and throw them down. The officers stopped and seized the packets which contained narcotics. Chesternut was then arrested. A subsequent search revealed more narcotics. The Court held in this case that Chesternut was not seized when he threw down the drugs, so there was no illegal search or seizure of the drugs. This case was strengthened in *Florida v. Bostick* (1991), which held that "a seizure does not occur simply because a police officer approaches an individual and asks a few questions. As long as a reasonable person would feel free 'to disregard the police and go about his business,' the encounter is consensual."

These rulings were strengthened in *California v. Hodari D.* (1991). In this case, two police officers were patrolling a high-crime area when they saw four or five youths huddled around a car. When the youths saw the police car approaching, they fled. One officer gave chase. The officer did not follow one of the youths directly; instead, the officer took another route that brought them face-to-face on a parallel street. Hodari was looking behind as he ran and did not turn to see the officer until they were upon each other; whereupon he tossed away a small rock. The officer tackled Hodari and recovered the rock, which turned out to be crack cocaine. The Court held in this case that a seizure only occurs under the Fourth Amendment when there is the use of physical force by an officer or submission by the suspect to the authority of the officer. As in this case, no seizure occurs when the officer attempts to make an arrest through a show of authority, but applies no physical force and the suspect does not willingly submit.

A seizure can occur, however, if the government's actions are such as to constitute a seizure. In *Brower v. County of Inyo* (1989), in an effort to stop Brower, who had stolen a car and eluded the police in a chase of over twenty miles, police placed an eighteen-wheeled truck across both lanes of a highway, behind a curve, with a police car's headlights pointed in a manner that would blind Brower. Brower was killed in the crash as a result of the roadblock. The Court held in this case that a seizure occurs when there is a "governmental termination of the freedom of movement through means intentionally applied." In this case, the roadblock set up to stop Brower was intentional and it did stop him, so a seizure did occur.

There are restrictions concerning where an arrest without a warrant can take place. The general rule is that officers cannot arrest a person in a private dwelling without a warrant or exigent circumstances [*Payton v. New York* (1980)]. The Supreme Court held in *United States v. Watson* (1976) that officers could arrest a person in a public place without a warrant; and the Court held that an arrest would be valid if it began in a public place but the arrestee fled to a private place before being arrested [*United States v. Santana* (1975)].

Other Seizures

A few issues of the Fourth Amendment do not fit into the other categories discussed. These are included here in the interest of providing additional information that might be important to a police officer's function.

One of the more interesting cases concerning the Fourth Amendment is *Winston v. Lee* (1985). In this case, a storeowner was wounded in the legs and the assailant appeared to be wounded in the left side of the body in a shoot-out resulting from a robbery. Some time later, officers responding to another call saw the suspect eight blocks from the store. He told the officers that he had been wounded when he himself was robbed. The suspect was taken to the same hospital as the storeowner. While at the hospital, Lee was identified by the storeowner as the man who had shot him. The state asked a court for an order directing Lee to undergo surgery to have the bullet removed. The doctors first said that there was some danger involved in the operation, but later stated that the bullet was lodged near the surface of the skin and could be easily removed with no danger. While Lee was being prepared for surgery, it was discovered that the bullet was deeper than originally thought and would require surgery under general anesthesia. Lee then moved for a rehearing in the state court that was denied. The case eventually went to the United States Supreme Court.

The Supreme Court had held previously, in *Schmerber v. California* (1966), that the drawing of blood from a suspect without his or her consent is not a violation of the Fourth Amendment as long as it is done by medical personnel using accepted medical practices. *Winston* took the issue further. In this case, there was an issue about how extensive the wound was and what it would take to remove the bullet. The Court held that if it was a simple operation, then seizing the bullet would not violate the Fourth Amendment. A major procedure using a general anesthetic, however, was beyond what would be reasonable under the Fourth Amendment—regardless of whether it would produce evidence of a crime.

In *Cupp v. Murphy* (1973), the Court dealt with the issue of making a warrantless seizure of evidence that was likely to disappear before a warrant could be obtained. In this case, Murphy voluntarily went to the police station for questioning following his wife's death. While at the station, police noticed a dark spot on Murphy's finger that appeared to be dried blood. Murphy refused an officer's request to take a sample from his fingernail, placed his hands behind his back and in his pockets, and appeared to be rubbing his hands to remove the spot. The officers then forcibly and without a warrant took scrapings from Murphy's fingernails. The scrapings were found to contain traces of skin and blood from the victim. The Court held that, given the facts of this case—the existence of probable cause, the limited detention of the suspect, and the destructibility of the evidence—the seizure was valid.

Finally, in *City of West Covina v. Perkins* (1999), the Court dealt with the issue of what actions are required by police when seizing evidence. In this case, pursuant to a valid search warrant, police officers searched Perkins's home and seized a number of items. The suspect in the crime was a boarder in the Perkins house. Items seized by the police incriminated the boarder, but some belonged to Perkins. Upon completing the seizure, officers left notice of the search and other information, such as the name of the judge who had issued the warrant, officers to contact for information, and an itemized list of property seized. The officers did not leave the warrant number because the case was ongoing and the information was sealed; however, that information was maintained by the court clerk in a file indexed by the address of the home searched. After attempts to secure the return of the property, Perkins filed suit. The Court held that the police are not required to provide the owner of property seized with detailed notice of the procedures for the return of the property.

FIFTH AMENDMENT ISSUES

The Fifth Amendment provides two sets of rights: the privilege against self-incrimination and the right to due process under the law. The Fourteenth Amendment also contains a provision for due process rights that was typically used to incorporate the Bill of Rights to the states. As such, the Fifth and Fourteenth Amendments are intimately linked, with the Fourteenth Amendment actually being the first application of self-incrimination protections. The key case in this section is *Miranda v. Arizona* (1966). Other cases in this section will be discussed as they support *Miranda* or are exceptions to it.

Miranda and Cases That Support It

The protection against self-incrimination was first incorporated to the states in *Brown v. Mississippi* (1936). In that case, the Supreme Court held that confessions obtained as a result of coercion or brutality were inadmissible. This case was actually decided under the Fourteenth Amendment rather than the Fifth Amendment; but the result was the same—police officers could no longer coerce confessions and have them admitted in court. This decision was eventually extended under the Fifth Amendment; culminating in the decision in *Miranda* and the many cases after it.

Some of the most easily recognized words of the Supreme Court are from *Miranda v. Arizona* (1966). In that case, the Court had to decide whether the police must inform a suspect who is subjected to a custodial interrogation of his or her constitutional rights involving self-incrimination and right to counsel. Of course, the Court held in favor of Miranda, and penned the rule now so well known:

1. that a suspect has the right to remain silent
2. that anything the suspect says may be used in a court of law
3. that the suspect has the right to have an attorney present during questioning
4. that if the suspect cannot afford an attorney, one will be appointed prior to questioning

It is this standard upon which all other cases of this type are based.

Once *Miranda* was decided, it became necessary to determine what conditions represented an interrogation. Two cases are instructive on this issue. In *Brewer v. Williams* (1977), after police arrested Williams in another jurisdiction on suspicion of murder, Williams's counsel was assured that Williams would be transported back to the original jurisdiction without being interrogated. During transport, and without advising Williams of his *Miranda* rights, an officer began a conversation with him concerning the whereabouts of the girl he was alleged to have murdered. This conversation came to be known as the "Christian burial speech," where the officer told Williams that he should tell the officer where the body was so it could receive a Christian burial before a snowstorm came that could prevent the body from being found. Ultimately, Williams agreed to take the officer to the child's body. The Court held in this case that what the officer did was equivalent to an interrogation without counsel. Since Williams was entitled to right to counsel at that time, the evidence had to be suppressed.

In a similar case, *Rhode Island v. Innis* (1980), the Supreme Court ruled that a conversation between two officers not directly speaking to the suspect that elicited the same kind of information as in *Williams* was not an interrogation; thus, the evidence did not have to be suppressed. The key here was that the officers were not talking directly to the suspect.

The extent to which the *Miranda* warnings apply was decided in *Edwards v. Arizona* (1981). In this case, Edwards was arrested pursuant to a warrant. At the police station, he was read his *Miranda* warnings and indicated that he understood them and would answer questions, but he later changed his mind and said that he wanted to speak to an attorney before answering further questions. At that point questioning ceased. The next morning, two different officers asked to see Edwards. He told the detention officer that he did not wish to speak to the officers, but was told that he had no choice in the matter. Edwards was again informed of his *Miranda* rights. Ultimately, Edwards made a statement implicating himself in the crime. The issue before the Court here was whether the police could contact Edwards again without the presence of his lawyer once he had invoked his *Miranda* rights. The Court held in this case that once a suspect invokes his or her *Miranda* rights, the interrogation must cease.

This standard exists regardless of whether the suspect actually speaks to an attorney or not. The rule is that once a suspect invokes his or her right to an attorney, one must be present at the questioning [see *Minnick v. Mississippi* (1990)]. Furthermore, the police may not later interrogate the suspect, even with another reading of the *Miranda* warnings or even for another crime [see *Arizona v. Robertson* (1988)], until the suspect has been provided counsel. The one exception to this rule is if the suspect initiates the communication with police; then it is acceptable to reread the *Miranda* warnings and proceed with an interrogation.

When *Miranda* warnings become necessary was the issue in *Berkemer v. McCarty* (1984). In this case, after following McCarty's car for two miles and observing it weave in and out of a lane, an officer stopped the car and asked McCarty to get out. McCarty had difficulty standing while getting out of the car. The officer decided to charge McCarty with a traffic offense, thus terminating his freedom to leave the scene. McCarty was not told he would be taken into custody but was required to take a field sobriety test, which he failed. While still at the scene of the stop, McCarty was asked if he had been using any intoxicants, to which he replied that he had consumed two beers and several marijuana cigarettes. McCarty was then formally arrested and taken to jail. At no point was McCarty given his *Miranda* warnings.

This case actually addressed two different issues in the continuum of whether *Miranda* warnings are necessary. These were whether the roadside questioning of a motorist detained for a traffic violation was an interrogation (thus requiring *Miranda* warnings), and whether suspects charged with misdemeanor traffic offenses (or greater) require *Miranda* warnings before interrogation. The Supreme Court held that simple questioning that is a part of traffic violations is not a custodial interrogation and, thus, does not require *Miranda* warnings be given. If the questioning (or anything else) leads to an arrest, however, whether it is for a felony or a misdemeanor, then *Miranda* warnings are required before interrogation.

Berkemer was further clarified years later in *Pennsylvania v. Muniz* (1990). In this case, an officer stopped Muniz's vehicle and directed him to perform three standard field sobriety tests, which he failed. The officer then arrested Muniz and took him into custody. At the police station, Muniz was processed through procedures for receiving persons suspected of driving while intoxicated. Without being given his *Miranda* warnings, he was asked seven questions regarding his name, address, height, weight, eye color, date of birth, and age. He was also asked, and was unable to give, the date of his sixth birthday.

After Muniz refused to submit to a breathalyzer test, he was read his *Miranda* warnings. He then waived his rights and admitted in further questioning that he had been driving while intoxicated. The Court held in this case that the police may ask *routine* questions of persons suspected of driving while intoxicated without giving *Miranda* warnings. This is not self-incriminating because it is not the answers to the questions (testimonial evidence) that are of interest to the police, it is the way the responses are made (physical evidence). Questions that are not routine, however (such as the date of Muniz's sixth birthday), and to which the correct answer would be used as testimonial evidence, require *Miranda* warnings.

Cases That Weakened Miranda

It took almost eighteen years before the Supreme Court decided a case that was a substantial blow to the protections provided by *Miranda*. That case was *New York v. Quarles* (1984). In this case, a woman claiming that an armed man had just raped her approached officers. She described him, and said that he had entered a nearby supermarket. The officers drove the woman to the supermarket and one officer went in while the other radioed for assistance. The officer in the supermarket quickly spotted Quarles, who matched the description provided by the woman, and a chase ensued. Once the officer apprehended Quarles, he frisked him and discovered an empty shoulder holster. After handcuffing Quarles, the officer asked him where the gun was. Quarles nodded in the direction of some empty cartons and responded, "The gun is over there." The gun was retrieved from the cartons and Quarles was placed under arrest and read his *Miranda* warnings.

The issue in this case was whether a question asked by a police officer that was prompted by concern for public safety could be admissible in court even if the officer did not read the suspect his or her *Miranda* warnings. The court ruled that there should be a "public safety exception" to *Miranda* where concern for public safety outweighs the rights of the suspect. Furthermore, the motivations of the officer are not called into question here. Regardless of why the officer might ask questions of concern to public safety, no *Miranda* warnings are necessary for that narrow line of questioning.

Another exception to *Miranda* is that responses to questioning made after the *Miranda* warnings are given are admissible in court regardless of any previous communication between the police and a suspect. In *Oregon v. Elstad* (1985), officers went to a burglary suspect's home with a warrant for his arrest. One officer waited with Elstad while the other explained his arrest to his mother. The officer told Elstad that he was implicated in the burglary, to which he responded, "Yes, I was there." Elstad was then taken to the police station, where he was advised of his *Miranda* rights for the first time. Elstad indicated that he understood his rights and wanted to talk to the officers. He then made a full statement, which was typed, reviewed, and read back to him for corrections, then signed by him and the officer. At trial, Elstad stated that his first confession should have been suppressed because it was prior to being given *Miranda* warnings, and the second confession should have been suppressed because there was no reason to not confess after being given *Miranda* warnings because he had already "let the cat out of the bag." The court held in this case that the confession made after the *Miranda* warnings were given and the rights waived was admissible. The Court noted that if the police had not taken the second confession, the previous, unwarned admission would not have been admissible.

In *Colorado v. Spring* (1987), the Supreme Court dealt with the issue of what could be discussed in an interrogation that results from a proper waiver of *Miranda* warnings. In this case, Spring and a companion shot a man during a hunting trip in Denver. After arresting Spring in Kansas City for interstate trafficking in stolen firearms, officers advised him of his *Miranda* rights. Spring signed a statement that he understood and waived his rights. Officers then asked Spring about his involvement in the firearms transactions leading to his arrest. He was also asked if he had ever shot a man, to which he responded affirmatively, but denied the shooting in question. Thereafter, Colorado officials questioned Spring. He was again read his *Miranda* warnings and again signed a statement asserting that he understood and waived his rights. This time, Spring confessed to the Colorado murder.

The Court held in this case that a suspect's waiver of *Miranda* rights is valid, regardless of what crimes are to be discussed. If the suspect believes that a set of minor crimes will be discussed, but the interrogation ultimately leads to questioning about a different and more serious set of crimes, the waiver is still valid (unless the suspect revokes the waiver) and the confession is admissible in court.

Related to this case is what actions the police are required to take after a valid waiver of *Miranda* protections. In *Davis v. United States* (1994), Davis and Shackleford were playing pool; Shackleford lost a game and a $30 wager but refused to pay. Shackleford was later beaten to death with a pool cue. An investigation into the murder revealed Davis's involvement in the crime. Davis was interviewed by agents who advised him of his *Miranda* rights. Davis waived his rights to remain silent and to counsel both orally and in writing. An hour and a half into the interview, Davis said, "Maybe I should talk to a lawyer." When the agents asked Davis whether he was asking for an attorney, he replied that he was not. After a short break, agents reminded Davis of his rights and the interview continued. After another hour, Davis said, "I think I want a lawyer before I say anything else." At that time, questioning ceased.

The issue in this case was when the officers had to cease questioning. The Court ruled that a request for an attorney subsequent to waiving *Miranda* rights must be unambiguous enough that the officers know that such a request is being made. This case is perfect for examining the issue. When Davis said, "Maybe I should talk to a lawyer," the officers asked directly if he was asking for an attorney. When Davis stated that he was not, the interrogation continued. When Davis finally stated, "I think I want a lawyer before I say anything else," the questioning ceased.

In *Arizona v. Mauro* (1987), the Supreme Court decided in favor of the police on what constituted an interrogation. In this case, Mauro admitted to killing his son. He was then arrested and advised of his *Miranda* rights, and stated that he did not wish to make any more statements until a lawyer was present. At that time all questioning ceased. Following questioning in another room, Mauro's wife insisted on speaking with him. Police allowed the meeting on the condition that an officer was present and tape the conversation. The tape was used to impeach Mauro's contention that he was insane at the time of the murder. The Court ruled in this case that the recorded conversation between Mauro and his spouse did not constitute an interrogation; thus, the evidence would be admissible in court.

The Court addressed the issue of whether a confession must be written to be admitted, in *Connecticut v. Barrett* (1987). In this case, Barrett was arrested and advised of his *Miranda* rights. Barrett stated that he would not give a written statement in the absence of counsel, but would talk to the police about the incident. In two subsequent interrogations, Barrett was again advised of his rights and signed a statement of understanding. On both occasions, he gave an oral statement admitting his involvement in the assault but refused to make a written statement. Because of a malfunction in the tape recorder, an officer reduced the confession to writing based on his recollection of the conversation.

The Court held in this case that oral statements made by a suspect are admissible even if the suspect tells police that he or she will not make any written statements without a lawyer present. In this case, the suspect was very specific about what he would and would not do after being read his *Miranda* warnings. Most suspects simply invoke their right to remain silent and/or request an attorney, which must be absolutely honored by police. This case was different, however, in that the suspect himself set the terms of the interrogation.

For over twenty years following *Miranda*, the police read almost verbatim those special words that the Supreme Court put into history and which were popularized in police movies and TV shows. In fact, several lower court opinions following *Miranda* required that the words be used verbatim, that police officers read the words off a card rather than cite them from memory, and that the warnings be in a written form that the suspect could read and sign. The issue of whether the warnings given a suspect must be exactly as stated in the *Miranda* case was finally addressed by the Supreme Court in *Duckworth v. Egan* (1989).

In this case, Duckworth, when questioned by police in connection with a stabbing, made incriminating statements after having signed a waiver form that provided, among other things, that if he could not afford a lawyer, one would be appointed for him "if and when you go to court." He challenged his confession as inadmissible, arguing that the waiver form did not comply with the requirements of *Miranda*. The Court held that the *Miranda* warnings need not be given in the exact form as stated in the decision. The only requirement is that they convey to a suspect his or her rights as stated in *Miranda*.

The issue of what is and is not waived in *Miranda* warnings was addressed in *Patterson v. Illinois* (1988). In this case, after being informed by the police that he had been charged with murder, Patterson twice indicated his willingness to discuss the crime. He was interviewed twice, and on both occasions was read a form waiving his *Miranda* rights. He initialed each of the five specific warnings on the form and then signed it. He then gave incriminating statements to the police about his participation in the crime. The question before the court was whether Patterson's waiver of his *Miranda* rights was a waiver of both his Fifth Amendment right to silence (discussed in this section) and his Sixth Amendment right to counsel (discussed in the next section). The Court held that a waiver of *Miranda* rights was a waiver of both Fifth and Sixth Amendment rights.

The invocation of the right to counsel, however (as addressed below), without actually invoking the *Miranda* rights does not also invoke Fifth Amendment rights. In *McNeil v. Wisconsin* (1991), McNeil asked for and received counsel at his bail hearing, a procedural request not associated with a reading of his *Miranda* warnings. Later, McNeil was approached by police and read his *Miranda* rights. He waived his rights and ultimately gave a confession to the police. At trial, McNeil sought to have the confession suppressed as a violation of his *Miranda* rights. The court in this case held that the request for a lawyer can be independent of *Miranda* if the request is not made pursuant to the reading of *Miranda* warnings.

SIXTH AMENDMENT ISSUES

The right of assistance of counsel protected by the Sixth Amendment has followed a historical track very similar to that of the Fifth Amendment. Like the Fifth Amendment, defendants in state proceedings were not guaranteed this protection until the 1930s. For the Sixth Amendment, this came in the case of *Powell v. Alabama* (1932). In this case, like many others of its type, the protection was aimed at the trial stage of criminal proceedings rather than at the police. The case did hold, however, that defendants on trial for a capital offense must be provided assistance of counsel. This ruling was eventually extended in *Gideon v. Wainwright* (1963) to apply at trial to all defendants charged with a felony.

The first case where the Sixth Amendment right to counsel affected the police was *Escobedo v. Illinois* (1964). In this case, Escobedo was arrested without a warrant and interrogated in connection with a murder. Escobedo stated that he wished to speak to an attorney. Shortly after Escobedo arrived at the police station, his retained lawyer arrived and asked permission from several officers to speak with his client. His requests were repeatedly denied. Escobedo also asked several times during an interrogation to speak to his attorney and was told that the attorney did not want to see him. Escobedo subsequently implicated himself as the murderer. The Court held in this case that a suspect who has been taken into police custody is entitled to a lawyer during interrogation. The problem with *Escobedo*, however, was that it raised as many questions as it answered. To correct this, the Supreme Court handed down the ruling in *Miranda* a few years later. As a result, much of the right to counsel law affecting the police as opposed to right to counsel at the trial stages of the process has been shifted to *Miranda* cases rather than Sixth Amendment cases.

The Court, however, did have to address whether statements obtained through means other than an interrogation would be a violation of the right to counsel. The primary case here is *Massiah v. United States* (1964). In this case, Customs officials received information that Massiah was transporting narcotics aboard a ship. Officers searched the ship and found 300 pounds of cocaine. Massiah was indicted for possession of narcotics. While out on bail, officers enlisted the aid of one of Massiah's friends. The friend allowed officers to install a transmitter under the front seat of his automobile, then engaged Massiah in a conversation that could be overheard by officers. These incriminating statements were admitted over Massiah's objection at trial and he was convicted. The Court ruled in this case that statements were not admissible if obtained in any manner after the suspect was formally charged and had obtained an attorney.

The final case that is pertinent to the police concerning right to counsel extends the decision in *Massiah*. This is *United States v. Henry* (1980). In this case, Henry was indicted for armed robbery and incarcerated. While Henry was in jail, officers contacted an informant who was a cellmate of his and instructed him to be alert to any statements made by Henry but not to initiate any conversations regarding the robbery. After the informant was released from jail, he met with officers who paid him for information concerning incriminating statements made by Henry. There was no indication that the informant would have been paid had he not provided such information. The issue here was whether the officers created a situation likely to elicit incriminating statement without Henry having his attorney present. Based on the ruling in *Massiah*, the Court ruled that it did violate Henry's right to counsel.

CONCLUSION

As this chapter has shown, a lot has changed in policing since the beginning of the twentieth century, in terms of both restrictions on police officers as well as restrictions lifted from them. Probable cause is a good example of this give-and-take of the law. Until the *Boyd* decision in 1914, there were very few restrictions on what the police could do in terms of searches. Over the years, however, the exclusionary rule placed more and more restrictions on the police in terms of what kind of evidence could be excluded if not properly seized. At the same time, however, the level of surety that police officers needed to establish probable cause was reduced, and the number of instances when reduced probable cause was required for a search steadily increased. Restrictions on the police in establishing probable cause has reached a point now where there is very little that officers cannot do if evidence is located in an automobile (as will be discussed in Chapter 2). On other issues, however, such as protections during custodial interrogations, the police are quite restricted. All an offender must do is to announce that he or she does not wish to speak to officers without a lawyer present and the police are nearly powerless in speaking to the offender.

This chapter provides a foundation for the legal issues that will be addressed in this text. Some of the topics discussed in this chapter will be addressed in more detail in the chapters that follow. In Chapter 2, Hemmens addresses the issue of search and seizure and other investigation issues of the Fourth Amendment as they relate to the war on drugs. Golden and VanHouten will then address Fourth Amendment issues concerning roadblocks. In Chapter 4, Stevens addresses legal issues that apply in a community policing environment, and examines some differences in legal issues between community policing and more traditional, order-maintenance policing. Golden and Walker then discuss Fourth Amendment issues in more detail as they relate to the use of narcotics detection dogs in police investigations. In the final chapter covering police operational issues, Chapter 6, Taylor and Morgan discuss legal and constitutional issues inherent in policing the Internet.

The text then turns to issues that were not directly addressed in this chapter. These are related to administrative functions of the police, but are no less important than the operational issues discussed in the first six chapters. In Chapter 7, Buerger establishes the transition between operational and administrative issues with a discussion of police agency responses to legal changes. Bloss then discusses legal issues from the police officer's perspective in an examination of the privacy rights of officers. In Chapter 9, Gaines and Schram discuss the legal issues and ramifications of affirmative action in policing. Pascarella follows on this discussion in Chapter 10 with an examination of the continuing debate over age limitations and discrimination in policing. In the final chapter of the text, Dantzker provides an integration and concluding discussion of the legal aspects of policing.

Cases Cited

- *Adams v. Williams*, 407 U.S. 143 (1972)
- *Aguilar v. Texas*, 378 U.S. 108 (1964)
- *Arizona v. Hicks*, 480 U.S. 321 (1987)
- *Arizona v. Mauro*, 481 U.S. 520 (1987)
- *Arizona v. Robertson*, 486 U.S. 675 (1988)

- *Berkemer v. McCarty*, 468 U.S. 420 (1984)
- *Boyd v. United States*, 116 U.S. 616 (1886)
- *Brewer v. Williams*, 420 U.S. 387 (1977)
- *Brinegar v. United States*, 338 U.S. 160 (1949)
- *Brower v. County of Inyo*, 489 U.S. 593 (1989)
- *Brown v. Mississippi*, 297 U.S. 278 (1936)
- *Bumper v. North Carolina*, 391 U.S. 543 (1968)
- *California v. Acevedo*, 500 U.S. 565 (1991)
- *California v. Carney*, 471 U.S. 386 (1985)
- *California v. Ciraolo*, 476 U.S. 207 (1986)
- *California v. Greenwood*, 486 U.S. 35 (1988)
- *California v. Hodari D.*, 499 U.S. 621 (1991)
- *Carroll v. United States*, 267 U.S. 132 (1925)
- *Chambers v. Maroney*, 399 U.S. 42 (1969)
- *Chimel v. California*, 395 U.S. 752 (1969)
- *City of West Covina v. Perkins*, 525 U.S. 234 (1999)
- *Colorado v. Bertine*, 479 U.S. 367 (1987)
- *Colorado v. Spring*, 479 U.S. 564 (1987)
- *Connecticut v. Barrett*, 479 U.S. 523 (1987)
- *Cupp v. Murphy*, 412 U.S. 291 (1973)
- *Davis v. United States*, 512 U.S. 452 (1994)
- *Delaware v. Prouse*, 440 U.S. 648 (1979)
- *Draper v. United States*, 358 U.S. 307 (1959)
- *Duckworth v. Egan*, 492 U.S. 195 (1989)
- *Dunaway v. New York*, 442 U.S. 200 (1979)
- *Edwards v. Arizona*, 451 U.S. 477 (1981)
- *Escobedo v. Illinois*, 378 U.S. 478 (1964)
- *Florida v. Bostick*, 501 U.S. 429 (1991)
- *Florida v. Wells*, 495 U.S. 1 (1989)
- *Gideon v. Wainwright*, 372 U.S. 355 (1963)
- *Illinois v. Gates*, 462 U.S. 213 (1983)
- *Illinois v. Rodriquez*, 497 U.S. 177 (1990)
- *Knowles v. Iowa*, 525 U.S. 113 (1998)
- *Mapp v. Ohio*, 367 U.S. 643 (1961)
- *Maryland v. Garrison*, 480 U.S. 79 (1987)
- *Massiah v. United States*, 377 U.S. 201 (1964)
- *McNeil v. Wisconsin*, 501 U.S. 171 (1991)
- *Michigan v. Chesternut*, 486 U.S. 567 (1988)
- *Michigan v. Long*, 463 U.S. 1032 (1983)
- *Michigan v. Summers*, 452 U.S. 692 (1981)
- *Minnesota v. Carter*, 525 U.S. 83 (1998)
- *Minnesota v. Dickerson*, 508 U.S. 366 (1993)
- *Minnesota v. Olson*, 495 U.S. 91 (1989)
- *Minnick v. Mississippi*, 498 U.S. 146 (1990)
- *Miranda v. Arizona*, 384 U.S. 436 (1966)
- *New Jersey v. TLO*, 469 U.S. 325 (1985)

2

Crime and the Supreme Court

The Impact of the War on Drugs on Judicial Review of Police Investigatory Practices

Craig Hemmens

INTRODUCTION

The United States has been engaged in a "war on drugs" since the mid-1980s. Federal and local police agencies have devoted increasing amounts of time and resources to fighting this war. More than $59 billion was spent on drug-related police criminal justice activities in 1998, a fourfold increase from the amount spent in 1981 (Kappeler, Blumberg, & Potter, 2000). As a result of the increased attention by the police to drug law violations, the number of persons arrested and incarcerated for drug-related crimes has increased exponentially. Between 1973 and 1996, the number of arrests for drug law violations increased from 328,670 to 1,506,200, a fourfold increase. In 1980, 8 percent of all inmates were incarcerated for drug law violations; by 1997, the percentage had increased to 23 percent of all inmates (Beckett & Sasson, 2000).

Part of the war on drugs has included calls to "get tough" on offenders and to place greater focus on protecting society and less emphasis on the individual rights of criminal suspects who are, in the minds of many, probably guilty anyway. Police agencies have responded to public demands to get tough on crime in part by developing and utilizing new investigatory practices, such as civility enforcement, community caretaking, order maintenance, and zero tolerance (Livingston, 1998). These activities, while effective in ferreting out some criminal activity and maintaining order, are also more intrusive than old-style reactive policing techniques, and allow the exercise of more discretion by individual police officers (Kahan & Meares, 1998; Meares & Kahan, 1998; Sklansky, 1998; Stuntz, 1998).

The Supreme Court in recent years has addressed the constitutionality of a number of these new police practices, and almost without exception has upheld the challenged police activity. In so doing the Court has increasingly relied on a balancing of public protection and individual rights, and determined that the individual interest is subordinate to public safety (Strossen, 1988; Stuntz, 1997; Sundby, 1994). The Court has accepted at face value assertions of danger to the police and public largely unsupported by social science research, while at the same time downplaying evidence that these police practices may have an effect on individual liberties. It appears that the Supreme Court, cognizant of public fear of crime and increasingly dominated by justices who stress efficiency, has relaxed the "reasonableness" standard in Fourth Amendment cases. It has yet to be determined whether this change will increase police effectiveness or simply restrict individual liberties (Cole, 1999; Schulhofer, 1998; Sklansky, 1998).

This chapter reviews a number of recent Supreme Court rulings in cases involving evidence obtained by the police during the course of an investigatory technique. These rulings are in the areas of the requirement that police "knock and announce" their presence before entering a dwelling and the use of traffic stops as a means of investigating potential criminal activity. Individually, these decisions may not appear significant, but when they are taken as a whole, a clear pattern of judicial deference to the police emerges.

THE SUPREME COURT AND THE POLICE: HISTORY

Historically, the Supreme Court paid little attention to the activities of state and local police agencies. There were three primary reasons for this lack of attention: police forces remained relatively small and unorganized until the twentieth century (Walker, 1998), defendants in criminal cases rarely challenged the means by which police obtained evidence (Kennedy, 1997), and the Fourth Amendment, which today is the primary tool for controlling police conduct, did not apply to the activities of state and local police (LaFave, 1996).

The Supreme Court in *Barron v. Baltimore* (1833) held that the Bill of Rights, of which the Fourth Amendment is a part, did not apply to the actions of state and local governmental agencies, but instead was intended to apply only to the activities of federal agencies. As the bulk of police work was conducted by state and local agencies, the decision in *Barron* meant that there were relatively few instances in which the Supreme Court was called upon to interpret the meaning of the Fourth Amendment.

In *Weeks v. United States* (1914), the Court held that evidence illegally obtained by federal police officers must be excluded in all federal criminal prosecutions. As the Court had not at that time applied the provisions of the Fourth Amendment to the states, this decision led to a practice commonly known as the "silver platter doctrine," in which federal courts admitted evidence illegally obtained by state police officers and then turned it over to federal agents. Under this doctrine, such evidence was deemed admissible because the illegal search and seizure was committed by state agents. In 1960, in *Elkins v. United States*, the Court put an end to this practice, prohibiting the introduction of illegally seized evidence in federal prosecutions regardless of whether the illegality was committed by state or federal agents.

It was not until 1949, in *Wolf v. Colorado*, that the Supreme Court determined that the Due Process Clause of the Fourteenth Amendment "incorporated" the Fourth Amendment and applied it to state action. Incorporation of the Fourth Amendment meant that the activities of state and local police agencies were now subject to the strictures of the Fourth Amendment. Finally, in 1961, in *Mapp v. Ohio,* the Court put the issue to rest and applied the exclusionary rule to the states through the due process clause of the Fourteenth Amendment.

During the 1960s, the Supreme Court handed down a number of decisions involving an interpretation of the meaning of the Fourth Amendment. While a complete discussion of these cases is beyond the scope of this chapter, a fair summary of these decisions is that they provided criminal suspects with a number of rights that the police were obliged to respect in their investigation of possible criminal activity (LaFave, 1996; Schwartz, 1983; Wiecek, 1988). These decisions were based in part on the civil rights movement, which has been credited with exposing to the members of the Court the realities of racial discrimination in the United States (Schwartz, 1983). Many of the Supreme Court's decisions in the area of criminal justice can be seen as attempts to reduce the impact of racial discrimination on the criminal justice process (Cole, 1999; Maclin, 1991; Stuntz, 1998).

While many of these decisions provided criminal defendants with greater protections, several decisions provided the police with tremendous power to investigate crime. These included, in particular, *Camara v. Municipal Court* (1967) and *Terry v. Ohio* (1968).

In *Camara v. Municipal Court*, the Supreme Court ruled that administrative search warrants may be issued on less than probable cause. The Court justified lowering the standard of probable cause by balancing the need to search against the limited invasion of privacy that an administrative search involved. Administrative searches are not concerned with uncovering evidence of criminal activity, but are designed to allow the government to ensure compliance with various health and safety regulations (del Carmen, 1998).

In *Terry v. Ohio*, the Supreme Court ruled that police could stop and frisk someone on the street based on "reasonable suspicion" that a crime had occurred. Reasonable suspicion, the Court acknowledged, was less than probable cause. The Court justified relaxing the probable cause requirement by again balancing the need to investigate crime against the limited invasion of privacy that a brief detention involved (Harris, 1994, 1998b).

Taken together, these two decisions provided police officers with a great deal of flexibility in their approach to the investigation of criminal activity. As the Supreme Court has become increasingly dominated by conservative, pro-police justices and public fear of crime has risen, the Court has repeatedly approved the use of these police practices and repeatedly narrowed the protections of the Fourth Amendment. The Court has accomplished this in large part by accepting at face value police claims of social necessity and expediency, and downplaying the impact of intrusive police activities on individual citizens. This inclination to endorse police activity has been heightened by the war on drugs.

THE WAR ON DRUGS

Drugs are a pervasive problem in American society, and police departments are fighting the war on drugs in all regions of the country. The war on drugs has created a virtual panic among public officials, which makes it easier for many to rationalize police activities that may impinge on civil liberties. Referring to the use of the drug war as an excuse to limit civil liberties, Yale Kamisar said: "Throughout history, the government has said we're in an unprecedented crisis and that we must live without civil liberties until the crisis is over . . . it's a hoax" (Morganthau, 1990, p. 23).

Those arrested on drug-related charges receive little sympathy from the public, police, or community leaders. In 1990, Los Angeles Police Department chief Darryl Gates told the Senate Judiciary Committee that casual drug users "ought to be taken out and shot" (Rowley, 1992, p. 605). Drug czar William Bennett suggested that beheading drug dealers was morally acceptable (Rowley, 1992). Comments of this sort, made by respected political leaders, indicate the tremendous sense of outrage and urgency to stem the tide of illegal drug use felt by many in this country. Such statements can be expected to have an impact on police departments attempting to prioritize operations with limited resources. Fyfe (1998) argues that research on police behavior indicates that the major determinant of the behavior of officers in the streets is the philosophy and policy of their chiefs.

Police officers on the street may become so convinced of the moral rightness of their actions that they are willing to sidestep legal requirements, such as the provisions of the Fourth Amendment, to get drugs off the streets. An American Bar Association committee on criminal justice found "evidence that . . . disregard for the Fourth Amendment, specifically in drug cases, may be an unavoidable by-product of a drug problem so pervasive that the police feel they sometimes must violate constitutional restraints in order to regain control of the streets" (Rowley, 1992, p. 605).

Related to the war on drugs is the endorsement and adoption of "zero tolerance" policing techniques. Under a zero tolerance approach, officers seek to prevent crime through order maintenance. This may take the form of enforcing vagrancy and curfew statutes and other laws or municipal ordinances intended to keep the streets clean and safe.

As standard investigative techniques fail to significantly reduce the drug problem and drug-related crime, police are employing new methods of detecting drugs. These methods have been largely endorsed by the Supreme Court. The Court has permitted the use of police sobriety checkpoints [*Michigan Department of State Police v. Sitz* (1990)], drug courier profiles [*Ornealas v. United States* (1996)], and random drug testing of adults [*National Treasury Employees Union v. von Raab* (1989)] and children [*Vernonia School District 47J v. Acton* (1995)]. The government may also examine telephone numbers called, check and deposit slips, a person's fenced backyard, and garbage placed on the curb for collection (Katz, 1990). All of this may occur without the protection of the Fourth Amendment because the Supreme Court has defined each of these activities as beyond the scope of the Amendment (Burkoff, 1984; Sundby, 1994).

Together, the public hue and cry to get tough on crime, the war on drugs, and the adoption of order maintenance strategies such as zero tolerance policing have resulted in police officers across the country pushing the envelope on the protections of the Fourth Amendment; and these actions have largely been sanctioned by the Supreme Court. The next section examines recent Supreme Court decisions involving police investigatory practices affecting persons in their home and in public.

RECENT SUPREME COURT DECISIONS INVOLVING POLICE INVESTIGATORY PRACTICES

The Fourth Amendment bars "unreasonable" searches and seizures by police. This seemingly simple statement provides tremendous room for maneuvering, however, as the courts attempt to determine what is and is not reasonable. In recent years, the Supreme Court has examined several aspects of police work that implicate the Fourth Amendment. In this chapter, the focus is on two: "knock and announce," and the activities of police officers during traffic stops.

Examining the cases in both of these areas provides background on the individual case as well as a brief recitation of the applicable law. The Supreme Court's decision is then analyzed, focusing on its rationale. In most of these cases, the Court utilized a balancing test to determine the reasonableness of the challenged police actions. Under this test, the Supreme Court does not determine what is unreasonable based solely on precedent or common sense; it also focuses on the competing public and individual interests, and whether there is a "reasonable expectation of privacy."

The Knock and Announce Rule

Police prefer to enter a structure they wish to search as quickly as possible for obvious reasons, such as to prevent suspects from escaping or destroying evidence or from harming police officers. Officers have long been required, however, to knock and announce before entering a building. The phrase "knock and announce" is shorthand for the requirement that police officers identify themselves and give notice of their purpose. Entry without notice is allowed only in certain exigent circumstances, such as danger to innocent occupants of the premises, danger to the officer seeking to enter the premises, the possibility of the destruction of evidence contained on the premises, and the possibility that the occupants will either escape or frustrate the intended arrest or search (Hemmens, 1997). Announcement is also unnecessary when it would be a useless gesture; that is, when the presence and purpose of the police is already known to the occupants. Entry by force is permissible after notice and announcement are given and refused, or if there is no response from within the dwelling.

The knock and announce rule was first reported in *Semayne's Case* in 1603. The earliest-known American case is *Read v. Case*, decided in 1822. During the twentieth century, a number of states enacted statutes dealing with the manner of warrant service. A majority of the states passed knock and announce statutes that generally required notice and announcement, but also codified common law exceptions to the general rule. Currently, at least forty states have either case law or statutes requiring police to knock and announce (Hemmens, 1997).

There have been only a handful of Supreme Court cases dealing with the knock and announce principle. In *Miller v. United States* (1958), the Supreme Court held that an entry and arrest by federal agents was illegal because they failed to first announce the purpose of their visit to Miller's apartment. The Court declined to expressly incorporate the knock and announce rule into the Fourth Amendment, however, preferring to decide the case on a non-constitutional ground.

In *Wong Sun v. United States* (1963) the Supreme Court ruled that evidence seized by federal agents who broke into a home without first identifying themselves and announcing their purpose should be suppressed because there were no facts to make the officers "virtually certain" that the suspect was aware of their purpose. The majority opinion suggested, in dicta, that some of the common law exceptions to the knock and announce rule might be applicable in the appropriate case.

In *Ker v. California* (1964), the Supreme Court held that police failure to knock and announce was acceptable only in certain circumstances, and that these circumstances should be judged based on the reasonableness clause of the Fourth Amendment. Unfortunately for lower courts looking for guidance, the Court's decision was badly splintered. Justice Brennan's plurality opinion held that unannounced entry into a home violated the Fourth Amendment except in three limited situations: (1) where the persons within are already aware of the officers' authority and purpose, (2) where the police believe that persons within are in imminent peril of bodily harm, or (3) where those within, made aware of the presence of someone outside (because, for example, there has been a knock on the door), are attempting to escape or destroy evidence.

Justice Clark's plurality opinion held that police could ignore the knock and announce rule whenever "exigent circumstances" existed. Clark did not specify what sort of activity would constitute exigent circumstances in general, focusing instead on the specific facts of the case. Some of the language of his opinion, however, suggested that the very nature of some contraband (such as narcotics) might create an exigency, absent any indication that the suspects were attempting to destroy it.

The Supreme Court did not hear a case involving the knock and announce rule for almost thirty years after *Ker*. In the last four years, however, the Court has rendered several decisions in cases involving challenges to the knock and announce rule. Three of these are described below.

Wilson v. Arkansas (1995)   In 1995, in *Wilson v. Arkansas*, the Supreme Court clarified the relationship of the knock and announce rule and the Fourth Amendment. Wilson was convicted of narcotics possession after police officers, armed with a search warrant, entered her home without knocking or announcing. When the police came to the house, they found the front door open and the screen door unlatched. Looking inside, they saw a man sitting on the living room sofa. They opened the screen door and entered, announcing only after they crossed the threshold. During the subsequent search of the house, contraband was seized and Wilson was arrested.

At a pretrial suppression hearing, Wilson sought unsuccessfully to have the evidence seized by the police during the search of her house excluded from trial on the grounds that the police had failed to knock and announce. Wilson was convicted, and her conviction was upheld on appeal.

The Supreme Court reversed the decision of the state court. In doing so, the Court for the first time squarely held that the common law knock and announce rule was a part of the Fourth Amendment's prohibition on unreasonable searches and seizures. The Court held that (1) the Fourth Amendment requirement that searches be reasonable includes as a factor whether the police gave notice and announcement prior to entry, and (2) that there are exceptions to the general rule that police should knock and announce. After examining the common law at the time of the framing of the Bill of Rights, the Court concluded that whether the police knocked and announced before entry was a factor in determining whether a search was reasonable.

The Supreme Court went on to say that just as the knock and announce principle was subsumed in the reasonableness clause of the Fourth Amendment, so too were possible exceptions to the general rule of notice and announcement. The Court declined to enumerate these possible exceptions, however, and instead chose to leave to the lower courts the task of determining when it might be appropriate to make an unannounced entry. The Court did indicate, however, that some of the more common exceptions to the knock and announce rule already existing in case law might well withstand constitutional scrutiny.

The decision in *Wilson* left lower courts in much the same position they were before the decision. In effect, all that *Wilson* did was to make explicit what many lower courts already assumed—that the "knock and announce" principle is a constitutional requirement, not just a common statutory provision or a common law principle, and that there are some exceptions to the general rule.

Richards v. Wisconsin (1997) *Richards v. Wisconsin* (1997) involved an attempt by police officers to execute a search warrant for a hotel room occupied by Richards. After Richards refused entry to a police officer disguised as a hotel employee and a wait of "four to five seconds," the officers kicked in the door and searched the room, finding a large amount of cash and cocaine in two plastic bags hidden above the ceiling tiles of the bathroom.

Richards was subsequently charged with two drug offenses. Richards sought to have the drugs seized during the search of his hotel room suppressed on the grounds that the police failed to knock and announce before entering his hotel room. The trial court denied his suppression motion.

On appeal the Wisconsin Supreme Court upheld the validity of the entry and search, relying on a prior state case in which it had created a blanket rule under which the police could ignore the requirement to knock and announce whenever the search involved a drug offense. The state supreme court based its endorsement of a blanket rule on two factors. First, it determined that there was a high risk of violence any time police attempt to execute search warrants involving felony drug possession, and that the public interest in officer safety outweighed what the court saw as a minimal intrusion into the privacy rights of citizens. Second, the court asserted that the nature of the evidence sought in drug possession cases also mandated abrogation of the knock and announce rule. Drugs, the court noted, are often easily disposed of, and thus fall under the destruction of the evidence exception to the knock and announce requirement. This reasoning adopted the approach apparently endorsed by Justice Clark in his *Ker* opinion.

The Supreme Court granted certiorari to decide whether the Fourth Amendment permits a blanket exception to the knock and announce rule if drugs are the object of a search warrant. The Court held that the Fourth Amendment does not permit a blanket exception to the knock and announce requirement for felony drug investigations, and struck down the Wisconsin Supreme Court's blanket rule as unconstitutional.

While this decision may at first blush seem a victory for individual liberties, closer examination of the opinion suggests otherwise. While the Supreme Court's opinion disapproved of the Wisconsin court's blanket rule, it did not eliminate no-knock entries. Instead, the Court held that a no-knock entry is justified when the police "have a reasonable suspicion that knocking and announcing their presence, under the particular circumstances, would be dangerous or futile, or that it would inhibit the effective investigation of crime." Requiring the police to demonstrate a reasonable suspicion of such exigent circumstances, the court felt, struck the appropriate balance between the interests of police and the individual privacy interests affected by no-knock entries.

The impact of the application of this relaxed standard is reflected in the outcome of the *Richards* case. The Supreme Court concluded that the circumstances in the case provided the officers with reasonable suspicion that Richards might destroy evidence, and that this justified their no-knock entry. The Court created a large window of opportunity for the police when it permitted the police to disregard the knock and announce rule upon the relatively low threshold of reasonable suspicion of danger to the police or destruction of evidence. Normally, reasonableness requires meeting the probable cause standard. In some instances, however, courts only require reasonable suspicion. By requiring only reasonable suspicion, the Court ensured that police will be able to more easily avoid the knock and announce rule.

It is a narrow view of the Fourth Amendment that suggests that the privacy interest at stake in unannounced entry situations is either nonexistent or negligible. The Fourth Amendment was created largely in response to official invasions of the home, and the Supreme Court has repeatedly upheld the sanctity of an individual's residence. Unannounced entry destroys this privacy interest; consequently, such entries should be limited to the most extraordinary of circumstances.

United States v. Ramirez (1998)   Finally, in *United States v. Ramirez* (1998) the Supreme Court unanimously overturned a Ninth Circuit rule that police officers must possess more than a reasonable suspicion of an exigent circumstance to execute a no-knock warrant in which property damage occurs. The Court declined to adopt the Ninth Circuit's "two-tier" mode of analysis and determined that minor property damage during entry did not transform an otherwise lawful entry into an unlawful one. Requiring the police to demonstrate a reasonable suspicion of exigent circumstances, the Court felt, struck an appropriate balance between the interests of police and individual privacy interests.

The impact of *Wilson*, *Richards,* and *Ramirez* on police tactics is significant. While the decision in *Wilson* that the knock and announce rule was constitutionally mandated was a victory for privacy interests, the endorsement in *Richards* of the reasonable suspicion standard for when unannounced entry is acceptable and the refusal in *Ramirez* to permit lower courts to hold police officers accountable for their unnecessary use of force during an unannounced entry effectively guts the victory (Hemmens, 1998).

This trio of knock and announce decisions opens the door (pardon the pun) to increased police use of unannounced entry. This is a clear victory for the police. Another area in which the police have recently been the beneficiaries of a deferential Supreme Court is traffic stop practices. The following section reviews several recent decisions involving police behavior during routine traffic stops.

Traffic Stop Practices

Travel by automobile is a fact of life in contemporary America. Almost as ubiquitous as the automobile are traffic laws and regulations. Traffic stops are routine occurrences. For many citizens, a traffic stop is the only time they will interact with a police officer. In recent years, some police officers have begun using otherwise valid traffic stops as a means of investigating possible criminal activity. As a result, courts have attempted to define the constitutional parameters of such encounters.

A seizure occurs when a police officer, by means of physical force or show of authority, restrains the liberty of a citizen [*Florida v. Bostick* (1991)]. Seizures come in several forms, from "Terry stops" to full arrest. To arrest someone, police must have probable cause that a crime has been committed. To conduct an investigative detention, or "Terry stop," the police must have an articulable, reasonable suspicion that a person has committed or is about to commit a crime [*Terry v. Ohio* (1968)].

A police officer who observes a motorist commit a traffic infraction has probable cause to conduct a traffic stop. During this stop, the officer may investigate the traffic violation and, if he or she so chooses, issue a traffic citation. Absent a reasonable, articulable suspicion of further criminal activity, the scope of the detention may not lawfully be expanded beyond the purpose of the initial stop. In addition, police officers may make an investigatory stop of a vehicle based on specific and articulable facts that create a reasonable suspicion of criminal activity on the part of the occupants of the vehicle. This "investigatory stop" is analogous to a "Terry stop" of a pedestrian.

A police officer may not conduct a full search of a vehicle or its occupants based on a traffic stop or an investigatory stop unless there exists probable cause to search. This is because the investigatory stop is based on less than probable cause, which is required to conduct a full search, and because a traffic infraction does not create probable cause to investigate for possible criminal activity. Only if the officer has probable cause as a result of the stop (for example, by discovering evidence in plain view) may a full search ensue (del Carmen, 1998).

To be considered reasonable, traffic stops and investigative stops must also be limited in duration. The Supreme Court has not provided a precise time limit, but has indicated that an investigative detention must be temporary, lasting no longer than is necessary to effectuate the purpose of the stop. The permissible length of a traffic stop is that which is necessary to investigate the infraction and issue the ticket. Once the reason for the traffic stop has been dealt with, either via issuance of a ticket or a warning, it is unreasonable to detain the driver to investigate possible criminal activity unless the police officer possesses specific and articulable facts to support the detention, or the driver voluntarily consents to further questioning.

As more than one commentator has noted, it is virtually impossible to travel by car for any appreciable length of time without committing a traffic infraction (Harris, 1998a; Maclin, 1998; Sklansky, 1998). The significance of this fact lies not in the small fine that may accompany a citation for a minor traffic violation, but in the use of traffic regulations by individual police officers as a pretext to conduct an investigation of criminal activity; an investigation not based on probable cause or even reasonable suspicion.

The Supreme Court has recently decided several cases involving traffic stops and the authority of police during these encounters, and has generally allowed the police to use the traffic stop as a means of investigating for possible unlawful activity. These recent cases are briefly described below.

Ohio v. Robinette (1996)   An increasingly popular investigative technique involves a police officer making a lawful traffic stop and then requesting permission to conduct a search of the vehicle (Harris, 1997). This request is made routinely, and is not based on any particularized suspicion of drug-related activity by the person being cited for a traffic infraction. Specialized drug interdiction patrols utilize this tactic, as do officers on routine patrol. In *Ohio v. Robinette* (1996), the Supreme Court upheld this practice, and did not require that police officers inform motorists of their Fourth Amendment right to refuse consent.

Citizens may waive their rights, including their Fourth Amendment rights. Generally, however, for consent to be considered valid it must be voluntary. There is no formula or "bright-line" rule for determining when consent is voluntary. Instead, courts look to the "totality of the circumstances" (LaFave, 1996).

While consent must be voluntary, it need not be "intelligent." That is, there is no requirement that the state show those who waive their Fourth Amendment rights and consent to a search be aware that they have a right to refuse consent. In *Schneckloth v. Bustamonte* (1973), the Supreme Court expressly rejected imposing a bright-line rule requiring knowledge of the right to refuse consent. In *Miranda v. Arizona* (1966) the Court determined that for a criminal suspect to validly waive the right to counsel and the privilege against self-incrimination, the waiver must not only be voluntary, but also intelligent—meaning that the police must inform the suspect of these rights before asking the suspect to waive them. The defendant in *Schneckloth* asked the Court to extend this requirement of "intelligent" waiver to the Fourth Amendment right to be free of unreasonable searches and seizures. The Court declined to extend the protections accorded the Fifth and Sixth Amendments to the Fourth Amendment.

While the Supreme Court made it clear in *Schneckloth* that the "totality of the circumstances" was the appropriate standard by which to determine voluntariness, it did not clarify the meaning of "voluntary." Subsequent cases have provided some guidance. In *United States v. Mendenhall* (1980) the Court determined that a seizure occurs when a reasonable person would not have felt free to leave. In *Florida v. Bostick* (1991), the Court held that a seizure occurs only when an officer, by means of physical force or show of authority, restrains the liberty of a citizen.

The cumulative effect of these decisions was that police officers began to routinely seek consent to search in more encounters with civilians, including routine traffic stops. In *Ohio v. Robinette* (1996), the Supreme Court, faced with an extreme example, nonetheless upheld the practice. A sheriff's deputy on drug interdiction patrol stopped Robinette for speeding, intending, he admitted later, to use the stop as an opportunity to seek consent to search Robinette's car. The deputy asked Robinette to step out of the car, examined his license, issued Robinette a verbal warning, and handed back the driver's license. At this point, the traffic stop was completed. The deputy did not stop there, however. He then asked: "Would you mind if I search your car? Make sure there's nothing in there?" Robinette gave his consent, a small amount of drugs was discovered, and he was subsequently convicted of drug possession.

On appeal Robinette contended that once the purpose of the traffic stop (the issuance of a warning for speeding) was satisfied, the deputy could not legally detain him further for the purpose of obtaining consent to search. The Supreme Court of Ohio agreed and reversed his conviction. The United States Supreme Court reversed the Ohio court, holding that the Fourth Amendment does not require that a lawfully seized defendant be warned that he or she is free to leave before consent to a search is recognized as voluntary. After outlining the facts of the case, the Court then reiterated the recent holding in *Whren v. United States* (1996) that a police officer's subjective intent is irrelevant so long as there is objective justification for the police officer's actions. Here, the deputy was clearly justified in detaining Robinette for speeding based on his observations, and additionally justified, under *Pennsylvania v. Mimms* (1977), in asking Robinette to step out of the car.

The Court asserted that "it would be unrealistic to require police officers to always inform detainees that they are free to go before a consent to search may be deemed voluntary." However, the Court did not explain why requiring an officer to make such a statement would be impractical, although it did acknowledge that such a requirement would not be in the interests of effective policeing (Hemmens & Maahs, 1996).

A traffic stop, while mild compared to a full-blown arrest, is nonetheless a traumatic experience for the average citizen. Lights, weapon, uniform, show of authority, and the embarrassment (or anger or frustration) of being caught all contribute to creating an unpleasant experience. Such an experience is unsettling at the least, and may impair the judgment of the average citizen. People may say or do things they would not normally say or do. They may feel compelled to submit to the displayed authority of the police officer. They may also think that refusing consent will not stop the officer from searching, but will only annoy him or her. As one Supreme Court justice has acknowledged, "few motorists would feel free to . . . leave the scene of a traffic stop without being told they might do so" [*Berkemer v. McCarty* (1979)].

Maryland v. Wilson (1997)   Wilson was a passenger in a car lawfully stopped for speeding. After ordering the driver out of the car and asking him for his driver's license and registration, the trooper noticed that the passenger, Wilson, was nervous and sweating. He then ordered Wilson out of the car. As Wilson exited the vehicle, he inadvertently dropped a package of crack cocaine. The trooper seized the drugs and arrested Wilson for drug possession. Wilson sought to have the drugs suppressed as the product of an unlawful seizure, arguing that the trooper had no authority to order Wilson, a passenger not suspected of any wrongdoing, out of the vehicle. The trial court suppressed the drugs and the Maryland Court of Special Appeals affirmed.

In *Maryland v. Wilson* (1997), the Supreme Court reversed the state court, and stated that a police officer who has lawfully stopped a vehicle for a traffic infraction may order passengers out of the car. This case extended the ruling of a prior case, *Pennsylvania v. Mimms* (1977), in which the Court determined that, as a matter of officer safety, police may order a driver out of a lawfully stopped vehicle. Police officers observed Mimms driving an automobile with an expired license plate and stopped him to issue a citation. The police officer approached the car and asked Mimms to exit the vehicle and produce his driver's license and registration. When Mimms got out of the car, the officer noticed a bulge in Mimms's jacket. Fearing the bulge might be a weapon, the officer conducted a

Terry-style frisk of Mimms, and determined that the bulge was a handgun. Mimms was then arrested for carrying a concealed weapon. Mimms challenged the admission of the handgun into evidence, claiming the officer had no right to order him out of the car, and that the handgun was only discovered as a result of this activity.

The Supreme Court decided that the police had probable cause to stop Mimms, based on the traffic violation, and that the request to exit the automobile was an "incremental intrusion" into the liberty of a lawfully stopped driver. The Court balanced the interests of the individual and society, and determined that the intrusion into the individual's liberty was "de minimus" and "a mere inconvenience," while the weight accorded officer safety was "too plain for argument."

The Court in *Mimms* concluded that police officers could routinely order a driver out of a lawfully stopped vehicle, regardless of the severity of the offense. This was based on balancing the interest in police safety against the privacy interests involved in being ordered out of a car. The Court in *Wilson* acknowledged that ordering a passenger out of a vehicle was an intrusion on the privacy interests of the passenger, but determined that, as in *Mimms*, this intrusion was minimal and outweighed by the public benefit in increased officer safety.

The result of the *Wilson* decision is that police are now free to order any and all passengers out of a lawfully stopped vehicle. The police may do this even though they have not observed the passenger commit a crime (or even a traffic infraction). Police need not have any articulable suspicion of wrongdoing on the part of the passenger.

Whren v. United States (1996)   District of Columbia police officers on drug interdiction patrol in an unmarked car observed a vehicle, driven by passenger Whren's co-defendant, stop at an intersection for approximately twenty seconds, then turn right without signaling. The police officers followed the vehicle and stopped it for the traffic violation, even though departmental regulations instructed undercover officers not to conduct traffic stops. The officers observed Whren in possession of crack cocaine in plain view during the stop, and he was arrested and subsequently convicted of drug possession.

On appeal, Whren claimed that the traffic stop was just a pretext to search for drugs, and that such pretextual stops constituted an unreasonable seizure for purposes of the Fourth Amendment. He argued that police officers used pretext stops to target members of minority groups for enforcement of drug laws, and cited a number of studies that indicated that black and Hispanic motorists were stopped more frequently for traffic offenses than white motorists (Harris, 1997, 1998a).

In *Whren v. United States* (1996), the Supreme Court upheld the validity of the traffic stop. In so doing, the Court resolved a conflict among lower federal and state courts and held that the subjective intent of police officers making a traffic stop is irrelevant, thus validating the use of pretext stops as a means of investigating crime. So long as police officers have a valid reason to stop a vehicle, the Court said, the fact that the officers used the violation of a traffic law as a pretext, or excuse, to stop a vehicle is irrelevant. The test is not whether an officer would have made the traffic stop, but whether an officer could have made the traffic stop. Since the traffic violation provided the police officers with an objective and lawful basis for making the traffic stop, inquiry into their subjective motivation for doing so is unnecessary. In addition, local police department regulations forbidding such traffic stops are not controlling because this would make the Fourth Amendment subject to local rather than national standards.

The Court gave short shrift to Whren's claim that minority motorists were unfairly targeted for pretext stops, stating in an aside that if a defendant has evidence of intentional discrimination in the application of the law, he should file an equal protection claim rather than allege a violation of the Fourth Amendment. Unfortunately, this is likely to be a toothless remedy, because proof of an equal protection violation requires both a discriminatory effect and a discriminatory purpose. Proving a discriminatory purpose, in the absence of officer admission, may be impossible, since no records are kept of traffic stops to document the anecdotal evidence of targeting (Maclin, 1998).

The result of the *Whren* decision is that police officers are free to stop anyone who commits a traffic violation, even if the officer does so not because of concern over the traffic violation, but to use the violation as an excuse to stop the vehicle to investigate other possible crimes. Given the comprehensive scope of state traffic codes, *Whren* is a decision that affords the police a great deal of power vis-à-vis individual citizens.

Wyoming v. Houghton (1999)   A trooper observed a car speeding, with a broken headlight. The trooper conducted a lawful traffic stop, and upon approaching the vehicle, noticed a syringe sticking out of the driver's shirt pocket. The driver was ordered out of the car and admitted to using the syringe to take drugs. Houghton, one of the passengers in the vehicle, was ordered out of the car and frisked, and the car was searched for drugs, based on the probable cause established when the driver admitted to illegal drug use and the automobile exception to the search warrant requirement. In the back seat of the vehicle, police officers found Houghton's purse and opened it. Inside they found drug paraphernalia and a syringe containing methamphetamine. Houghton was arrested and convicted of drug possession.

At trial and on appeal Houghton asserted that the search of her purse violated the Fourth Amendment because the police had no probable cause to suspect her of carrying drugs, and therefore they had no probable cause to search her purse. The Wyoming Supreme Court reversed her conviction, acknowledging while that the officer had probable cause to search the car, there was no authority to examine items in the car that clearly did not belong to the driver.

In *Wyoming v. Houghton* (1999), the Supreme Court reversed the decision of the state court, and held that a police officer who has lawfully stopped a vehicle for a traffic violation and subsequently developed probable cause to believe the vehicle contains contraband may search the belongings of a passenger in the vehicle. After admitting that the common law at the time of the framing of the Fourth Amendment did not provide a clear answer to the lawfulness of this search, the Court turned to a reasonableness analysis, balancing the interests of the individual passenger against the interests of society. In this context, the Court held, there is no reason to limit the search of a vehicle to only those containers clearly in the possession of the driver. Passengers have a reduced expectation of privacy with regard to the property they transport in automobiles, and the degree of intrusiveness here is minimal. On the other side of the equation, society has a significant interest in permitting police officers to examine the belongings of passengers of a vehicle when there is probable cause to believe there is contraband somewhere within the vehicle.

The impact of *Robinette*, *Wilson*, *Whren*, and *Houghton* is that citizens are now afforded fewer Fourth Amendment protections while driving. This loss of individual liberties has occurred in large part because of the Supreme Court's increased reliance on the balancing of individual and police interests. The result is a significant increase in the power of the police.

DISCUSSION

As the above cases reveal, the police have become more proactive in investigating criminal activity, particularly that which is drug-related. The Supreme Court has repeatedly endorsed these police practices and shown great deference to police interests. It has done so in a variety of ways, including creating flexible exceptions to a rule, making bright-line rules vague, and limiting the opportunities for meaningful post-conviction review (Smith, 1997). The Supreme Court repeatedly endorses the existence of a constitutional right, but in a manner which effectively protects that right only for the privileged few, while as a practical matter denying it for the less privileged (Cole, 1999). This leads to a gap between rhetoric and reality in criminal procedure decisions. This so-called symbolization of rights (Smith, 1997), in essence, allows the Court to have its cake and eat it too—it is still seen as the guardian of individual rights while actually advancing pro-police preferences.

An example of how the Supreme Court has accepted as necessary more intrusive police practices is its refusal to require police officers to notify a suspect that he or she has the right to refuse consent. As the Ohio supreme court in *Robinette* and the dissent in *Florida v. Bostick* pointed out, people routinely give consent when doing so is clearly not in their best interest. The Court in *Miranda v. Arizona* required police to give a detailed explanation of a suspect's rights, and subsequent studies revealed that this requirement neither reduced the confession rate nor significantly impeded the investigatory process. The Court in *Robinette*, however, claimed that requiring a police officer to inform someone that a detention was over, or that there was a constitutional right to refuse to consent to a search, was "impractical." This in spite of the *Miranda* rationale and the reality that such a warning would take a few seconds at most. Clearly what the Court means by impractical is that it fears that if the police tell suspects they can refuse consent, the suspects will not feel as if they have to consent, and this will reduce the number of occasions on which consent is given. This may be true, but it is troubling that the Court would base a decision in large part on whether or not the result will make the police officer's job a little more difficult.

Additionally, the Supreme Court is refusing to recognize, legally, the inequality inherent in modern American society. An example is the Court's continued claims that warrants are preferred in all but a few limited, exigent circumstances. While continuing to maintain a preference for warrants, the Court has repeatedly held that it is permissible for police officers to seek consent to search at any time, without probable cause or even reasonable suspicion of involvement in criminal activity. This tactic is disproportionately employed against young black men (Harris, 1998a). The Court rhetoric is that it protects the rights of all citizens, but the reality is that police prerogatives generally prevail over the rights of minorities and the poor (Cole, 1999). The result, again, is that the police have more freedom to conduct the war on drugs as they see fit, often supported by the courts. And the police are getting the message.

It should be noted that the police do not always win in the Supreme Court. On occasion, the Supreme Court has held that the police have exceeded the scope of their authority. An example is *Knowles v. Iowa* (1998). In this case, a police officer stopped Knowles for speeding. After issuing a speeding ticket, the officer ordered Knowles out of the car and searched it, finding marijuana. Knowles was then charged and convicted of drug possession. The officer searched the car under the authority of two state statutes: one that authorized police to either arrest or issue a citation for traffic offenses, and one that authorized police to conduct a search incident to an arrest even in situations where the officer chose not to actually take a person into custody but instead merely issued a traffic citation. The trial court and state supreme court upheld the search on the grounds that a search incident to arrest was appropriate in any situation where an officer was authorized to arrest, even if an arrest did not actually take place.

The Supreme Court struck down the Iowa law as violative of the Fourth Amendment. The Court acknowledged that the "search incident to an arrest" was a continuing exception to the rule requiring a warrant, but noted that the exception was created for two reasons: (1) to protect officers from a potentially armed person about to be taken into custody; and (2) to preserve evidence for later use at trial. Neither of these two justifications existed in this case. First, Knowles was not in custody. Second, it was unlikely that the search would turn up any evidence of speeding, the offense that Knowles was charged with when the search commenced.

Undecided by the Court was the situation where a state eliminated citations altogether and mandated custodial arrests for minor traffic offenses. Would the search incident rationale then be extended to these types of custodial arrests? Also unanswered was whether the court might extend the search incident to an arrest exception to other situations where there is only the issuance of a citation, such as offenses more serious than a traffic offense, where a stronger case can be made that the person might be a danger to the officer. The opinion left these issues unresolved. Thus while the Court in *Knowles* forbade searches incident to citations for traffic offenses, it left the door open for searches incident to other minor, traditionally non-arrestable offenses.

CONCLUSION

While the Supreme Court is the ultimate decision-making body with regard to criminal procedure, it is limited in its ability to implement its decisions (Horowitz, 1977). Courts are the interpreting population, while the police are the "implementing population" (Canon & Johnson, 1999), the group whose behavior is reinforced or sanctioned by the interpreting population. The police are receiving the message from the Supreme Court that all is fair in the drug war—most of the criminal procedure decisions of the past decade have been an endorsement of police practices, even as these practices have become increasingly intrusive. Consequently, the police continue to push the envelope in the drug war, trying new and more intrusive practices. Where this movement will end is anybody's guess.

According to the current Supreme Court, reasonableness is the "touchstone" of the Fourth Amendment [*Florida v. Jimeno* (1998)]. This simply means that the Amendment requires that police officers act rationally and pursue reasonable goals when they intrude upon individuals (Maclin, 1993). There is no requirement that police officers always have a warrant, or even probable cause in some instances. The Court determines what constitutes reasonable police behavior by weighing the individual's privacy interest against the legitimate interests of police. Unfortunately, such a balancing test is inherently subjective, and thus tends to deprive the Fourth Amendment of its meaning and weakens it, as well as producing inconsistent results (Strossen, 1998).

The result of the Court's increased reliance on a relaxed application of the balancing test to determine the reasonableness of police action has been a pronounced tendency by the Court to uphold most police investigatory practices, based on the necessity of fighting the drug war and expediency. This is unfortunate, as the Fourth Amendment, in the words of Justice Frankfurter, "reflects experience with police excesses" [*Davis v. United States* (1944)]. The Fourth Amendment makes plain, perhaps more directly than any other amendment, that the Constitution does not tolerate a police state.

The Warren Court, during the civil rights era, was concerned with the treatment of blacks in the criminal justice system. This concern with race relations served as the "unspoken subtext" (Sklansky, 1998) of many criminal procedure decisions. Today, this concern has disappeared from Fourth Amendment jurisprudence. Current cases show little or no concern for the intangible damage of police investigatory practices (Maclin, 1998). Racial issues, as the *Whren* opinion makes clear, are essentially irrelevant to the determination of reasonableness under the Fourth Amendment. This is especially disturbing when considered in the context of several studies and much anecdotal evidence that some police misuse traffic regulations as a means of investigating crime, and when they do so, they target minority drivers. Indeed, the practice has become so common that it has its own slang description, DWB, or "Driving While Black" (Cole, 1999; Harris, 1998a).

Scholarly complaints about the Supreme Court's treatment of the Fourth Amendment have generally fallen on deaf ears outside the legal academic community. This may be because society has become so unified in its fear of crime, and has increased its trust of the police since the tumultuous 1960s. As Justice Douglas noted in dissent in *Terry v. Ohio* in 1968: "There have been powerful hydraulic pressures throughout our history that bear heavily on the Court to water down constitutional guarantees and give the police the upper hand."

The war on drugs and the get tough on crime movement have contributed to the reluctance of an increasingly conservative Supreme Court to restrain police. Consequently, it appears that Justice Douglas's fear has been largely realized. This chapter has reviewed how the Supreme Court has deferred to the wishes of the police in two areas, the knock and announce requirement and traffic stops. The cases in these two areas indicate a clear tendency on the part of the Court to let the police intrude into the privacy rights of the individual citizen. How far this intrusion will go remains to be seen.

REFERENCES

BECKETT, K., & SASSON, T. 2000. *The politics of injustice: Crime and punishment in America.* Thousand Oaks, CA: Pine Forge Press.

BURKOFF, J. M. 1984. When is a search not a search? Fourth amendment doublethink. *University of Toledo Law Review, 15,* 515–560.

CANON, B. C., & JOHNSON, C. A. 1999. *Judicial policies: Implementation and impact.* Washington, DC: Congressional Quarterly Press.

COLE, D. 1999. *No equal justice.* New York: Free Press.

DEL CARMEN, R. V. 1998. *Criminal procedure: Law and practice.* Belmont, CA: Wadsworth.

FYFE, J. J. 1998. *Terry*: An ex-cop's view. *St. John's Law Review, 72,* 1231–1248.

HARRIS, D. A. 1994. Factors for reasonable suspicion: When black and poor means stopped and frisked. *Indiana Law Journal, 69,* 659–688.

HARRIS, D. A. 1997. "Driving while black" and all other traffic offenses: The Supreme Court and pretextual traffic stops. *Journal of Criminal Law and Criminology, 87,* 544–582.

HARRIS, D. A. 1998a. Car wars: The Fourth Amendment's death on the highway. *The George Washington Law Review, 66,* 557–591.

HARRIS, D. A. 1998b. Particularized suspicion, categorical judgment: Supreme Court rhetoric versus lower court reality under *Terry v. Ohio. St. John's Law Review, 72,* 1231–1248.

HEMMENS, C. 1997. The police, the Fourth Amendment, and unannounced entry: *Wilson v. Arkansas. Criminal Law Bulletin, 33,* 29–58.

HEMMENS, C. 1998. I hear you knocking: The Supreme Court revisits the knock and announce rule. *University of Missouri-Kansas City Law Review, 66,* 559–602.

HEMMENS, C., & MAAHS, J. R. 1996. Reason to believe: *Ohio v. Robinette. Ohio Northern University Law Review, 23,* 309–346.

HOROWITZ, D. L. 1997. *The courts and social policy.* Washington, DC: Brookings Institution.

KAHAN, D. M., & MEARES, T. L. 1998. The coming crisis of criminal procedure. *Georgetown Law Journal, 86,* 1153–1184.

KAPPELER, V. E., BLUMBERG, M., & POTTER, G. W. 2000. *The mythology of crime and criminal justice (3rd ed.).* Prospect Heights, IL: Waveland Press.

KATZ, L. A. 1990. In search of a Fourth Amendment for the twenty-first century. *Indiana Law Journal, 65,* 549–590.

KENNEDY, R. 1997. *Race, crime and the law.* New York: Pantheon Books.

LAFAVE, W. R. 1996. *Search and seizure: A treatise on the Fourth Amendment.* St. Paul, MN: West.

LIVINGSTON, D. 1998. Police, community caretaking, and the Fourth Amendment. *University of Chicago Legal Forum,* 261–314.

MACLIN, T. 1991. Black and blue encounters—some preliminary thoughts about Fourth Amendment seizures: Should race matter? *Valparaiso University Law Review, 26,* 243–279.

MACLIN, T. 1993. The central meaning of the Fourth Amendment. *William and Mary Law Review, 35,* 197–249.

MACLIN, T. 1998. Race and the Fourth Amendment. *Vanderbilt Law Review, 51,* 333–393.

MEARES, T. L., & KAHAN, D. M. 1998. Law and (norms of) order in the inner city. *Law and Society Review, 32,* 805–838.

MORGANTHAU, T. 1990. Uncivil liberties? *Newsweek,* April 23, 1990.

ROWLEY, C. J. 1992. *Florida v. Bostick*: The Fourth Amendment: Another casualty of the war on drugs. *Utah Law Review,* 601–645.

SCHULHOFER, S. J. 1998. The constitution and the police: Individual rights and law enforcement. *Washington University Law Quarterly, 66,* 11–32.

SCHWARTZ, B. 1983. *Super chief: Earl Warren and his Supreme Court—A judicial biography.* New York: New York University Press.

SKLANSKY, D. A. 1998. Traffic stops, minority motorists, and the future of the Fourth Amendment. In D. J. Hutchinson, D. A. Strauss, & G. R. Stone (Eds.), *The Supreme Court Review, 1997,* pp. 271–330. Chicago: University of Chicago Press.

SMITH, C. E. 1997. Turning rights into symbols: The U.S. Supreme Court and criminal justice. *Criminal Justice Policy Review, 8,* 99–117.

STROSSEN, N. 1998. The Fourth Amendment in the balance: Accurately setting the scales through the least intrusive alternative analysis. *New York University Law Review, 63,* 1173–1267.

STUNTZ, W. J. 1997. The uneasy relationship between criminal procedure and criminal justice. *Yale Law Journal, 107,* 1–76.

STUNTZ, W. J. 1998. Race, class, and drugs. *Columbia Law Review, 98,* 1795–1842.

SUNDBY, S. E. 1994. Everyman's Fourth Amendment: Privacy or mutual trust between government and citizen? *Columbia Law Review, 94,* 1751–1812.

WALKER, S. 1998. *The police in America.* New York: McGraw-Hill.

WIECEK, W. M. 1988. *Liberty under law: The Supreme Court in American life.* Baltimore: Johns Hopkins University Press.

Cases Cited

- *Barron v. Baltimore,* 32 U.S. 243 (1833).
- *Berkemer v. McCarty,* 468 U.S. 420 (1979).
- *Camera v. Municipal Court,* 387 U.S. 523 (1967).
- *Davis v. United States,* 328 U.S. 582 (1944).
- *Elkins v. United States,* 364 U.S. 206 (1960).
- *Florida v. Bostick,* 501 U.S. 429 (1991).
- *Florida v. Jimeno,* 499 U.S. 934 (1991).
- *Ker v. California,* 374 U.S. 23 (1963).
- *Knowles v. Iowa,* 525 U.S. 113 (1998).
- *Mapp v. Ohio,* 367 U.S. 643 (1961).
- *Maryland v. Wilson,* 519 U.S. 408 (1997).
- *Michigan Department of State Police v. Sitz,* 496 U.S. 444 (1990).
- *Miller v. United States,* 357 U.S. 301 (1958).
- *Miranda v. Arizona,* 384 U.S. 436 (1966).
- *National Treasury Employees Union v. von Raab,* 489 U.S. 656 (1989).
- *Ohio v. Robinette,* 519 U.S. 33 (1996).
- *Ornealas v. United States,* 517 U.S. 690 (1996).
- *Pennsylvania v. Mimms,* 434 U.S. 106 (1977).
- *Read v. Case,* 4 Conn. 166 (1822).
- *Richards v. Wisconsin,* 520 U.S. 385 (1997).
- *Schneckloth v. Bustamonte,* 412 U.S. 218 (1973).
- *Semayne's case,* 77 Eng. Rep. 194 (1603).
- *Terry v. Ohio,* 392 U.S. 1 (1968).
- *United States v. Mendenhall,* 446 U.S. 544 (1980).
- *United States v. Ramirez,* 523 U.S. 65 (1998).
- *Vernonia School District 47J v. Acton,* 515 U.S. 646 (1995).
- *Weeks v. United States,* 232 U.S. 383 (1914).
- *Whren v. United States,* 517 U.S. 806 (1996).
- *Wilson v. Arkansas,* 514 U.S. 927 (1995).
- *Wolf v. Colorado,* 338 U.S. 25 (1949).
- *Wong Sun v. United States,* 371 U.S. 471 (1963).
- *Wyoming v. Houghton,* 526 U.S. 295 (1999).

3

The Supreme Court Puts Up Roadblocks to Drug Enforcement

James W. Golden

Amy C. VanHouten

INTRODUCTION

Once introduced into American society and culture, the automobile was quickly found to be a valuable tool in policing. The first use of the patrol car was just prior to World War I; and it was in widespread use by the 1920s (Walker, 1999). With citizens and some criminals driving cars, police were forced to keep up with the times to provide the level of service demanded by the public (Walker, 1999).

As the automobile became more a part of the popular culture, it also began to be increasingly used in criminal activity. This required the police to develop tactics and procedures for dealing with cars used by criminals in the commission of crimes or as means of transportation. The Supreme Court weighed in on the issue in 1925 when it allowed the police to make warrantless searches of automobiles thought to contain the evidence of a crime. This "automobile exception" has been expanded over the years as police developed new tactics and as the use of automobiles by criminals expanded.

More recently, police began to use roadblocks in attempts to detect and control crime. Roadblocks have been used for such purposes as detecting illegal aliens, identifying and stopping drivers suspected of driving under the influence of alcohol, and attempting to stop the flow of drugs smuggled in cars.

This chapter will examine the legal issues involved in the police use of roadblocks as an enforcement technique. Following a brief history of the automobile exception, police use of roadblocks for general purposes and specifically in controlling the smuggling of drugs will be discussed. The chapter will then discuss the latest Supreme Court ruling on roadblocks (*City of Indianapolis v. Edmond*). It will conclude with a statement on the effect of *Edmond* and the current state of the law concerning police use of roadblocks.

HISTORY OF THE AUTOMOBILE EXCEPTION

In 1925, the Supreme Court heard its first case on automobile stops and seizures, *Carroll v. United States* (1925). In *Carroll*, the Court set forth an automobile exception to the Fourth Amendment based on the mobility of the automobile. The automobile exception allows officers to search a vehicle based on probable cause without a warrant because of the mobility of the vehicle. The Court, however, clearly did not intend that police should stop any or all vehicles on the chance that contraband substances would be found, noting that "those lawfully within the country, entitled to use the public highways, have a right to free passage without interruption or search unless there is known to a competent official, authorized to search, probable cause for believing that their vehicles are carrying contraband or illegal merchandise" (267 U.S. 132, at 155).

The automobile exception was further refined by the Court in *Robbins v. California* (1981), where it listed five considerations determining whether a set of circumstances fell under the automobile exception. The first was if it was impractical to obtain a warrant because of the mobility of the motor vehicle. Second there was a diminished expectation of privacy surrounding automobiles. The third consideration was that a car is used primarily for transportation, not as one's residence or a place to store personal effects. The fourth consideration was that the occupants and contents of an automobile travel in plain view. Finally, there was a substantial governmental interest in the regulation of automobiles.

In addition to these considerations, officers must have reasonable suspicion of involvement in criminal activity before stopping a vehicle [see *United States v. Cortez* (1981)]. Checkpoints or roadblocks are an exception to the rule that there must be a reasonable suspicion of criminal activity to make a vehicle stop [see *United States v. Martinez-Forte* (1976); *Michigan Department of State Police v. Sitz* (1990)]. Whitebread and Slobogin (2000, p. 304) suggested that "checkpoints are useful as a means of investigating a large number of people in an efficient manner." Historically, checkpoints have been used to control the flow of illegal immigrants at the borders or during transportation inland, to detect drunk drivers and other traffic violators, and as a means to check for driver's licenses and registration. Even so, a small number of people stopped at a checkpoint are likely to be found in violation of the law.

In the cases discussed above, the Supreme Court addressed the constitutionality of such checkpoints, finding in each of these instances an exception to the requirement of individualized suspicion of criminal activity. Recently, in *City of Indianapolis et al. v. Edmond et al.* (2000), the Court examined the use of roadblocks or checkpoints to detect and interdict the use of narcotics.

INDIANAPOLIS v. EDMOND

In *City of Indianapolis et al. v. Edmond et al.* (2000), the Supreme Court addressed the legality of a checkpoint whose primary purpose was the discovery and interdiction of illegal narcotics. The Court held that the checkpoint program established by the Indianapolis Police Department was operating only from a general interest in crime control, and was therefore in violation of the Fourth Amendment.

The Indianapolis Police Department conducted six drug-interdiction checkpoints between August and November, 1998. Checkpoints were selected weeks in advance of the actual roadblock, and were based on numbers and types of crimes in the area and on traffic flow. The checkpoints were clearly identified as narcotics checkpoints, and drivers were warned that a narcotics-detection dog would be in use. The police stopped a predetermined number of vehicles for processing and allowed other traffic to proceed. The average stop for a vehicle, absent further processing, was two to three minutes. They stopped 1,161 vehicles and arrested 104 motorists. Of those arrests, only 55 were for drug-related crimes. Thus, the overall "drug hit rate" for the program was approximately 5 percent.

During a stop, the police inspected the driver's license and vehicle registration, and subjected the outside of the vehicle to a sniff by a narcotics-detection dog. The officer also was instructed to observe the driver for signs of impairment and to conduct a walk-around inspection of the outside of the vehicle. Directives issued by the police department instructed officers that they could only search a vehicle with the owner's consent or with the appropriate reasonable suspicion.

James Edmond and Joell Palmer were stopped at a narcotics checkpoint. They subsequently filed a class action lawsuit claiming that the roadblock violated the Fourth Amendment. The Supreme Court granted certiorari to address the issue of narcotics roadblocks. It held that the checkpoint's primary purpose was that of a general interest in crime control, and was not conducted for a specific purpose previously approved by the Court. The three major exceptions allowed by the Court are checkpoints designed to halt the flow of illegal immigrants [*United States v. Martinez-Forte* (1976)], sobriety checkpoints [*Michigan Department of State Police v. Sitz* (1990)], and checkpoint stops for license and registration inspection [*Delaware v. Prouse* (1979)]. Thus, the checkpoint program conducted in Indianapolis violated the seizure provisions of the Fourth Amendment because the checkpoint was not conducted for one of the purposes previously determined to be constitutional. The Court did note, however, that this ruling did not affect previous decisions where specific purposes were addressed.

The finding in this case prohibited checkpoints whose purpose was general in nature and designed only to detect evidence of ordinary criminal wrongdoing. The direction for police personnel is clear: a roadblock can only be used to target a specific type of offense and cannot be used as a general sweep for any type of criminal activity, including narcotics. To more fully understand the court's decision in *Edmond*, an examination of the exceptions to the general requirement of probable cause for illegal immigrants is appropriate.

ILLEGAL IMMIGRANTS

Much of the case law on checkpoints is based on decisions concerning enforcement to control illegal immigration. This relationship is based on the extensive use of roadblocks for such enforcement. Historically, three types of roadblocks have been used to detect illegal aliens: permanent checkpoints, temporary checkpoints, and roving patrols. Permanent checkpoints are located along major highways at nodal intersections where other major highways intersect the main road leading from the border. Temporary checkpoints are established for short periods of time at various locations along highways leading from the border. Roving patrols are units that patrol the highways leading from the border and stop vehicles suspected of carrying illegal aliens.

Cases involving search and seizure of illegal immigrants hinge on two major issues. The first is whether the stop can be justified within the framework of an administrative inspection, border search, or functional equivalent. The second is the related issue of a privacy interest in an automobile as it relates to the Fourth Amendment.

In *Almeida-Sanchez v. United States* (1973), the Court addressed these issues. Almeida-Sanchez, a Mexican citizen with a valid U.S. work permit, was stopped by the Border Patrol. A search of his vehicle yielded a large quantity of marijuana. On appeal, he contended that the search of his automobile was illegal. The government argued that the vehicle search, although made without a warrant and without probable cause, was valid under the Immigration and Nationality Act, which provides for warrantless searches of automobiles within a reasonable distance from any external boundary. The attorney general's regulation defines reasonable as being 100 miles from a U.S. border. The appeals court upheld the search on the basis of the act and the attorney general's regulation.

The Supreme Court determined that the search could not be considered valid under any previous decision of the Court involving the search of automobiles, as it did not meet the minimal requirements of probable cause set forth in *Carroll*. In effect, the stopping of a vehicle by a roving patrol is not the functional equivalent of a checkpoint. Searches at international airports after a nonstop flight from a foreign country or searches at an established station near the border along a road leading from the border may be considered functional equivalents of border searches. In this case, however, the search of an automobile on a road that did not extend to the border without probable cause or consent was unreasonable. The Court's decision in *Edmond* is an extension of this principle applied to a situation where there was no substantive rationale, other than general policing, to stop a vehicle. Police officers may not institute a checkpoint for narcotics in the interior of the country and consider it the functional equivalent of a border checkpoint designed to stop the flow of narcotics into the country.

The government also argued that the stopping of a vehicle suspected of carrying illegal aliens was an administrative inspection. Previously, in *Camara v. Municipal Court* (1967), the Supreme Court held that administrative inspections to enforce community health and welfare regulations could be made on reasonable suspicion, but the officer must obtain either a warrant or consent. The Court found in *Almeida-Sanchez* that the search was at "the unfettered discretion of the members of the Border Patrol, who did not have a warrant, probable cause, or consent" (413 U.S. 266, 270). Based on this line of reasoning by the Court and its ruling in *Edmond*, police should not attempt to use an administrative-inspection checkpoint as a pretext to search a vehicle for contraband.

Two years later, the Supreme Court again dealt with the issue of border searches at a checkpoint where there was no probable cause or consent. In *United States v. Ortiz* (1975), the Court was asked to determine the issue of whether vehicle searches at traffic checkpoints must be based on probable cause.

The United States Border Patrol had a permanent checkpoint station set up in San Clemente, California. In November, 1973, a car driven by Ortiz was stopped at the checkpoint for a routine immigration search. During that search, three illegal aliens were found hiding in the trunk.

The government's position in this case was that the characteristics of the checkpoint justified the search without probable cause. First, the checkpoint site was selected by high-ranking Border Patrol officials, using criteria based on a balancing of the Border Patrol mission and the potential for inconveniencing motorists. Second, checkpoint stops were less intrusive than roving-patrol stops because of the extensive notification by roadway signs, the presence of uniformed officers, and the bright lighting of the checkpoints. Finally, the government argued that the discretion of the officers manning the checkpoint was limited by the checkpoint location.

The Court ruled the search unconstitutional, holding that checkpoints should not be afforded a lesser constitutional protection with respect to searches than other types of vehicle searches. The major issue for the Court was the issue of discretion. The use of checkpoints did not seem to offer any limits on which vehicles the officer chose to inspect further. For that reason, the Court chose to consider checkpoints in the same light as roving patrols to stop illegal immigrants: both require probable cause, consent, or a warrant to search the stopped vehicle.

A case involving similar circumstances was decided at the same time as *Ortiz*. In *United States v. Brignoni-Ponce* (1975), the Court examined the Border Patrol's authority to stop automobiles and question their occupants near the border. This case differed from *Almeida-Sanchez* and *Ortiz* in that it only dealt with the issue of questioning occupants about their citizenship and immigration status.

In *Brignoni-Ponce*, officers were observing northbound traffic from a patrol car because the checkpoint was closed due to inclement weather. The road was dark, and the only illumination was from the headlights of the patrol car. Officers observed a vehicle heading north with three occupants who appeared to be of Mexican descent. The officers subsequently stopped the vehicle and found two illegal aliens. Brignoni-Ponce was convicted at trial and appealed. On appeal, the Supreme Court held that suspicion that the occupants appear to be of Mexican descent is not enough to establish probable cause for a search.

A stop by a roving patrol for the purpose of determining residency is a limited intrusion, not requiring a search. Because of the limited intrusion, less than probable cause may justify the stop. The Court, however, was not willing to allow the Border Patrol to dispense with the need for reasonable suspicion that the law was being violated. Thus, based on the *Terry* doctrine, the importance of the governmental interest in stopping the flow of illegal immigrants, the minimal intrusions of a brief stop, and the lack of policing the border, the Court held that a stop may be made on reasonable suspicion if officers can point to specific and articulable facts that caused them to make the stop. Later, the Court used a similar line of reasoning in considering a checkpoint a limited intrusion requiring less than probable cause. The Court, however, did not grant police unlimited discretion, and restricted the government to cases where the primary purpose for the checkpoint was clearly not a means to evade the Court's prohibition against using checkpoints for the detection of ordinary criminal wrongdoing.

In *Brignoni-Ponce*, the officers relied on a single factor, the apparent Mexican descent of the occupants, as the reason for the stop. After glimpsing the occupants under poor illumination, they stopped the car. In its analysis, the Court determined that this factor did not rise to the level of reasonable suspicion required for a traffic stop, as mandated by *Carroll* and subsequent cases, including *Almeida-Sanchez* and *Ortiz*. The Court suggested that a number of factors may be used to develop reasonable suspicion. Among these are the characteristics of the area, previous experience with alien traffic, driving behavior, certain types of vehicles known to be used in smuggling aliens, and a number of other factors based on the training and experience of the officer (422 U.S. 873 at 885). The Court, however, clearly stated that a single factor presented by the officers for reasonable suspicion would not be acceptable.

A year later, the Court again addressed the issue of Border Patrol checkpoints in *United States v. Martinez-Fuerte* (1976). The Border Patrol checkpoint in this case was a permanent checkpoint complete with signs, lights, and a permanent building housing both Border Patrol offices and a temporary detention facility. At the checkpoint, traffic was brought to a virtual halt. An agent standing between two lanes of traffic visually screened northbound vehicles. Most of them were allowed to resume progress without interruption. Others were directed to a secondary inspection area where the occupants were asked to verify their citizenship and immigration status. The average length of time spent in secondary inspection was three to five minutes. This checkpoint was operating under a warrant of inspection issued by a magistrate, authorizing the Border Patrol to conduct a routine stop and inspection at the San Clemente checkpoint. The Supreme Court granted certiorari to address the issue of whether permanent routine checkpoints are a constitutionally valid law enforcement technique for suppressing illegal immigration and whether a warrant is necessary to operate a checkpoint.

The Supreme Court took note of the immigration policy of the United States and the difficulty of interdicting the flow of illegal aliens from Mexico, recognizing it as a legitimate law enforcement interest. As a legitimate and specific law enforcement issue, the Court is more likely to grant the government some leeway in conducting traffic stops and using checkpoints. The Court in *Almeida-Sanchez* required roving patrols to use probable cause as their basis for searching a vehicle. In *Ortiz*, the Court placed the same limitations on vehicle searches at permanent checkpoints. In *Brignoni-Ponce,* the Court modified this requirement by holding that a roving patrol stop could be made on reasonable suspicion rather than probable cause. The Court then turned to the issues in the current case.

First, checkpoints constituted seizures within the meaning of the Fourth Amendment. The government argued the necessity of a traffic-checking program in the interior because the flow of illegal aliens cannot be effectively controlled at the border, as previously discussed in *Brignoni-Ponce*. The Court agreed, and held that the requirement of probable cause for a stop at a permanent checkpoint would be impractical because the traffic flow would be too great to allow officers to develop the particularized suspicion or probable cause required by previous decisions since the creation of the automobile exception in *Carroll* and its extension in *Robbins*.

The Court then turned to the issue of intrusion on the Fourth Amendment, finding that a checkpoint stop, due to its circumstances, poses less of an intrusion than a stop by a roving patrol. Motorists using the highways are not taken by surprise, as the checkpoint is known or knowledge about it is available. In addition, locations are chosen by officials who are responsible for making decisions regarding the allocation of scarce resources, not by the officers running the checkpoint. Noting these facts in addition to the lesser expectation of privacy in an automobile, the Court held that stops and questioning of motorists may be made in the absence of any individualized suspicion at reasonably located checkpoints, and that the stops be made without a warrant.

These cases provide some background for continued discussion of the *Edmond* case. The Court, particularly with respect to the legitimate law enforcement interest in halting the flow of illegal aliens, has set some clear guidelines. First, the government must be exercising a reasonable law enforcement interest in using vehicular checkpoints to stop traffic, and a warrant is not needed to operate the checkpoint; however, vehicles diverted to a secondary area for further investigation must be diverted based on reasonable suspicion, not the higher standard of probable cause [*United States v. Martinez-Fuerte* (1976)]. Searches of these vehicles must be made on individualized suspicion that they will yield the evidence of criminal activity [*United States v. Martinez-Fuerte* (1976)]. Finally, officers in roving patrols stopping vehicles to check the citizenship and immigration status of the occupants must have individualized suspicion or probable cause to make the stop, and cannot rely on a single articulable rationale [*United States v. Brignoni-Ponce* (1975)].

SOBRIETY CHECKPOINTS

In *Edmond,* the Supreme Court discussed a second exception for stopping vehicles at checkpoints: sobriety checkpoints. The Court addressed the issue of sobriety checkpoints in *Michigan Department of State Police v. Sitz et al.* (1990), holding that the state's use of sobriety checkpoints did not violate the Fourth and Fourteenth Amendments to the Constitution.

The Michigan State Police established a sobriety checkpoint program, complete with advisory committee, to govern the use of sobriety checkpoints in the state. The committee created guidelines for checkpoint operations, site selection, and publicity. Every vehicle at the site of a checkpoint was stopped and its driver briefly observed for signs of intoxication. If the officer at the checkpoint saw signs of intoxication, the driver was directed out of the traffic flow for examination of license and registration and a field sobriety test. Other drivers were permitted to pass through the checkpoint with minimal delay. During the 75-minute operation by the Saginaw County Sheriff's Department, 126 vehicles were checked. The average delay per vehicle was 25 seconds. Two drivers were detained and subsequently arrested for driving under the influence. A third driver drove through the checkpoint without stopping and was subsequently arrested for driving under the influence.

Sitz and others filed suit seeking an injunction to prohibit the checkpoint program from being implemented. The issue before the Supreme Court was whether a sobriety checkpoint violated the Fourth Amendment. In deciding this issue, the Court considered two issues: privacy and governmental interest.

In *Sitz,* the Court found that police had a governmental interest in eliminating drunken driving. Applying the balancing test in *Martinez-Forte* to the facts in *Sitz,* the Court saw "virtually no difference between the levels of intrusion on law-abiding motorists from the brief stops necessary to the effectuation of these two types of checkpoints, which to the average motorist would seem identical save for the nature of the questions the checkpoint officers might ask" (496 U.S. 444, at 452, 453). The Court held that sobriety checkpoints did not violate the Fourth and Fourteenth Amendments, as the sole intention of the checkpoint was highway safety, and the small intrusion upon those stopped was insignificant and, therefore, constitutional.

The privacy issue raised by the Court in *Sitz* involved balancing the government's interest in the prevention of drunk driving and the level of intrusion on motorist privacy caused by the checkpoint. Extending the rationale discussed in *Martinez-Fuerte,* the Court determined that there was very little difference in the two types of checkpoints, one for illegal aliens and the other for sobriety, other than the questions asked of the driver. As such, the Court ruled that the invasion of a motorist's privacy was minimal, and therefore constitutional.

RANDOM CHECKS FOR LICENSE AND REGISTRATION

The final issue discussed by the Court in *Edmond* was random police checks for driver's licenses and vehicle registration. The leading case for this issue is *Delaware v. Prouse* (1979).

A police officer stopped an automobile occupied by Prouse. As he walked toward the stopped vehicle, the officer smelled marijuana smoke. Investigating further, he found marijuana in plain view on the vehicle floorboard. At trial, the officer testified that he did not note any traffic or equipment violations prior to stopping Prouse's vehicle. He only stopped Prouse to check his license and registration.

The issue before the Court was a balancing test between legitimate governmental interests and the individual's privacy with respect to the Fourth Amendment. In *Prouse,* the government argued that officers should be given the greatest latitude in stopping cars without probable cause, since the government's interest in roadway safety outweighed the resulting intrusion on individual privacy.

The Court, relying on its previous decision in *Ortiz*, reiterated that roving patrol stops by Border Patrol officers on any type of roadway without reasonable suspicion were not permissible. While the state had an interest in traffic and roadway safety, the Court stated that with "alternative mechanisms available, both those in use and those which might be adopted, we are unconvinced that the incremental contribution to highway safety of the random spot check justifies the practice under the Fourth Amendment" (440 U.S. 648 at 659).

The Court held that police must have at least articulable and reasonable suspicion that the motorist is unlicensed, the automobile is not registered, or the vehicle or occupant is subject to seizure for violation of the law before the automobile can be stopped for a license or registration check. The Court, however, declared that states may develop methods for spot checks that involve either less intrusion or constrained discretion. Specifically, the Court suggested that questioning of all traffic at a checkpoint was one possible alternative to a random traffic stop.

A later Supreme Court case, *New York v. Class* (1986), dealt with a routine traffic stop where police officers found a weapon. Officers observed a car that was traveling over the speed limit with a cracked windshield. After they pulled the car over, the driver produced proof of insurance and registration, but was unable to produce a valid driver's license. In an effort to locate the Vehicle Identification Number (VIN), the officer opened the left door of the car and then moved papers from the dashboard to view the VIN. In the process, the officer saw a gun, seized it, and charged the driver with illegal possession of a firearm.

The Supreme Court held in this case that the officer acted within the bounds of the Fourth Amendment. The Court held that it is within an officer's right to obtain the VIN; and if the occupant had remained in the car, he would have been required to produce it. This case is consistent with *Edmond*, which does not prohibit an examination of the vehicle provided the police have reasonable suspicion to make the stop. *Edmond* only prohibits checkpoints used for general crime control purposes.

RATIONALE

The Fourth Amendment does not prohibit searches and seizures. It does, however, prohibit unreasonable searches and seizures, including the seizure of an automobile at a traffic stop or vehicle checkpoint without probable cause or particularized suspicion, absent the three major circumstances previously discussed (immigration, sobriety, license and registration).

The Court in *Edmond* paid particular attention to the reason for the stop, noting that walking "a narcotics detection dog around the exterior of each car . . . does not transform the seizure into a search." In *United States v. Place* (1983), the Court upheld checkpoints for the purposes of a sniff by a narcotics-detection dog. What is different in *Edmond* is the primary purpose of the checkpoint. The government argued that the checkpoints were designed primarily to interdict the flow of illegal drugs in Indianapolis, which the government saw as a compelling state interest. The Court disagreed, finding that the primary purpose of the program was to uncover evidence of ordinary criminal conduct.

The Court further distinguished *Edmond* from *Sitz*. In *Sitz*, the government clearly articulated a need for sobriety checkpoints. In *Edmond*, the government could not make the same argument. The Court found that drug interdiction broadly served the safety of the community, but did not present the immediate, vehicular threat to life and limb seen in the case of drunk driving.

The Court, in further distinguishing *Edmond*, focused on the primary purpose of the checkpoint program. The government argued that the secondary purpose of the checkpoint was to keep impaired motorists off the road and to check vehicle licenses and registration. The Court found the primary purpose to be "generally indistinguishable from the general interest in crime control." The Court's decision, therefore, was that roadblocks with only a general interest are in violation of the Fourth Amendment.

SUMMARY AND CONCLUSION

The Supreme Court was forthright in its holding in *Edmond*. There must be a legitimate governmental interest beyond a general interest in crime control to hold a vehicle checkpoint. The Court was careful to point out that the holding in *Edmond* does not affect border searches, sobriety checkpoints, or checkpoints related to vehicular and driver safety. At any of these types of checkpoints, arrests can be made on individualized suspicion that the actors are involved in criminal activity.

Each of these checkpoints was designed to serve a purpose closely related to halting the flow of illegal immigrants or ensuring roadway safety. The facts and circumstances in *Edmond* did not fall within the exemption parameters stated by the Court. The government, in *Edmond,* conceded that the primary purpose of the checkpoints were to interdict illegal narcotics, even to the point of referring to the checkpoints as drug checkpoints.

Edmond prohibited two types of checkpoints. First, the Court prohibited a checkpoint that has only a general crime control function rather than a specific purpose. Second, the Court placed police officers on notice that it will examine the purpose of a vehicular registration checkpoint to ensure that it is not being used as a pretext for generalized intrusion.

REFERENCES

WALKER, S. 1999. *The police in America: An introduction* (3rd ed.). Boston: McGraw-Hill.

WHITEBREAD, C. H., & SLOBOGIN, C. 2000. *Criminal procedure: An analysis of cases and concepts* (4th ed.). New York: Foundation Press.

Cases Cited

- *Almeida-Sanchez v. United States*, 413 U.S. 266 (1973)
- *Camara v. Municipal Court*, 387 U.S. 523 (1967)
- *Carroll v. United States*, 267 U.S. 132 (1925)
- *Delaware v. Prouse,* 440 U.S. 648 (1979)
- *Indianapolis v. Edmond,* 99-1030 (2000)
- *Michigan Department of State Police v. Sitz*, 496 U.S. 444 (1990)
- *New York v. Class*, 475 U.S. 106 (1986)
- *Robbins v. California*, 453 U.S. 420 (1981)
- *United States v. Brignoni-Ponce*, 422 U.S. 873 (1975)
- *United States v. Cortez,* 449 U.S. 411(1981)
- *United States v. Martinez-Fuerte*, 428 U.S. 543 (1976)
- *United States v. Ortiz*, 422 U.S. 891 (1975)

4

Civil Liabilities and Arrest Decisions

Dennis J. Stevens

❖

INTRODUCTION

What do these incidents have in common?

- In December 1996, in a period of two weeks, two men died in handcuffs while in custody of Palm Beach County sheriff's deputies in Florida. One died of asphyxia from pepper spray while handcuffed behind the back in a prone position. Several days earlier, another person died after being restrained by a deputy.
- In January 1997, a man was shot and killed by a Pawtucket, Rhode Island, police officer after a low-speed car chase. The man, who was unarmed, was suspected of driving a stolen car.
- In February 1997, an unarmed motorist was kicked and punched by three Hartford, Connecticut, police officers after a brief chase that ended in front of a Bloomfield, Connecticut, police station. The beating was so severe that Bloomfield police officers intervened.
- In January 2000, a San Antonio, Texas, officer, while working part-time as a security officer for Dillard's, was implicated in the choke-hold death of a man who reportedly was in violation of disorderly conduct. Dillard's settled the claim for $1.1 million.[1]
- In September 2000, the sheriff of Tulia, Texas, while involved in an undercover drug bust, arrested almost 10 percent of the African-American population of the

---

[1]Aired on CBS, *20/20,* March 26, 2001.

city, a rural farming and ranching community of about 5,000. The sheriff prepared a list of people he considered "undesirables" before enacting a policy to strong-arm them out of Swisher County.[2]

In each of the preceding cases, the police officers involved were subject to civil and possibly criminal litigation that could have, among other things, resulted in their being suspended or even terminated from the job.

Whether reality or conjecture, there is a popular conception that the American public possesses a litigious nature. Suing police officers has become much more frequent, fueled in part by the pursuit of a corruption-free government by means of exaggerated regulations, ambiguous judicial control, and misinformed intervention (IACP, 1994a; Kappeler, 1997; Sullivan, 1994). This chapter does not debate the temperament of the American public or the merits of substantive laws. The question is: are uniformed officers less likely to do their duty in certain situations if they have a perception that they may be defendants in a civil liability suit (del Carmen, 1991, 1994)?

Almost every aspect of police work may result in an incident that can lead to civil litigation (IACP, 1994a). There is also a potential for criminal liability under federal law for certain deprivations of constitutional rights. One estimate suggests that police are currently involved in more than 30,000 civil actions annually, and that the frequency of plaintiffs prevailing in their suits is on the rise (Kappeler, 1997; Silver, 1996). Police officers often report that civil litigation was irrational and excessive (Scogin & Brodsky, 1991). Nonetheless, the fear of being named a defendant in a suit seeking punitive damages is not unreasonable. The possibility of litigation may cause an officer to question his or her abilities, second-guess decisions, and hesitate before taking appropriate police initiatives (Stewart & Hart, 1993). For some officers, therefore, the threat of litigation could translate into poor police service, which ultimately might compromise public safety.

This chapter examines these issues and brings evidence to the notion that the threat of civil litigation can influence the decision an officer might make concerning an arrest. Specifically, the chapter addresses the issue of whether the threat of police officer litigation influences arrest decisions. Should evidence from the study reported here support this idea, it could be argued with some degree of confidence that the variables of arrest rate and the threat of police officer litigation are more related than previously thought.

BACKGROUND ON CIVIL LIABILITY ISSUES

Suits filed against police officers alleging a constitutional violation are generally founded on 42 U.S.C., Section 1983, a statute which imposes civil liability on any person acting under state laws who deprives another person of his or her constitutional rights. The constitutional protection claimed to have been violated is frequently either the Fourth Amendment (alleged unlawful arrest or search), the Fifth Amendment (alleged improperly obtained confession or deprivation of liberty or property without proper due process), the Sixth Amendment (violating the right to counsel), or the Eighth Amendment (incarceration of a plaintiff claiming to have been subjected to cruel and unusual punishment). The defenses available are technical in nature, including improper service and venue and lack

---

[2]For more detail, see ACLU [On-line]. Available: http://www.aclu.org/library/ycl00/law.html.

of jurisdiction. In addition, the first argument to be made is that the plaintiff failed to state a claim against the police officer upon which relief can be granted. The second avenue is the qualified immunity defense, which shields the police officer from liability (Higginbotham, 1985).

Police officers acting illegally and outside their scope of authority may be liable under Section 1983 despite the requirement that they had to have been acting under "color of state law" (del Carmen, 1991).[3] According to Title 42 U.S.C., Section 1983, the words "color of state law" include all conduct of police officers even when they are acting under statute, ordinance, regulation, custom, or usage of any law.[4] One way to interpret the statute is that any person who causes another person to be subjected to the deprivation of any rights, privileges, or immunities guaranteed by the Constitution may be liable even if that person is conducting police business. Most suits brought against police officers fall within Section 1983 of Title 42.

In recent years, the U.S. Supreme Court has demonstrated a tendency to narrow Section 1983 liability (McCormack, 1993; Smith, 1995). For instance, the Court tried to balance the needs of police personnel and criminal suspects by developing two types of immunity—absolute and qualified—for police officials who are sued for alleged constitutional violations (McCormack, 1993). These developments have undoubtedly pleased police agencies that face the specter of civil liability while having to make quick decisions under difficult circumstances; however, limiting police officer exposure to Section 1983 claims is a double-edged sword. Over time, it may increase the incidence of unlawful police actions, and foster protectionism, police cover-ups, and divisiveness between the police and the community (Kappeler, 1997; Schofield, 1990). To the extent that civil remedies for constitutional violations are reduced, the rationale for retaining the exclusionary rule remains. Nonetheless, this chapter will argue that the threat of civil liabilities shapes police officer conduct.

CIVIL LIABILITY CONCERNS

The past two decades have shown a tremendous increase in the propensity of citizens to sue police officers (Anechiarico & Jacobs, 1996; del Carmen, 1991; IACP, 1994b). Civil suits against officers and the desire for a corruption-free government may have produced unanticipated outcomes (Stevens, 2001). For instance, arrests have fallen sharply in New York City since four officers were indicted in the fatal shooting of Amadou Diallo (Barstow, 1999). According to figures recently released by the New York City Police Department, the number of people arrested in April 1999 fell to 30,134, from 35,813 in

---

[3]See Smith (1995). Section 1983 creates no substantive rights; rather, it is a vehicle for suing defendants acting under the color of state law for violating another person's federal rights. By its very terms, Section 1983 applies only to persons acting under the color of state law. Thus, it is applicable only to state and local law enforcement officers who exert authority derived from state law. To state a claim under Section 1983, a plaintiff must allege that he or she was deprived of a federal right and that the person who deprived the plaintiff of that right acted under the color of state or territorial law.

[4]For a more detailed discussion, see *Thomas v. Reagan*, USDC Cr. No. 84-3552 [On-line]. Available: http://www.prop1.org/legal/843552/870108a2.htm.

March, a 14 percent decline. Police officials attributed the decline in arrests to fewer crimes reported. They noted that complaints of crime were down 12 percent in the first four months of 1999 compared with the same period the preceding year. The April 1999 drop-off was considerably more pronounced than in previous months; but crime rates have been falling for years, even as the number of arrests have risen. This has some police officials searching for other explanations, including the possibility of fallout from the death of Diallo (Barstow, 1999). Clearly, criminal prosecution is far different from a civil liability suit, but a concern held by many officers is whether the department would back them in the event of a suit regardless of its nature. Certainly, high-profile cases can help shape public opinion, including among police officers. The president of the NYPD's Patrolmen's Benevolent Association, the city's largest police union, urged officers to use "maximum discretion" when citing people for minor offenses (Barstow, 1999). He said that the city's crackdown on minor violations, such as drinking alcohol in public, had harmed relations between the police and the public.

Another example comes from the Los Angeles Police Department, which reported that litigation against police officers cost the city more than $322 million from 1992 to 1997 (Newton, 1996). The suits ranged from police shootings to civil rights violations. Arrests by the Los Angeles Police Department dropped precipitously during that period, from 290,000 to 189,000. This trend exceeded the modest dip in reported crimes, and appears at odds with the LAPD's growth over the same period (Newton, 1996). Police officials said they were alarmed about the lower arrest rates, and feared that the decline was evidence that police officers were no longer pursuing their jobs with the same vigor as before the Rodney King beating (Newton, 1996). For example, after Timothy Edward Wind and Theodore Joseph Brisino were fired despite their acquittals in criminal cases and being found not liable for damages in a civil case concerning the Rodney King beating (Cannon, 1999), some officers might feel that keeping their jobs took priority over police intervention.

Furthermore, police officers in a national study indicated that they were unclear about how their commanders or the criminal justice system would support them if they were named a defendant in a suit (Stevens, 1999a). Some police officers reported that they did not trust their commanders or the public (Stevens, 1999a, 1999b, 1999c). There are many court decisions that erode officers' confidence in the system. For example, New York has no responsibility to pay the fees of an attorney to defend an officer if that officer violated city departmental rules [*Schwartz v. City of New York* (1999)]. Also, in California, an appeals court ruled that a city has no responsibility to provide legal defense for an officer accused of an alleged crime [*San Diego Police Officers Association v. City of San Diego* (1999)]. Furthermore, a California county has no duty to provide individual sheriff's deputies with independent counsel in civil rights lawsuits [*Laws v. County of San Diego* (1990)]. The threat of an ever-escalating award of attorney's fees in a Section 1983 lawsuit can force some police officer defendants to settle suits before trial, even when the validity of the suit is suspect (McCormack, 1994).

The department, too, may be unclear about civil liability expectations. For example, a plaintiff's son had been shot four times at close range by a police officer during a street disturbance, and died ("City liable," 1999). The plaintiff settled claims against the officer before trial, and the jury considered only federal civil rights claims against the city. The jury awarded \$330,000 in damages, finding that the department's training program, which consisted of only a movie and a lecture on the use of deadly force, was constitutionally inadequate. A federal appeals court upheld the result, finding that the inadequate training provided indicated that the city was "deliberately indifferent" to the need for more training on the use of deadly force ("City liable," 1999). The court found sufficient evidence in the record to show that the officer's use of deadly force was unjustified, including testimony that the officer had his weapon out while the defendant was facing away from him with his hands in the air. The appeals court also criticized the city's lack of live drills providing practice on when to shoot or not to shoot, in addition to movies and lectures ("City liable," 1999). In another case, a jury awarded the plaintiffs \$1.6 million against an off-duty officer and the city. The court found that the officer, although off-duty, was an agent of the city acting within the scope of his duty, and therefore the city could be held liable for the officer's actions ("Off duty," 1999).

It can be argued that lawsuit prerogatives are often confusing. For instance, a service station clerk held as a hostage brought suit against the Tampa Police Department, claiming mistakes by the police caused her to be held at gunpoint for four hours (Gettleman, 1998). The hostage's attorney said, "The police were negligent several times that day, and that's why Stephanie was injured. We have enormous sympathy for the detectives who were killed, but that doesn't mean we can't say that mistakes were made" (Gettleman, 1998, p. 3). On the other hand, federal prosecutors decided not to charge one of the hostage-takers with violating federal firearms laws in concert with her boyfriend, who had killed her son and three police officers (Gettleman, 1998).

Furthermore, some researchers have surprisingly discovered, in a comparison between constitutional appellate decisions and trial court outcomes in shaping police policy, that civil liability lawsuits have led to police policy changes more frequently than decisions by the U.S. Supreme Court in recent years (Smith & Hurst, 1997). There is a tendency, however, among police officers to resist new police policy, such as community policing directives (Dicker, 1998).[5] Continuing along this thought, therefore, one might argue that there could be some resistance toward conducting a probable cause arrest. When an officer is making a decision between a stop and a probable cause arrest, this chapter argues that the threat of a lawsuit against the officer will influence his or her decision. This conclusion is based on a survey of police officers representing twenty-one police departments in eleven states.

METHODOLOGY

To examine the attitudes of police officers on the threat of civil liability potential and probable cause arrests, 711 sworn officers from twenty-one police agencies in all states were surveyed. The agencies were selected based on their ongoing cooperation with the writer in other research endeavors.

---

[5]For a closer look at the causes of officer resistance, see Dicker (1998), who suggests that supervision trust, satisfaction with the amount of control of one's work environment, rank, organizational trust, and level of pride in the department play the largest role toward resistance. See also chapter 7 in this text.

Sample and Administration

A survey was developed and e-mailed to police agencies in eleven states. These police agencies and their web site coordinators were known to the researcher due to having obtained data about their departments for other research. Many of the web site coordinators, who were sworn officers themselves, duplicated the questionnaire, distributed it to the sworn officers in their jurisdiction, collected it, and mailed the surveys to the researcher. The survey showed the home address of the researcher for respondents who wished to mail their completed questionnaire directly to the researcher rather than returning it to the web site coordinator. Approximately 220 completed questionnaires were mailed directly to the researcher by the respondents, and 491 were mailed to the researcher by web site coordinators. Of the 711 received, 53 were less than one-half completed and/or were illegible and were disregarded. The data from the remaining 658 questionnaires were transcribed and used in this study.

Questionnaire

The questionnaire consisted of thirty-five questions. Nine of the questions asked for demographic information. One question asked the respondents to rank-order three of the most serious problems facing officers. Another question asked respondents to write-in a rank-ordered response as to why the typical officer would not take a suspect into custody when both the suspect and the evidence were present. A series of questions asked about the officer's past in the sense of confronting violators and arresting them. One of the arrest questions asked for a scaled response concerning experiences with arrest rates. Another question asked what type of training should be emphasized at police academies. Seventeen questions were in a scale that asked respondents to select numerically how often a typical officer might not take a suspect into custody when both the offender and the evidence were present.

Analysis Procedures

Frequency distributions were reviewed to eliminate errors in the data. Often the frequency counts were used to better understand the data and the links between the independent variables (including civil liability suits) and the dependent variable (a probable cause arrest). The primary methods of examination were correlation tests, crosstabs, and Chi Square. Since the data were all ordinal, regression was utilized to help the researcher further an understanding of the links between the variables, but was not used in the final analysis. Most would argue that regression is not appropriate for ordinal level data.

FINDINGS

When the data were pooled and examined, distinctive patterns lent support to the hypothesis that the threat of litigation influenced arrest decisions. That is, the possibility of becoming a defendant in a civil liability suit interfered with an officer's decision to conduct a probable cause arrest of a violator.

Demographic Information

The demographic and other characteristics of the respondents to the sample are shown in Table 4.1. The average sworn officer in this study had ten years of experience as a police officer, with a range from one year to twenty-five years, and generally held the rank of patrol officer or deputy sheriff, although there were also eight deputy chiefs among the respondents. Fifty-one percent (334) of the participants reported that they were white, 25 percent (166) reported that they were black, 14 percent (93) were Hispanic, 9 percent (57) were Asian, and 1 percent (8) were "other." The typical officer was thirty-five years of age with an age range from twenty-one to fifty-three. Twenty-nine percent (193) of the respondents reported that they were married, 45 percent (295) were single, 20 percent (129) were divorced, 4 percent (28) were separated, and 1 percent (4) were widowed. The average respondent reported two dependent children living at home, with a range from zero to four. The typical respondent reported thirteen years of education with a range from twelve years to eighteen years; and 7 percent (45) of the respondents reported that they held a master's degree.

From the twenty-one agencies involved, 21 percent (135) of the respondents reported that they worked for a police agency in Massachusetts, 16 percent (105) worked in North Carolina, 11 percent (70) in Florida, 10 percent (66) in California, 9 percent (62) in Wisconsin, 9 percent (61) in Virginia, 6 percent (42) in Michigan, 6 percent (40) in Tennessee, 5 percent (36) in Ohio, 4 percent (25) in Texas, and 2 percent (16) in Oklahoma. It was estimated that the involved agencies employed approximately 11,000 sworn officers at the time of this research. Therefore, the 658 respondents appear to represent approximately 8 percent of the officers employed in all those agencies.

Serious Challenges

In one question, participants were asked to rank-order three serious challenges from a list of ten items (the combinations selected totaled 1,782 different responses). From this list, 21 percent (367 of 1,782) of the respondents reported drug dealers as the most serious problem facing the typical police officer (see Table 4.2). Eighteen percent (315) of the respondents reported that police officer training was the second-most-serious problem encountered by officers. A tie for third place was reported by 15 percent (262) of the respondents, who stated that civil liabilities and paperwork were the next-most-serious problems for police officers. At first glance, therefore, it might appear that the threat of a civil suit plays only a small role in an officer's decision to take a suspect into custody.

Arrest Experiences

When the officers were asked about their experiences with arrests today as compared to three years ago, 59 percent (346) of the participants reported that they made fewer arrests today (sixty-nine respondents had not been employed as officers for more than two years). When the officers were asked about their arrest experiences five years ago as compared to today, 62 percent (324) of them reported that they made fewer arrests today (there were 138 missing cases, largely due to 116 respondents who did not work in policing five years ago); however, in another question, 71 percent (369) of the respondents reported that they

TABLE 4.1   Characteristics of Sample (N = 658)

Category	Mean/Percent[a]	Range/Number
Years of service	10 years	1–25
Rank	Patrol	Patrol–Deputy Chief
Duties	Patrol	Patrol–Administration
Race		
White	51%	334
Black	25%	166
Hispanic	14%	93
Asian	9%	57
Other	1%	8
Age	35	21–53
Gender		
Male	88%	580
Female	12%	77
Marital status		
Married	29%	193
Single	45%	295
Divorced	20%	129
Separated	4%	28
Widowed	1%	4
Dependent children	2	0–4
Years of education	13	12–18
4-year degree	7%	45
Location of Sample		
Massachusetts	21%	135
North Carolina	16%	105
Florida	11%	70
California	10%	66
Wisconsin	9%	62
Virginia	9%	61
Michigan	6%	42
Tennessee	6%	40
Ohio	5%	36
Texas	4%	25
Oklahoma	2%	16

[a]Missing cases are not shown; all percents are rounded.

TABLE 4.2   Serious Challenges (N = 658)

Serious challenges	Percent of selections[a]	Number of selections[b]
Drug traders	21%	367
Police officer training	18%	315
Civil liabilities	15%	262
Paperwork	15%	260
Gangs	13%	228
Weapons and equipment	7%	116
Cooperation between agencies	4%	73
Training of prosecutors	3%	57
Supervisors	2%	41
Lack of staff/backup	1%	30
Other	2%	33
Totals	100%	1782

[a]Rounded, missing cases not shown.
[b]Each respondent had up to three choices.

confronted more suspects today than they had in the past three and/or five years as police officers. Further examination shows that the more experienced officers reported fewer arrests today than in the past but were more frequently confronted with suspects in situations where a probable cause arrest could be conducted. This is consistent with earlier studies reporting that narcotics officers felt that they confronted more offenders today than in the past, yet also reported that they arrested fewer drug abusers and drug dealers than previously (Stevens, 1999c). In both studies, one predictor of fewer arrests was the officer's experience.

Arrest Obstacles

When the participants were asked to write-in three reasons (totaling 1,941 answers) why a typical officer would not take an individual into custody when evidence suggested an arrest should be conducted, distinctive patterns again arose. To analyze these results, responses were placed into ten categories (see Table 4.3). Twenty percent (379) of the 1,941 responses written-in by the participants reported that paperwork and/or booking time was the greatest obstacle against taking a suspect into custody even when the evidence suggested an officer should. Eighteen percent of the respondents (354) reported that training and/or skills were the second barrier to a probable cause arrest. Fourteen percent (277) reported that waiting on warrants and/or writing a citation shaped officer decisions concerning an arrest, while 11 percent (222) of the respondents reported that minor crimes and/or victimless crimes were barriers to an arrest. Another 11 percent (216) of the respondents reported that civil liabilities promoted alternatives to arrest even when the evidence suggested that an officer should take the suspect into custody. Nine percent (170) of the respondents characterized complaints as a barrier to an arrest, 7 percent (127) of the respondents reported that police supervisors, judges, and prosecutors were roadblocks to an arrest, while another 4 percent (68) of the respondents reported that a lack of staff and/or backup influenced a decision to arrest. Three percent (65) of the responses reported that officer laziness and/or little incentive were obstacles in conducting an arrest, and 2 percent (33) of the responses reported that community policing initiatives and/or an officer's changing job assignments led to other avenues of action. Lastly, 2 percent (30) of the responses reported such influences as departmental politics, advancement considerations, state attorney's directives, peer pressure, and no jail space as factors motivating officers into other courses of action. To be considered a separate category, at least twenty respondents had to respond in a similar manner. Of the responses that were not categorized separately, respondents indicated that officers were working in a lower crime rate area than in the past, such as police trainers who rarely confronted suspects. Other reasons reported by the participants included an inefficient court system, "directed not to" because of other actions pending, and that the offense carried stricter penalties than the respondents felt matched the crime, such as drug possession.

Overall, the sample reported that paperwork, training/skills, and warrants/citations were the three most important reasons why the typical officer did not take a suspect into custody. This finding does not necessarily show that a strong relationship exists between civil liabilities and arrest decisions, yet it does indicate that one in ten arrests could be influenced by civil liability issues. Nonetheless, while minor crime/victimless crimes and civil liabilities were tied for fourth place, further examination showed that there was a strong relationship between training and civil liabilities.

TABLE 4.3   Arrest Obstacles (N = 658)

Obstacles	Percent of selections[a]	Number of selections[b]
Paperwork	20%	379
Training/skills	18%	354
Warrants/citations	14%	277
Minor crime	11%	222
Civil liabilities	11%	216
Complaints	9%	170
Supervisor/judge/prosecutor	7%	127
Lack of staff/backup	4%	68
Laziness/no incentive	3%	65
Community policing/change	2%	33
Other	2%	30
Totals	100%	1941

[a]Rounded, missing cases represented as a zero response.
[b]Each respondent had up to three choices.

Training

When the respondents were asked which topics should be emphasized at police training academies, 38 percent (248) of the participants reported that civil liabilities should be accentuated. Twenty-four percent (159) reported that community policing initiatives should be emphasized. Twelve percent (81) reported that tactical efforts should be emphasized, while 8 percent (51) reported that supervision courses should take precedence. Seven percent (43) of the participants reported that drug and alcohol programs might be best, while 5 percent (31) reported that traffic courses should be accented. Four percent (24) reported that administration-type programs would be the most welcome, and 3 percent (21) of the sample either reported "other" as their best choice or did not answer the question.

One implication from the selections of the respondents is that civil liability issues appear to be an important yet misunderstood concern among police officers. Furthermore, it could be argued with some degree of confidence that if police officers are thinking about liability skills under favorable conditions, such as while taking a survey, it is equally likely that they think about liability issues when confronted by an offender. The argument can be made, then, that when the respondents are in the field, civil suits are a more salient issue, especially among experienced officers, who have probably witnessed the consequences of officer litigation more often than less-experienced officers. As stated above, it was the more-experienced officers who reported fewer arrests today than in the past but were confronted with more probable cause arrest situations. Lastly, as noted in the "Serious Challenges" section of this chapter, the respondents ranked training as the second-most-serious challenge among officers.

Arrest Rates and Training

Further examination of arrest rates and obstacles to training showed that of the 283 participants who reported that they made fewer arrests today as compared to three and/or five years ago, 41 percent (116) of them also reported that the major focus of police academies should be on civil liabilities. Cross tabulation shows a Chi Square score of 78.604, DF 35, and significant at .000 (21 missing responses). This finding is consistent with the research of the North Carolina Department of Justice (1997), which discovered that 47 percent of the narcotics officers in a statewide survey stated that legal courses were what they required to accomplish their jobs.

On the other hand, of the 181 respondents who reported that they were making a similar number of arrests today as compared with previous years, the highest percentage (55 or 31 percent) reported that community policing initiatives were responsible for their decisions not to take a suspect into custody. As a matter of record, the respondents reported that on a typical shift an average officer might have five interactions with individuals where the officer believes there is probable cause for an arrest. The participants added, however, that on average, only one arrest would be typically conducted.

Offenses Committed and Frequency of Arrest

Of further interest were the reported responses by the participants to the scale concerning the likelihood of arrest when a typical officer might have both the suspect and the evidence present at the same time. When the data were examined, distinctive patterns of attitudinal characteristics of the participants emerged, centered on the offender's gender, age, citizen status, affiliation, and the level of respect shown the officer at the time of the encounter. That is, young and elderly people were less likely to be taken into custody than adults, males were subject to arrest more often than females, and immigrants were very often if not always subject to an arrest. More specifically, youths who shoplifted, sold a joint, drank a beer, and smoked cigarettes or a joint were less likely to be taken into custody than an adult male or female who was driving while intoxicated (see Table 4.4). These arrests are consistent with governmental reports (Bureau of Justice Statistics, 1999). On the other hand, domestic violence calls produced arrests 78 percent of the time (always or very often), probably due to mandatory arrest laws. Furthermore, elderly shoplifters, females with illegal weapons, male middle managers, and females working for hospice units were less often arrested even when evidence was presented that they should be. Suspects cussing at an officer at an altercation site were sometimes subject to arrest, while a domestic dispute between a police officer and his or her spouse, or crime between gang members were just as likely to lead to an arrest. Almost all of the time (95 percent), immigrants were always or very often arrested during an eviction process or for fighting when an officer confronted them.

One implication of these results is that officers tend to arrest more often in situations where the threat of a civil liability suit is less likely, due to outside influences on the arrest decision as opposed to subjective influences. That is, driving while intoxicated violators (measurements of intoxication are objective), immigrants (may have less confidence in bringing suit against the police than others), and domestic violence calls (mandated intervention) produced arrests more often. Thus, it can be inferred that officers make arrests when they are less likely to be defendants in a civil suit than when they are more likely to become defendants.

LIMITATIONS

Research provides reason to believe that police officers, like those in many other occupations, cannot give valid inferences about factors that influence their decisions at work (Nisbett & Wilson, 1977). Other findings suggest that there is an important distinction between the self-image of the police and the day-to-day reality of routine policing, suggesting that some officers might embellish work-related experiences (Goldstein, 1977; Parks, Mastrofski, Dejong, & Gray 1999; Walker, 1999). For instance, the emphasis on crime control is and has been largely a matter of what the police say they are doing about crime as opposed to what is actually being done about crime (Dantzker, 2000; Manning, 1997; Walker, 1999). One implication is that some officers manipulate reports and findings to advance their professional and political autonomy. For instance, one study shows that there is a moderate acceptance of deviant lies for legitimate purposes among a sample of officers (Barker, Friery, & Carter, 1994). These researchers reported that a high proportion of their sample used "white lies" regularly in response to situations in which discretion was needed to resolve a problem. The researchers concluded that the root cause of the lies may have been frustration with the criminal justice system and the concerns officers have about apprehending lawbreakers. Thus, two points about the integrity of the responses of the officers in this chapter are: (1) this study does not relate to questions about resolving problems; and, (2) the

TABLE 4.4   Frequency of Arrest (N = 658)

Situation	Always	Very often	Some-times	Seldom	Never	Mean	Standard deviation
Youth shoplifting	0	14%	75%	11%	0	3.03	.52
Youth selling joint	1%	1%	38%	41%	20%	2.20	.79
One youth drinking beer	1%	6%	35%	40%	18%	2.31	.85
Female youth smoking	0	1%	21%	48%	30%	1.94	.75
Female youth smoking a joint	0	1%	5%	93%	1%	2.05	.30
Adult white male DWI	41%	58%	1%	0	0	4.40	.52
Adult white female DWI	36%	58%	4%	1%	0	4.29	.61
Domestic violence	29%	49%	11%	11%	1%	3.93	.96
Elderly female shop-lifting	1%	2%	35%	44%	19%	2.23	.81
Adult female illegal weapon	2%	4%	45%	31%	19%	2.39	.89
Adult professional male drug possession	19%	38%	25%	18%	0	3.58	1.00
Adult female hospice worker drug possession	0	1%	64%	34%	1%	2.63	.55
Suspect cussing at officer at scene	19%	40%	35%	6%	0	3.72	.84
Officer engaged in do-mestic violence	2%	43%	25%	29%	0	3.18	.89
Gang members versus gang members	8%	37%	30%	25%	0	3.29	.93
Immigrant eviction	32%	63%	4%	2%	0	4.24	.61
Immigrants fighting together	26%	69%	3%	1%	0	4.17	.71

Note: Rounded, missing variables not shown.
Scale: 5 = Always, 4 = Very Often, 3 = Sometimes, 2 = Seldom, 1 = Never

participants had no idea about the hypothesis; therefore it is unlikely that they would have lied to advance their professional and political autonomy.

CONCLUSION

The findings of this research suggest that many police officers do not conduct probable cause arrests when both offenders and evidence suggest they should. The individuals they were more likely to arrest were, in part, persons who were less likely than other offenders to bring a suit against them—driving while intoxicated offenders, whose credibility is suspect; politically powerless (or fearful) immigrants; and domestic violence participants due to mandated arrest regulations. The evidence implies that, as a result of the influence of civil liability suits, experienced officers made fewer probable cause arrests than other officers. Overall, one could argue that some officers are more concerned with the potential of personal litigation than in controlling societal crime.

This is not to say that liability questions played a key role in these decisions, since many factors influence an arrest decision, but they certainly were part of the decision, as is evident from the findings. A rival influence of civil liability influences as a predictor of probable cause arrest might relate to street justice. This thought is congruent with Sykes (1986), who confirms that street justice exists to provide an order-maintenance strategy used by the police as a central function of policing at the local level; therefore, arrests, even when evidence is present, would be less likely. Street justice is justified by some officers on moral grounds as part of their community-building and -maintaining functions. This idea is also consistent with Klockars (1999), who suggests that street justice is utilized by officers when they think the system is not administering appropriate justice or guidance to offenders. If we accept these notions, then civil liability concerns may be less of an influence on arrests than street justice strategies.

Nonetheless, as we look at the relationship between the threat of civil suits and arrest decisions, several implications link these two variables. For instance, it may be that liability concerns are doing exactly what they are supposed to do, which is to make police officers be concerned about their official actions with an eye on the law. This idea suggests that liability does provide a deterrent effect and protection for individuals in a democratic society. Also, if the participants in this study resemble the typical sworn officer in the United States, then it would be safe to argue that arrests are down not necessarily because crime is down, because these officers face more offenders than in the past, but largely because they are more likely to avoid an arrest than to make one, depending on the circumstances and the offender.

On the other hand, police executives need to be aware that newly recruited police officers are usually not familiar with the civil liability problem, and that even experienced officers have many misconceptions that need to be corrected (IACP, 1994b). In addition, the law of civil liability is constantly changing. Moreover, proper training in civil liability principles at all departmental levels reduces a police agency's civil liability exposure (IACP, 1994b). For instance, training and qualification programs on use of force can provide training and practice in both cognitive and manipulative skills that pertain to use of force, and protect officers against making decisions that will enhance the potential of a lawsuit (Stewart & Hart, 1993). Officer training in anger management and interpersonal communication is also recommended to de-escalate verbal challenges without risking First Amendment liability (Vaughn, 1996). Other writers seem to take a different approach. For instance, Kappeler (1997, p. 14) argues that "without consequences for unsanctioned behavior, there is no deterrence. The possibility of litigation has also created better training and more responsible practices."

Perhaps, training, incentives, and professional supervision are answers to quality police service. Of course, not all officers are crime-free, but my experience is that most police officers work hard at being good police officers and positive role-models, within limitations. However, it seems as if policing is responsible for certain behavioral outcomes within defined limitations in a pluralistic free society. Often the realities of policing include many difficult questions, producing some hard yet contradictory answers. Furthermore, the expectations of the American public and policy-makers concerning police work may be far different from the realities of the job, the resources, and the authority provided the men and the women who perform these tasks.

One hope of this research is to bridge the gap in the literature concerning police lawsuits and officer arrest decisions. Since only a very few studies link these two variables (del Carmen, 1991). A word of caution, however, is offered concerning this chapter. As stated earlier, it should be recognized that there are many influences which shape probable cause arrest decisions, many of which are beyond the scope of this work. The results of this study are congruent with Durkheim (1933, 1984), who argued some time ago that there is more than one cause for every effect. The findings of this study suggest that arrest decisions as final outcomes are influenced by numerous factors. One of the principal factors influencing arrests, based on the respondents in this study, is the threat of civil liabilities; therefore, the results relate only to the respondents, and may not reflect the attitudes of policing as a whole.

One concern the researcher realized after studying the results produced by the survey is that there should have been some procedure to gauge whether the risk of civil liability suits among the sample was greater today (i.e., when the participants completed the questionnaire) than years ago. In this respect, however, since the number of civil liability suits has increased from year to year, it is likely that the threat of civil liability suits has also increased. Thus, this chapter calls for future research to be conducted on the relationship between the threat of civil liability in previous years and the current threat of civil liability in today's world of policing.

REFERENCES

ANECHIARICO, F., & JACOBS, J. B. 1996. *The pursuit of absolute integrity*. Chicago: University of Chicago Press.

BARKER, T., FRIERY, R. N., & CARTER, D. L. 1994. After L.A., would your local police lie? In Thomas Barker and David L. Carter (Eds.), *Police deviance* (pp. 155–168). Cincinnati: Anderson.

BARSTOW, D. 1999. After officers' indictment in Diallo case, arrests drop in New York City. *New York Times*. May 6, p. 1.

BUREAU OF JUSTICE STATISTICS. 1999. *Sourcebook of criminal justice statistics* [On-line]. Available: http://www.albany.edu.

CANNON, L. 1999. American travesty: How justice failed the Rodney King cops. *National Review, 51,* 30.

"CITY LIABLE." 1999. *Liability reporter* [On-line]. Available: http://aele.org/lrsam.html.

DEL CARMEN, R. V. 1991. *Civil liabilities in American policing: A text for law enforcement personnel.* Englewood Cliffs, NJ: Prentice Hall.

DEL CARMEN, R. V. 1994. Civil and criminal liabilities of police officers. In Thomas Barker and David L. Carter (Eds.), *Police deviance* (pp. 409–429). Cincinnati: Anderson.

DANTZKER, M. L. 2000. *Understanding today's police* (2nd ed.). Upper Saddle River, NJ: Prentice Hall.

DICKER, T. J. 1998. Tension on the thin blue line: Police officer resistance to community oriented policing. *American Journal of Criminal Justice, 23*(1), 59–82.

DURKHEIM, E. 1984. *The division of labor in society.* Translated by W. D. Hall. New York: Free Press.

GETTLEMAN, J. 1998. Former hostage to sue police. *St. Petersburg Times.* June 26, p. 3.

GOLDSTEIN, H. 1977. *Policing a free society.* Cambridge, MA: Ballinger.

HIGGINBOTHAM, J. 1985. Defending law enforcement officers against personal liability in constitutional tort litigation (Part 1). *FBI Law Enforcement Bulletin, 54*(4), 24–31.

IACP (International Association of Chiefs of Police). 1994a. *Civil liability part II: Civil liability avoidance.* NCJ 50512. [On-line]. Available: http://excalib1.aspensys.com

IACP (International Association of Chiefs of Police). 1994b. *Civil liability part I: Basic principles of civil liability.* NCJ 50511. [On-line]. Available: http://excalib1.aspensys.com.

KAPPELER, V. E. 1997. *Critical issues in police civil liability.* Prospect Heights, IL: Waveland Press.

KLOCKARS, C. B. 1999. Street justice: some micro moral reservations. Comment on Sykes. In Victor E. Kappeler (Ed.), *The police and society* (pp. 150–154). Prospect Heights, IL: Waveland Press.

MANNING, P. 1997. *Police work.* Prospect Heights, IL: Waveland Press.

McCORMACK, W. U. 1993. Civil liability and police prosecutor relations. *FBI Law Enforcement Bulletin, 62*(2), 28–32.

McCORMACK, W. U. 1994. Attorney's fees in civil litigation—controlling the costs. *FBI Law Enforcement Bulletin, 63*(4), 28–32.

NEWTON, J. 1996. Number of arrests by LAPD plunges since '91. *Los Angeles Times.* March 13, p. 1.

NISBETT, J., & WILSON, R. 1977. Telling more than we can know: Verbal reports on mental processes. *Psychological Review, 84*(3), 231–259.

"OFF DUTY COLOR OF LAW." 1999. *Liability reporter* [On-line]. Available: http://www.aele.org/lrsm.html.

PARKS, R. B., MASTROFSKI, S. D., DEJONG, C., & GRAY, M. K. 1999. How officers spend their time with the community. *Justice Quarterly, 16*(3), 483–517.

SCHOFIELD, D. L. 1990. Personal liability: The qualified immunity defense. *FBI Law Enforcement Bulletin, 59*(3), 26–32.

SCOGIN, F., & BRODSKY, S. L. 1991. Fear of litigation among law enforcement officers. *American Journal of Police, 10*(1), 41–45.

SILVER, I. 1996. *Police civil liability.* New York: Matthew Bender.

SMITH, C. E., & HURST, J. 1997. The forms of judicial policymaking: Civil liability and criminal justice policy. *Justice System Journal, 19*(3), 341–354.

SMITH M. R. 1995. Law enforcement liability under Section 1983. *Criminal Law Bulletin, 31*(2), 128–150.

STEVENS, D. J. 1999a. American police resolutions and community response. *Police Journal, 72* (2), 140–150.

STEVENS, D. J. 1999b. Corruption among narcotic officers: A study of innocence and integrity. *Journal of Police and Criminal Psychology, 14*(23), 1–10.

STEVENS, D. J. 1999c. Stress and the American police officer. *Police Journal, 72*(3), 247–259.

STEVENS, D. J. 2001. *Case studies in community policing.* Upper Saddle River, NJ: Prentice Hall.

STEWART, S., & HART, B. 1993. Reducing the cost of civil litigation: Use of force incidents. *Law and Order, 41*(5), 31–34.

SYKES, G. W. 1986. Street justice: A moral defense of order maintenance policing. *Justice Quarterly, 3*(4), 497–512.

SULLIVAN, J. J. 1994. *Guide to the laws of civil liabilities for New York law enforcement officers: Key data you need to know to protect your career.* NCJ 154176.

TELEMASP BULLETIN. 1999, January. Why the drop in crime? *Texas Law Enforcement Management and Administrative Statistic Program.* Huntsville, TX: Bill Blackwood Law Enforcement Management Institute of Texas, Sam Houston State University.

VAUGHN, M. S. 1996. Police civil liability and the First Amendment: Retaliation against citizens who criticize and challenge the police. *Crime & Delinquency, 42*(1), 50–75.

WALKER, S. 1999. *The police in america.* (2nd ed.). Boston: McGraw Hill College.

WILSON, J. Q. 1960. *Varieties of police behavior.* Cambridge: Harvard University Press.

Cases Cited

- *Laws v. County of San Diego*, 267 Cal. Rptr. 921 (1990).
- *San Diego Police Officers Association v. City of San Diego,* 29 Cal. App. 4th 1736 (1994).
- *Schwartz v. City of New York,* 57 F.3d 236 (2nd Cir. 1995).

5

That Dog *Will* Hunt

Canine-Assisted Search and Seizure

James W. Golden

Jeffery T. Walker

INTRODUCTION

The use of dogs to assist police officers in their duties is not a new phenomenon. Dogs are said to have helped the Egyptian forerunners of modern police in patrolling and protecting the pyramids as early as 2500 B.C. (Trojan, 1986). Shanahan (1985) noted that dogs had a variety of uses as early as the 1960s, including patrol, searches, apprehension of criminals, recovering stolen property, and finding missing persons. O'Block, Doeran, and True (1979) suggested that police dogs are cost-effective crime control measures, particularly in the area of general patrol, protection of their handler against attack, and in situations involving the detection of drugs. This chapter will focus on the legal implications of the use of police dogs in the detection of narcotics, concentrating specifically on the area of search and seizure.

An alert by a police drug dog has been held by the courts to be a proper application of probable cause to justify a search or a seizure. In *Florida v. Royer* (1983), no narcotics-sniffing dog was used to establish probable cause. The Supreme Court argued, however, that if a dog had been used in *Royer*, officers could have quickly determined the presence of contraband items. If so, the Court stated, "a positive result would have resulted in his justifiable arrest on probable cause" (460 U.S. at 508). The lower courts, however, have not unanimously supported narcotics-sniffing dogs. Opinions are divided as to the weight that should be given to the use of the dogs in the development of probable cause; and some courts are reluctant to consider an alerting canine as conclusive proof of possession of a controlled substance or other contraband.

Tackling the issues of search and seizure using police narcotics-detection dogs can be a daunting task without an explorative framework. To that end, this chapter will examine searches and seizures with the use of a canine from four major classifications: packages in transit, places and people, public transportation (such as buses, trains, and airplanes), and automobiles. Prior to discussing specific issues pertaining to the use of police narcotics-detection dogs, a general discussion of court decisions involving search and seizure is required to establish the foundation upon which these dogs work.

GENERAL ISSUES

The first consideration is the issue of whether the use of a police narcotics-detection dog is a search under the Fourth Amendment to the Constitution. The Supreme Court addressed this question with its decision in *United States v. Place* (1983). The decision in *Place* held that the use of a canine to sniff out odors from an inanimate object was not a search.

Place's behavior attracted the attention of authorities at Miami International Airport as he purchased a ticket to New York. Officers approached him while he was waiting in line, and he granted them permission to search his luggage. They decided not to search the luggage, however, because it was almost time for his flight to depart. After finding discrepancies in the address tags on the luggage, officers contacted New York authorities and two DEA agents met Place at La Guardia Airport. They transported his luggage to Kennedy Airport, where it was sniffed by a narcotics dog. When the dog alerted, the officers obtained a warrant to open the bags. Cocaine was discovered in the luggage, and Place was charged with possession of cocaine with intent to deliver.

Place was convicted after his motion to suppress the evidence arising from the search was denied. The district court held that the sniff of his luggage by a narcotics-detection dog was sufficient probable cause for the warrant, and that the subsequent seizure of cocaine was justified. On appeal, his conviction was overturned, with the court of appeals holding that the length of time his luggage was held (approximately 90 minutes) exceeded the limits for an investigative stop as defined by *Terry v. United States* (1968), and thus should have been viewed as a seizure without probable cause.

On appeal, the Supreme Court addressed the issue of whether the use of a canine to sniff out narcotics is a search under the Fourth Amendment. The Court argued that because of the transient nature of drug couriers, police should be allowed to make brief stops based on reasonable suspicion. The Court indicated that immediate exposure of luggage to a narcotics dog or transportation to another location was permissible. The Court held:

> A "canine sniff" by a well-trained narcotics detection dog, however, does not require opening the luggage. . . . Thus, the manner in which information is obtained through this investigative technique is much less intrusive than a typical search. Moreover, the sniff discloses only the presence or absence of narcotics, a contraband item. Thus, despite the fact that the sniff tells the authorities something about the contents of the luggage, the information is limited. . . . In these respects, the canine sniff is *sui generis*. We are aware of no other investigative procedure that is so limited both in the manner in which the information is obtained and in the

content of the information revealed by the procedure. Therefore, we conclude that the particular course of investigation that the agents intended to pursue here—exposure of the respondent's luggage, which was located in a public place, to a trained canine—did not constitute a "search" within the meaning of the Fourth Amendment. (462 U.S. at 707)

The rationale for the decision was based on the defendant's reasonable expectation of privacy [see *United States v. Chadwick* (1977)]. A person has a reasonable expectation of privacy with respect to the contents of personal luggage. The use of a narcotics-detection dog, however, does not entail opening the luggage. The use of a dog to sniff the luggage is minimally intrusive since it does not disclose the contents of the luggage but only the presence or absence of a contraband item. The Court concluded that the investigative procedure was so limited in manner and content of information that it did not constitute a search within the meaning of the Fourth Amendment.

The Court did, however, determine that the length of time exceeded the normal time frame of an investigative stop under *Terry*, noting that "the brevity of the invasion of the individual's Fourth Amendment interests is an important factor in determining whether the seizure is so minimally intrusive as to be justifiable on reasonable suspicion" (462 U.S. at 708). While not setting a specific time frame in *Place*, the court nonetheless reinforced the standard that the object of the stop would be to keep the suspect in place long enough to have the narcotics-detection dog sniff the item, thus accomplishing the law enforcement objective with a minimum of intrusion. The Court stated, however, that it has never approved the seizure of a person for as long a time as the 90 minutes that Place was detained. In its reversal of *Place*, the Court held that its reason for reversal was based on the length of detention of Place's luggage, the failure of police to inform him where the luggage was to be transported, the failure of police to tell Place how long he might be indisposed, and what arrangements would be made for the return of the luggage if no contraband was found, rather than on the sniff of the dog.

What can be concluded from the decisions presented here is the Court's recognition of police narcotics dogs as a bona fide method for establishing reasonable suspicion and probable cause for governmental intrusion into areas protected by the Fourth Amendment. It should be pointed out, however, that the court focuses not on the use of the canine's sniffing ability, but the facts and circumstances that lead to the development of reasonable suspicion and probable cause to make such an intrusion. With that foundation in mind, the discussion now turns to the first of the four categories of canine uses: examining packages in transit.

PACKAGES IN TRANSIT

In keeping with the Court's decision in *Place*, it is permissible to use a police narcotics dog to sniff a package in transit. Detaining a package, however, requires police to reasonably articulate the reason for the detention. Although *United States v. Van Leeuwen* (1970), does not specifically deal with the use of a canine, it does illustrate the requirement for reasonable suspicion in detaining a package that may subsequently be sniffed by a narcotics dog. Van Leeuwen mailed two packages of coins under circumstances that made authorities suspicious. Since the packages, which contained gold coins, were mailed first class, they were not subject to discretionary inspection. The police, however, did delay the delivery of the coins for 29 hours while they obtained a search warrant. At trial, Van Leeuwen was convicted of il-legally importing gold coins. The Supreme Court held that the significant Fourth Amend-ment interest was in the privacy of this first-class mail; and that privacy had not been disturbed or invaded until the approval of the magistrate was obtained. The finding in this case appears to be consistent with *Place* in that a package sniffed while in transit would not violate the Fourth Amendment if a minimally intrusive method, such as the limited intrusion by a narcotics-detection dog, were to be used.

Lower courts have also held that it is permissible to delay a package for inspection by a narcotics canine, provided that officers move expeditiously in bringing the package and the dog together. In *United States v. Aldaz* (9th Cir. 1990), the Court of Appeals exam-ined circumstances where the Postal Inspection Service held a package until a drug dog could be brought to the package. In this case, a package mailed from a remote village in Alaska was intercepted and rerouted to the Postal Inspection Service in Anchorage. The court held that there was no requirement for officials to station a narcotics dog in a remote section of Alaska, and that the delay in bringing the package to Anchorage, where dogs were available, was not unreasonable. Nor was the search rendered unreasonable by the delay resulting from the fact that the package was held overnight, since the authorities re-ceived the package at the end of a workday and immediately called for a drug dog, but none was available until the next morning.

A similar finding was issued by the court in *United States v. Butler* (10th Cir. 1990). In *Butler*, narcotics-detection dogs alerted on a package in overseas mail addressed to Butler. Upon opening the box, U.S. Customs officials found a wooden jewelry box with a letter and several pieces of costume jewelry. Under a false bottom of the box, officials found 45 grams of hashish. The package was rewrapped and a controlled delivery of the package to Butler was arranged. Butler retrieved the package under the control of offi-cials, who followed him to several houses. On some of these stops, the jewelry box was taken into the residence, on others it was left on the seat of the car. Agents arrested Butler as he reached the third house, and he was convicted of misdemeanor possession of hashish.

On appeal, the district court examined the issue of controlled delivery based on the standard of *Illinois v. Andreas* (1983). In *Butler,* as in *Andreas*, the package had been opened, inspected, and resealed. The court argued that it would be virtually impossible for the police to be so perfect in their timing as to arrest the owner and re-seize the container the moment he took possession; therefore, the issue was whether there was a substantial likelihood that the contents of the container would change between the time the owner took possession and the time the police made the arrest. The court declared that "because the jewelry box was designed for the specialized purpose of transporting contraband, it was likely that the jewelry box contained contraband as long as Butler still possessed it" (904 F.2d at 1486), and affirmed Butler's conviction. In this instance, the court did not re-quire that a second canine sniff be conducted by police before arresting Butler. The origi-nal probable cause, based on the canine sniff, was still in effect since there was a high probability that the jewelry box still contained contraband because it was designed specif-ically for transporting contraband.

It can be argued that the courts attach a minimal expectation of privacy to a pack-age in transit, particularly when the package is subject to a minimally intrusive form of investigation, such as a sniff from a narcotics dog. What is also apparent is that the courts will examine the circumstances in each case to determine whether the detention of the package constitutes a seizure because of unreasonable delay on the part of authorities. In cases of controlled delivery, the case will hinge on issues arising from both the limited intrusion sniff and the circumstances surrounding the delivery and subsequent arrest.

PLACES AND PEOPLE

With respect to places or people to be sniffed, *Horton v. Goose Creek Independent School District* (5th Cir. 1982) provides the greatest guidance. In *Horton*, the court dealt with a canine sniff in a school building, outside in the parking lot, and sniffs of individual students. The Goose Creek Independent School District (GCISD), responding to a growing problem of drugs in its schools, contracted with a private firm to provide drug-detection dogs for use in schools. Junior and senior high students were informed of the program, and the GCISD conducted assemblies in the elementary schools to acquaint students with the dogs.

On a random basis, unannounced inspections were conducted where the dogs sniffed student lockers and automobiles. On leashes, the dogs were taken into the classrooms to sniff students. If a dog alerted on a locker, the locker was searched without consent. If the dog alerted on an automobile, the student was asked to open the doors and trunk. If the student refused, the parents were notified. If the dog alerted on a person, the student was taken to the office and subjected to a search of pockets, purse, and outer garments.

At trial, the district court held that the sniff was a search, but not an unreasonable one. The standard of proof was reasonable cause based on the rationale that schools were searching *in loco parentis*, and the alerting dog provided reasonable cause for the searches. The district court also held that the search subjected the students to minimal intrusion, humiliation, and fear; thus it did not violate the student's due process.

On appeal, the issues before the court of appeals were whether the sniff of a drug-detecting dog was a search under the Fourth Amendment and what were the Fourth Amendment protections against unreasonable actions by a school administration. The court noted that there was very little guidance on these issues. With respect to the sniff of a school building or an automobile, the court held that courts generally have "in effect, adopted a doctrine of 'public smell' analogous to the exclusion from Fourth Amendment coverage of things exposed to the public view" (690 F.2d at 477). The court, relying primarily on *United States v. Goldstein* (cert denied 1981) (see below), held that a search using a canine to detect marijuana odors was no different from the principal strolling the hallways and smelling the aroma of marijuana. Thus, the sniff of the lockers or cars was not a search under the Fourth Amendment.

The use of narcotic dogs to sniff students, however, required a different approach, given that the Fourth Amendment protects people and effects, not places [see *Katz v United States* (1967)]. In *Horton*, the court determined that a dog's sniff of a person, "particularly where the dogs actually touch the person as they do in the GCISD program may be analogous to the warrantless 'stop and frisk' upheld by the Supreme Court on the basis of a suspicion that fell short of probable cause" (690 F.2d at 479). This determination, based on the *Terry* doctrine, requires that the school district provide evidence of reasonable suspicion before the person is sniffed. Thus, the court, relying in part on *Katz* and in part on *Terry*, determined that "the intrusion on dignity and personal security that goes with the type of canine inspection of a student's person involved in this case cannot be justified by the need to prevent abuse of drugs and alcohol where there is no individualized suspicion, and we hold it unconstitutional" (690 F.2d at 481, 482).

The Seventh Circuit in *Doe v. Renfrow* (7th Cir. 1979), however, held that the sniff of students by a dog is not a violation of a student's Fourth Amendment rights. Other courts in other circuits [see, e.g., *Jones v. Latexo Independent School District* (1980)] determined that, absent individualized suspicion, and using large animals trained to attack, the detection of odors outside the range of human senses, and the intrusiveness of a search of individual students, the sniffing of students by narcotics-detection dogs is not reasonable.

It can be argued in summary that, with respect to places to be sniffed by narcotics-detection dogs, the courts have determined that there is minimal intrusion into the privacy rights of an individual if the canine does not intrude upon the personal space of the individual. Thus it would be appropriate for a canine to walk the halls of a school and sniff lockers, or to sniff cars in a parking lot. However, when the sniff is of a person, some courts have held that the sniff is not a violation of the student's Fourth Amendment rights, whereas others have held that the sniffing of students is not reasonable under the Fourth Amendment. Officials contemplating this kind of action, therefore, should determine the prevailing law in their jurisdiction prior to any sniffs of any persons.

PUBLIC TRANSPORTATION

Public transportation creates unique issues in the use of narcotics-detection dogs. On the one hand, persons using public transportation often have a diminished expectation of privacy, especially on luggage that they check for transportation by the carrier. This lower expectation of privacy is not universal, however; and the person and possessions of people on public transportation have Fourth Amendment rights that must be recognized by the police.

Trains and Buses

Courts have determined that narcotics-detection dogs may be used in the passageway of a sleeper compartment on a train for the purpose of sniffing for narcotics. In *United States v. Colyer* (D.C. Cir. 1989), the court of appeals ruled that canine sniffs of a compartment from a public corridor were not a search under the Fourth Amendment. The court further held that a lawful canine sniff could be used with other information to provide probable cause for seizing and searching the bags of a passenger.

Colyer aroused the suspicions of a drug investigator because the circumstances surrounding the purchase of his ticket were suspicious. He was traveling from Palm Beach, Florida (a "source city"), to New York City (a "use" city), having made his reservation the day before departure. Also, Colyer purchased the one-way ticket with cash only a few minutes before departure, although a round-trip ticket could have been purchased for the same amount. The Amtrak agent contacted DEA and requested that a detail meet the train in Washington's Union Station, where it had a short stop.

When the train stopped at Union Station, it was met by authorities and a narcotics-detection dog. The dog sniffed the 8- × 10-inch mesh ventilation holes of several compartments prior to alerting at the ventilation grate in Colyer's compartment. A search of his luggage revealed a green vinyl pouch containing cocaine.

The court of appeals examined the sniff of the compartment and found that a train compartment did not hold the same expectation of privacy as a hotel room. This determination was based on its recognition of the decision in *United States v. Whitehead* (4th Cir. 1988), which rejected the argument that a sleeping compartment is a temporary home under the Fourth Amendment. Since the sniff in *Colyer* was conducted via the passageway, it was a reasonable act, and the court held that it was not a search, in keeping with the Supreme Court's decision in *Place*.

An overhead compartment, much like a rooming compartment, is also not considered by the courts to have a privacy interest if the luggage is removed for canine inspection. In *United States v. Graham* (8th Cir. 1992), the court held that removing a suitcase from the overhead rack and placing it in the aisle for the canine to sniff was not a seizure. The bus Graham was traveling on made a routine stop for fueling. While the passengers were inside the bus depot taking a break, officers boarded the bus with their narcotics-detection dog. When the dog began to "air scent" (an indication that he smelled something in a higher location), the officers removed several pieces of luggage. The narcotics-detection dog alerted on a bag with a tag identifying the owner as Katherine Graham. When the passengers reboarded the bus, officers identified themselves and asked for tickets and personal identification. Graham produced her ticket, but stated that her name was Jones and that she did not have any identification. When asked if she had any luggage, she identified two pieces, including the one the dog had alerted on. When Graham refused consent to search her luggage, she was taken off the bus, advised of her *Miranda* warnings, and advised of the positive notification of narcotics by the dog. After obtaining a search warrant, officers discovered over 5 kilograms of cocaine in the luggage. On appeal of her conviction, the court of appeals was asked to address the issue of whether moving the suitcase from the overhead rack to the aisle so the dog could sniff it was a violation of the Fourth Amendment. In a *per curiam* decision, the court upheld the lower court's decision that moving the bag did not constitute a Fourth Amendment violation.

Police officers, however, cannot manipulate the bag prior to removing it from the overhead compartment [*Bond v. United States* (No. 98-9349)]. In *Bond*, a Border Patrol agent boarded a bus to check the immigration status of passengers. While walking off the bus, he squeezed the soft luggage in the overhead storage compartment. On squeezing a canvas bag over Bond's head, he felt a "brick-like" object. Bond admitted owning the bag and consented to its search. When a brick of methamphetamine was found inside, Bond was arrested. At trial, he argued that the Border Patrol agent had conducted an illegal search. The district court denied his motion and found him guilty, holding that the manipulation of the bag by the agent was not a search under the Fourth Amendment.

On appeal, the Supreme Court determined that the physical manipulation of the bag was a violation of the Fourth Amendment. The Court took notice of two major themes in search and seizure case law. First, the Court held that personal luggage is an "effect" which is protected by the Fourth Amendment, and that a person has a privacy interest in his or her luggage. The second issue was that the Border Patrol agent's intrusion was physically inva-sive. The Court held that an individual has a limited expectation of privacy, given that other passengers or busline employees may move the luggage for one reason or another. However, when the government's intrusion was more than the casual contact that would have been ex-pected from passengers, the intrusion was an unlawful search under the Fourth Amendment.

It can be concluded from this discussion that the courts are willing to allow nar-cotics dogs to sniff luggage on trains or buses. The intrusion, however, must follow the standards set in *Place,* where the intrusion is limited to a sniff for contraband, not a ma-nipulation by the handler or other police officer followed by a canine sniff. Officers may remove baggage from overhead luggage racks, especially if a narcotics-detection dog has signaled an air scent. Officers must not manipulate the luggage, however, beyond what would be reasonable manipulation by other passengers or transportation officials.

Airplanes

The courts have dealt with issues of search and seizure involving airports and airplanes a number of times. We begin our discussion with *United States v. Goldstein* (5th Cir. 1981). Goldstein and Kern were detained in the Orlando airport after a narcotics-detection dog sniffed their baggage and alerted. The sniff occurred in the airline baggage area after offi-cers became suspicious of Goldstein and Kern's conduct prior to checking their baggage with the airline. At the airport police office, Goldstein refused to consent to a search of his baggage, but Kern did consent. Kern's bag was searched, and drug paraphernalia was found. Both were jailed, and a warrant was obtained to search Goldstein's bag. At trial, defendants were convicted of possession of cocaine.

On appeal, the Fifth Circuit Court of Appeals determined that a passenger enjoys a reasonable expectation of privacy with respect to the contents of checked luggage, but does not have any reasonable expectation of privacy for odors emanating from the luggage that could be sniffed by a narcotics dog in the airspace surrounding the luggage. Further, the court held that passengers have a diminished expectation of privacy in luggage, as they cannot control who handles their bags once in the control of the airline. In this case, the sniff that led to the probable cause was conducted in a place where the officer had a legal right to be, as he had permission from the airline. Kern's luggage was then searched with consent, Goldstein's with a warrant.

In 1984, the Ninth Circuit Court of Appeals was faced with a similar issue in *United States v. Beale* (9th Cir. 1984). In this case, Beale and Pulvano checked three pieces of luggage with a skycap, then proceeded inside to obtain tickets and seating arrangements. They took seats together in the boarding area, where agents approached and questioned them. Pulvano, showing signs of abnormal anxiety, admitted a previous narcotics arrest.

Detectives then used a narcotics-detection dog to sniff Pulvano's luggage in the checked-baggage area. After the dog alerted, agents kept the suspects under surveillance until they reached San Diego. In San Diego, another narcotics-detection dog alerted to Beale's luggage and shoulder bag. Beale's bags were searched pursuant to a warrant and narcotics were found. He was convicted in district court for possession of cocaine.

On appeal, the court held that Beal was not detained or inconvenienced while the in-vestigators built their case. Any interference with his luggage was minimal. The court held, therefore, that the sniff did not constitute a search under the Fourth Amendment because the suspect was not detained or otherwise inconvenienced, his travel plans were not interfered with, and there was only minimal interference with his luggage.

The Fifth Circuit Court of Appeals placed limitations on the police, however, in *United States v Cagle* (5th Cir. 1988). Cagle appeared at the El Paso International Airport, obtained his ticket, checked his luggage, and proceeded to the departure gate, appearing to be nervous and looking around the area the whole time. This action aroused the suspicion of Border Patrol agents, who went to the baggage area, removed Cagle's hard-sided suitcase from the baggage area, and shook it. Nothing inside rattled, but the agents noticed a substance that was later identified as baby powder coming from the suitcase seams. Agents went to Cagle and asked to see his baggage claim check, which he refused. When he refused to accompany them to the office, Cagle was informed that he was free to leave; he subsequently boarded his flight.

After Cagle's flight departed, agents had a narcotics-detection dog sniff the luggage. The dog alerted, and the Border Patrol contacted the DEA. DEA agents confiscated the suitcase, obtained a warrant, and opened the suitcase to find 11 pounds of marijuana. At trial, the district court determined that a seizure occurred when agents kept the luggage from departing with the plane and suppressed the evidence.

The court of appeals held that the sniff of the suitcase by a narcotics dog was not a seizure within the meaning of the Fourth Amendment. The seizure occurred when officers removed the suitcase from the flight. The court affirmed the exclusion of evidence by the trial court, finding that the detention of the suitcase without probable cause was unreasonable when there were more diligent and less intrusive investigatory techniques available. The decision was a combination of two factors: that there was no probable cause for the detention of the luggage, and there was an unreasonable delay of 90 minutes between the time the luggage was removed and when the sniff occurred.

If the police have reasonable and articulable suspicion, they may ask for passenger consent to a drug sniff by a narcotics-detection dog [*United States v. Ayarza* (9th Cir.1989)]. In *Ayarza*, officers in the Anchorage airport first noticed the suspect on a previous occasion, when an airline denied him access to a flight because he was thought to be under the influence of a controlled substance. One month later, Ayarza departed for New York, intending to return to Anchorage, with his ground time in New York scheduled to be less than eight hours. He checked no luggage, carrying only a small carry-on bag. Officers were waiting for Ayarza when he deplaned in Anchorage after completing his trip. They noticed that he was carrying a large garment bag, not the small carry-on bag he had departed with. Once Ayarza was outside the terminal, the officers approached him, identified themselves, and then advised him that he was not under arrest and could leave at any time. After a short discussion, the officers asked if he would allow his bag to be exposed to a narcotics-detection dog. Ayarza was allowed to contact his attorney while the bag remained in view of the officers. After the phone call, Ayarza stated that he would not submit to a search unless he was arrested. The officers advised him that he could go but the bag would be detained. When offered a receipt for the bag, Ayarza refused. The bag was exposed to two different narcotics-detection dogs, both of which alerted to the presence of narcotics. Officers obtained a search warrant, and 1005.7 grams of cocaine were found.

On appeal, the court stated that the detention of the luggage required reasonable suspicion, which was present in this case because of nine separate and articulable facts that matched a drug courier profile. With reasonable suspicion to detain the bag, it could then properly be sniffed by a narcotics-detection dog, whose alert was then used for probable cause for a warrant.

In *Brower v. County of Inyo* (1989) the Supreme Court held that a seizure occurs when the government terminates a person's movement through means intentionally applied. Although *Brower* was an unrelated case it can be applied here in the argument that any disruption of an airline passenger's travel that is caused by the government will be scrutinized in the light of the Fourth Amendment. Following the decision in *Place*, the detention of passengers or their luggage should be for a minimal amount of time with the minimal amount of disruption to the passengers. From a practical standpoint, *Place* seems to suggest that the use of police narcotics dogs would be acceptable to the courts if the police have the canines readily available and there is no unreasonable delay in searching either the passenger or the luggage. The difficulty comes in determining what the Supreme Court will deem a reasonable delay. In *Place*, the police knew the defendant's arrival time and could have procured a canine and been standing by when he arrived at baggage claim, rather than waiting some 90 minutes. In *United States v. Sharpe* (1985) the Court concluded that 30 to 40 minutes spent on the highway was not time enough to move a situation from an investigative *Terry* stop if officers "diligently pursued a means of investigation that was likely to confirm or dispel their suspicions quickly, during which time it was necessary to detain the defendant" (470 U.S. 675 at 686). It is clear that the Court will consider the totality of the circumstances, rather than specify a concrete time frame for the duration of an investigative *Terry* stop.

In 1990, time became an issue for the Seventh Circuit Court of Appeals in *United States v. Sterling* (7th Cir. 1990). DEA agents were monitoring arriving flights in Chicago when they noticed suspicious activity on the part of Sterling. After she picked up her suitcase, she was approached by plainclothes officers who identified themselves and asked to speak with her. They advised her that she was not under arrest, did not have to speak with them, and was free to leave. During this conversation, the officers were standing to the side and not blocking her way. During the subsequent five- to ten-minute conversation, Sterling was evasive and could not produce any identification. The officers then asked to search her luggage and she refused. The officers backed off about 30 feet and observed her make a phone call. Several minutes later, an unidentified woman approached Sterling, carried on a short conversation, and left. Upon inquiring about the woman, Sterling advised that she had come to pick her up, but offered no explanation why she did not go with the woman. Officers asked again to search her luggage; she refused, but did allow them to search her purse. A female agent was summoned; Sterling was patted down and her purse was searched. No drugs were found. Agents gave Sterling a receipt for the suitcase and made arrangements for the return of the luggage if the narcotics dog did not alert. The luggage was moved to the DEA office and a narcotics dog was summoned. When the dog alerted, officers obtained a warrant before opening the luggage. Two kilograms of cocaine were found.

The appeals court first examined the initial questioning of Sterling, finding that it was not an unreasonable *Terry* stop. What was first a consensual encounter turned into a *Terry* stop shortly after the unidentified woman left the airport and agents approached Sterling for the second time. Three crucial events occurred: the agents again requested the opportunity to search the suitcase, which Sterling refused; Sterling was informed of the agent's intention to detain the luggage; and a female officer was summoned for a pat-down. The court held that during the course of the consensual questioning, enough reasonable suspicion was raised to permit the subsequent investigative detention. Also at issue was whether the duration of the detention was reasonable. The court felt it was, noting that both agents were needed and the officers acted diligently to complete the investigation without due delay. The key points for police in this case are that officers complied with both the requirements set forth in *Place*; the sniff was in a reasonable and timely manner, and, since the detention was to be excessively long, the requirements of diligence without undue delay were met.

The final case to be discussed in the examination of search and seizure using narcotics-detection dogs in an airport environment is *United States v. Baro* (6th Cir. 1994). The Baro brothers and five others were charged with conspiracy to possess with intent to distribute cocaine. On one occasion, an undercover officer observed Baro purchase a one-way ticket with cash, separate from his companion, and walk to the departure gate. The officer then identified himself and asked to speak with Baro, requesting his ticket and identification. After securing Baro's consent to search his person and carry-on bag, he removed two bundles of cash from the bag and a third bundle from Baro's waistband. The officer advised him that the money was to be taken to the DEA office and would be subjected to a canine sniff. Baro was informed that he was not under arrest, and could catch his flight and wait for a receipt for the money to arrive in the mail, or he could accompany the officer to the DEA office. At the DEA office, a narcotics-detection dog alerted positively for drugs on the money, and a total of $14,190 was seized.

The Sixth Circuit Court of Appeals held that a seizure of Baro's person and cash occurred when his flight was scheduled for imminent departure and the DEA confiscated his money. The court also held that Baro did not consent to the seizure of his money; rather, the DEA agent stated that the currency was going to be seized and made the subject of a canine sniff. The court concluded that at the time of the seizure, the agent did not have sufficient probable cause to seize the currency. Thus, an improper seizure cannot be turned into a proper seizure merely because the police used a narcotics dog to develop probable cause subsequent to the improper seizure.

In an airline situation, the problems are different from a traditional police encounter with a mobile defendant. When traveling by airplane, not everyone carries his or her baggage on the plane. Although the traveler is contracting with a private company, airline travel is controlled for security reasons, and the government has a compelling interest to ensure that drugs are not transported from place to place via commercial airplanes. Thus, the courts must balance the government's desire to reduce the flow of drugs across the country with the individual's right to travel. One result of the balancing test is the court's determination that seizure of a defendant's luggage for the purposes of a canine sniff is essentially the same as seizing the defendant. Given the courts' totality of the circumstances test when applying *Terry* to airline passengers, officers must consider a number of options short of unreasonably detaining either the traveler or the luggage. For example, officers could expose checked luggage to a narcotics-detection dog, as long as the exposure was based on reasonable suspicion or was done without delay to the luggage. If officers remove luggage from a scheduled flight without reasonable suspicion, however, the fact that it is subsequently exposed to a narcotics-detection dog does not overcome its possibly unreasonable seizure. Also, if officers have reasonable suspicion, they may ask for passenger consent to have luggage sniffed by a narcotics-detection dog. Again, however, any detention that prevents a passenger or luggage from proceeding as scheduled must be accompanied by articulable suspicion or else it may violate the Fourth Amendment.

AUTOMOBILES

Police may use a narcotics-detection dog in the search of a vehicle in one of three circumstances: where the owner of the vehicle has given consent to search and the canine augments the officer's search; if the officer has probable cause to search a vehicle and the canine augments the officer's search; or if the officer uses the canine to develop probable cause to search a vehicle. Cases where consent to search is given and the canine augments the search will not be discussed here, as consent to search establishes reasonableness irrespective of the use of a dog in the search. Care must be taken, however, by the police officer to ensure that the consent is valid before searching.

We next turn to the discussion of probable cause to search augmented by a canine. As del Carmen (1998) notes, the Supreme Court carved out an automobile exception to the Fourth Amendment a number of years ago; however, questions regarding the relationship between automobiles and the Fourth Amendment will occupy the courts for years. Introducing an additional factor, such as the use of a narcotics-detection dog, adds to the number of questions ultimately to be answered by the courts.

The Foundations of Automobile Searches

In 1925, the Supreme Court, in *Carroll v. United States* (1925), determined that police do not need a warrant to search an automobile if it is not practical to obtain a warrant because the vehicle could be quickly moved out of the jurisdiction. The Court did, however, require that the officers show probable cause to make the search. Thus, the Court set down two requirements for a warrantless search: there must be probable cause, and the vehicle must be mobile. In *Pennsylvania v. Labron* (1996), the Court affirmed *Carroll* when it ruled that the Fourth Amendment did not require the police to obtain a warrant to search a motor vehicle, even if there was time for them to do so.

Additional factors to be considered in maintaining the automobile exception were discussed in *Robbins v. California* (1981). The Court laid out five rationales for the automobile exception: vehicle mobility; a diminished expectation of privacy; the use of a vehicle for transportation, not for storage of personal effects; plain view of persons traveling in a motor vehicle; and high regulation of motor vehicles by the government. It is the issue of diminished expectation of privacy that has consistently led the discussion when courts consider a non-intrusive sniff by a narcotics-detection dog.

The issue for this discussion hinges not on the automobile itself. Rather, it hinges on the probable cause necessary for the stop and the resulting probable cause that allows the search of the automobile. The issue is similar to the one raised in the previous discussion regarding airline passengers and the amount of permissible delay. As with airline passengers, the courts will consider the reason for delay of a motorist who travels the highway. It is imperative that police officers understand that in cases involving automobile searches, probable cause for the stop is critical, and cannot be gained solely by the use of a canine sniff after the stop.

In *Delaware v. Prouse* (1979), the Supreme Court held that a vehicular stop is a seizure under the Fourth Amendment, even if the purpose of the stop is limited and the detention brief. In *Berkemer v. McCarty* (1984), the Court held that a roadside stop may, depending on the circumstances, give rise to the belief that the person was, in fact, in custody. Thus, the length of the stop and how one is treated by the police may have a bearing on the admissibility of evidence gathered by a canine-assisted search. The officer must exercise caution not to unnecessarily delay a motorist through the use of a canine, thereby turning a simple vehicular stop into a much more complex case.

Canine-Involved Automobile Searches

One method of involving narcotics-detection dogs is in conjunction with an investigatory stop. There are a number of factors that should be considered in determining whether there is reasonable suspicion to stop a vehicle. If there is reasonable suspicion, then a subsequent sniff by a narcotics-detection dog is permissible; if there is no reasonable suspicion for the stop, the sniff is impermissible. An example of this principle can be found in *United States v. Monsisvais* (10th Cir. 1990). Border Patrol agents stopped Monsisvais after a sensor alarm alerted them to the presence of a vehicle traveling along a route often used to bypass the border checkpoint. Agents noted that the vehicle was a pickup truck bearing Arizona plates and equipped with a camper shell. The truck appeared to be heavily loaded. When officers stopped the vehicle, one noted the very strong odor of marijuana coming from the camper shell. After placing the two occupants under arrest for possession of marijuana, a dog was brought in and alerted to the presence of drugs.

On appeal, the Tenth Circuit Court of Appeals reversed the conviction, finding that there was no reasonable suspicion to stop the Monsisvais vehicle. The test used by the court was the totality of the circumstances that predicated the traffic stop. Two factors were considered key in this case (although more were articulable): the vehicle had a camper shell and was riding heavily. In this case, the court invalidated the conviction because the canine sniff was used in a situation where there was no probable cause for the stop.

Two years later, the Tenth Circuit Court revisited the issue in *United States v. Barbee* (10th Cir. 1992). In *Barbee*, Border Patrol agents observed a vehicle with out-of-state plates traveling on a highway routinely used by individuals smuggling aliens because it bypasses the checkpoint. The agents were able to reasonably articulate other reasons building probable cause for the stop: it was after dark; the vehicle was traveling in a month in which only a little traffic typically travels that road; and when headlights illuminated the vehicle, passengers in the back crouched down. The vehicle was stopped, and Mexican nationals without visas were found in the rear seat. When the vehicle was taken to the checkpoint, a dog alerted on the trunk of the car. Upon the removal of the luggage from the car, the dog again alerted. Opening the luggage, officers found a semiautomatic machine pistol, large amounts of cash, and over 35 grams of cocaine. On appeal, the court concluded that the stop was based on reasonable suspicion; therefore, the dog sniff of the vehicle for narcotics was not unlawful, as the vehicle had already been lawfully seized.

Although a vehicle stop amounts to a seizure under *Prouse*, simply having a canine sniff the exterior of a vehicle does not constitute a search. This issue was addressed by the Tenth Circuit Court of Appeals in *United States v. Morales-Zamora* (10th Circuit 1990).

Zamora was stopped by a police roadblock where she was required to produce her license and registration. While one officer checked the documents, a police narcotics dog sniffed the exterior without touching her car. When the dog alerted, a search of the car revealed marijuana. On appeal, the issue before the court was whether Zamora was unlawfully detained after a lawful initial stop for the purpose of facilitating the canine sniff. The court held that the narcotics dog alerted before the document inspection was completed, and thus there was no seizure of the vehicle for the purpose of facilitating a canine sniff. Relying on previous decisions in *United States v. Jacobsen* (1984) and *Place*, the court determined that "there is no intrusion on legitimate privacy interests (and hence no 'search') where the only information revealed is limited to contraband items" (914 F.2d at 205).

The Eighth Circuit Court of Appeals faced a similar situation in *United States v. Bloomfield* (8th Cir. 1994). In this case, an officer noticed a rental truck driving in an erratic manner and followed it for approximately 2 miles. After stopping the truck, the officer noted that Bloomfield appeared to be very nervous, his eyes were red, he only rolled the window part-way down, and he would not look at the officer. The officer also observed two radar detectors on the dash. When the officer asked Bloomfield to sit in the patrol car, he opened the truck door only partway, squeezing himself out. As the truck door opened, the officer noted that the defendant was wearing a pager and there was a masking odor of deodorant coming from the truck.

When the officer obtained inconsistent answers to his questions and the defendant continued to act in a suspicious manner, the officer called for a drug dog to be sent from the nearest available source. When Bloomfield asked if he was under arrest, he was advised that he was not. During the wait, Bloomfield asked to be taken to a place where he could use the bathroom, but not to a police station where other officers would be present. The officers agreed, and Bloomfield drove his truck to the Highway Patrol Zone Office, where there were no other officers present.

While there, Bloomfield inquired as to the length of time of his wait for the dog. The officers told him that they would wait until the arrival of the dog, unless he felt the waiting period was becoming unreasonably long. About an hour after the original stop, the dog arrived and alerted. Officers placed Bloomfield under arrest and searched the truck, finding a range of deodorant products, dog repellent, pet deodorizer, ammonia, and 797 pounds of marijuana.

On appeal, the court of appeals held that there was a legitimate reason for the traffic stop; and it was therefore reasonable to ask Bloomfield for his license and registration, to request that he sit in the patrol car, and to ask him about his destination and purpose. The court also found that the officer acted diligently to verify suspicions, including radioing for the dog within six minutes of the beginning of the stop, and asking for the nearest dog. In addition, the one-hour wait was not unreasonable, Bloomfield was not subjected to any intrusion or restraint other than what was necessary for the investigation, he was allowed to drive his truck to a second location where he could use restroom facilities, and the officers did not search the truck until after the dog provided the requisite probable cause for the search. Finally, after the drug dog alerted, the truck could be searched under the automobile exception to the Fourth Amendment.

The *Bloomfield* case was supported by *United States v. Frost* (3rd Cir. 1993). The court in this case also ruled that a one-hour wait was not unreasonable given the diligence of the officers to obtain probable cause for the search. These cases support an argument that courts are reluctant to name a specific time frame, and approach each case on an individual basis. Factors considered by the courts include the diligence of the officers and the location of the traffic stop.

In cases where the police unlawfully seize a vehicle, a police narcotics-detection dog cannot be used to justify a search of the vehicle [*United States v. Hogan* (8th Cir. 1994)]. In *Hogan*, a confidential informant advised police that Hogan would be in possession of drugs either in his residence or in a white 1990 Dodge pickup truck. Officers, armed with a search warrant for Hogan's house and the truck, went to the residence and set up surveillance. Approximately an hour and a half later, Hogan left in a 1987 Oldsmobile Cutlass, which was stopped by an officer. When Hogan declined permission to search the vehicle, the officer impounded it. A narcotics dog alerted on the vehicle, which was subsequently removed to a storage facility where it was searched pursuant to a warrant specifically for that vehicle.

The court held that the vehicle was seized without a warrant when the officer impounded the car. The seizure was unlawful because there was no probable cause to believe that Hogan was transporting narcotics in that particular vehicle, since it was not named in the search warrant for the house and truck. Of particular interest in this case was that the informant bought drugs from Hogan at work and expressly stated that the drugs would be brought to the plant in the truck, which the informant stated was the sole vehicle used by Hogan when traveling to and from work.

In *Merrett v. Moore* (11th Cir. 1995), the Eleventh Circuit Court of Appeals ruled that the use of dogs to sniff the exterior of vehicles during a license and registration checkpoint was not an unconstitutional search, even though there was no reasonable suspicion of drug activity attached to parties stopped by the roadblock. In *Merrett*, drivers were stopped at a roadblock, and a narcotics-detection dog sniffed the outside of the vehicle at the same time that officers were examining license and registration documents. Most people experienced only a slight delay, as the dogs usually completed their sniff by the time the officers completed the document examination. The court held that the occupants did not have a reasonable expectation of privacy in possessing illegal drugs (see *United States v. Morales-Zamora,* above) and that the sniffs only alerted officers to the potential presence of drugs rather than exposing the vehicular contents to public view. The court did caution police, however, not to use canines in a way that caused unreasonable delay, and to pay special attention to traffic backups at roadblock sites, since these areas carried significant potential constitutional violations.

In 1997, the Eleventh Circuit Court of Appeals was faced with a derivative of the roadblock decision in *Merritt* in *United States v. Holloman* (11th Cir. 1997). Police established an interdiction operation in which northbound vehicles were stopped if violations of the motor vehicle code, except minor speeding, were observed. When a vehicle was stopped, detectives would approach it, ask the driver to exit, explain the reason for the stop, and request consent to search. If consent was given, one officer would search the vehicle while another ran a computerized check on the driver. If consent was denied, a narcotics dog would sniff the automobile while the computerized check was being run.

Holloman was stopped for failure to display an illuminated license tag. He refused consent to search his automobile and a narcotics dog then sniffed the car. When the dog alerted, the car was searched and a sneaker box containing 694 grams of crack cocaine was found. On appeal, the court followed the Supreme Court's framework in *Whren v. United States* (1996), where the Court held that reasonableness of the stop must be determined irrespective of intent. Given that any seizure of an automobile based on probable cause will invariably be determined as reasonable, the court of appeals made two final points in concluding its decision. First, the stop was made with probable cause for a violation of traffic law, regardless of what the driver thought was the reason for the stop. Also, Holloman was not delayed in his travels, since the narcotics-detection dog was available at the scene and promptly sniffed the vehicle after his refusal to a consent search of his vehicle.

If a vehicle is stopped on the highway in need of assistance, however, officers may have to conduct their inquiry in a different manner. In *United States v. Buchanon* (6th Cir. 1995), the court of appeals examined whether a seizure could occur if police officers had not stopped the vehicle. An officer offered to assist two vehicles stopped on the side of the road, one behind the other. Buchanon told the officer that he was having mechanical trouble, and asked if he would call a tow truck. The officer did so, and advised Buchanon that it would take about 45 minutes for the tow truck to arrive. During the wait, the officer began to be uneasy about the situation, citing the nervousness of the men and the fact that one kept staring at his service weapon. As a result, he called an officer with a narcotics-detection dog. The five men standing alongside the disabled vehicles were asked twice by officers to move onto the grass and away from the vehicles. A narcotics dog was walked around the vehicles, and he alerted to the presence of contraband. The officers then considered the men to be in investigative custody and patted them down. The vehicles were searched without a warrant, with the officers finding 13.146 grams of cocaine, four handguns, and four empty aerosol cans with false bottoms in Buchanon's vehicle. The other vehicle also contained drugs.

On appeal of their convictions, the court of appeals reversed. The key issue for the court was the point at which the course of events turned investigatory, finding that when the officer "had instructed the men to move onto the grass, the troopers' questions became investigatory" (72 F.3d. at 1221). The court focused on the issue of motion, finding that, pursuant to *United States v. Mendenhall* (1980), a person could be detained when not in motion and not proceeding to a destination. Even though the appellants in Buchanon were not in motion, their freedom to leave was removed, or a reasonable person would believe the freedom was removed, when the officers directed them to a particular location so that a canine sniff could take place. The appeals court concluded that as long as the canine was to be used "on an unattended vehicle or unattended personal property, or so long as the canine sniff is performed on legally seized personal property pursuant to a legal seizure of a person, the canine sniff would not be unconstitutional" (72 F.3d.at 1228). That was not the case here, however.

From the preceding analysis of cases, an argument can be made that the courts have begun to adopt a standard consistent with the view of a dog sniff as analogous to a sniff by a human officer (the public smell doctrine). That is, if the officer is in a place where he or she is legally entitled to be, a police narcotics dog accompanying the officer may be used as an extension of the officer's persona. It is imperative to note, however, that a canine cannot be used as a pretext for a generalized search without reasonable suspicion.

CONCLUSION

The purpose of the Fourth Amendment is to protect persons from unreasonable governmental intrusion into their personal privacy [*Katz v. United States* (1967)]. The Fourth Amendment was not designed to protect individuals from all searches and seizures, only those that are considered unreasonable. The focus of this protection is on the investigative technique that is used for the intrusion; if it is reasonable, then the intrusion is reasonable. If the investigative technique is not reasonable, the courts will declare the intrusion to be in violation of the individual's constitutional rights. Therefore, any governmental intrusion using a narcotics-detection dog must meet the test of reasonableness.

Shahin (1993) noted the Supreme Court's willingness to expand police authority to conduct searches. This willingness is exemplified in *Place*, where the Court determined that canine sniffs are not searches because the sniff only reveals evidence of criminality and does not intrude into areas expected to be kept private.

This is based on the Court's public smell doctrine, which is very similar to the public view doctrine. Based on this doctrine, an officer can seize anything that can be smelled from any place the officer has a legal right to be (such as a principal smelling the odor of marijuana in the halls of a school as discussed in *Horton*). If an officer has the right to establish probable cause based on a public smell, then a police narcotics-detection dog has the same right, even if the dog is much better able to carry out the task.

Pollack (1994) cautioned that the courts require that the intrusiveness of the sniff be balanced with the individual expectation of privacy. This is particularly important because the primary use of canines for search and seizure is in the area of narcotics detection. As a result, police should take care to use narcotics-detection dogs in a manner consistent with established constitutional safeguards, particularly in the area of privacy. Hall (1994) echoes the previous assertion, noting that the Supreme Court has failed to provide clear and convincing guidelines for canine sniffs.

As a result of this lack of guidelines, there is a tremendous amount of latitude with respect to canine sniffs. Courts, as we have seen, are divided on the proper application of *Place*. It is possible that some lower courts may abandon the decision in *Place*, and focus more on the privacy issues enumerated in *Katz*. Since the sensitivity of the canine's nose is almost tailor-made for the war on drugs, there are some who advocate finding new and innovative ways to bring the canine into contact with suspects. Others advocate taking a conservative approach and restricting the use of canines.

We advocate a middle ground. Courts have clearly decided that a sniff is not a search. Other issues, however, have not been clearly delineated. It would be impossible for courts to specify each and every action that might constitute a seizure. As we have seen in this discussion, courts prefer to examine issues in light of the reasonableness of the police officer and within the framework of the totality of the circumstances. Due diligence and ensuring that one is on solid legal footing when using police narcotics-detection dogs should preserve the ability of police officials to use canines as valuable members of the police team.

REFERENCES

DEL CARMEN, R. 1998. *Criminal procedure: Law and practice* (4th ed.). Belmont, CA: Wadsworth.

HALL, H. W. 1994. Sniffing out the Fourth Amendment: *United States v. Place*—dog sniffs—ten years later. *Maine Law Review, 46,* 151–188.

O'BLOCK, R., DOERAN, S. E., & TRUE, N. J. 1979. The benefits of canine squads. *Journal of Police Science and Administration*, *7*(2), 155–160.

POLLACK, K. L. 1994. Stretching the Terry doctrine to the search for evidence of crime: Canine sniffs, state constitutions, and the reasonable suspicion standard. *Vanderbilt Law Review, 47,* 803–855.

SHAHIN, L. 1993. The constitutional posture of canine sniffs. *Touro Law Review*, *9*, 645–697.

SHANAHAN, D. 1985. *Patrol administration: Management by objectives* (3rd ed.). Boston: Allyn & Bacon.

TROJAN, C. 1986. Egypt: Evolution of a modern police state. *CJ International, 2* (1): 15–18.

Cases Cited

- *Berkemer v. McCarty,* 468 US 429 (1984)
- *Bond v. United States* (No. 98-9349)
- *Brower v. County of Inyo*, 489 U.S. 593 (1989)
- *Carroll v. United States*, 267 U.S. 132 (1925)
- *Delaware v. Prouse*, 440 U.S. 648 (1979)
- *Doe v. Renfrow*, 631 F.2d. 91 (7th Cir. 1979) cert denied, 451 U.S. 1022 (1981)
- *Florida v. Royer*, 460 U.S. 491 (1983)
- *Horton v. Goose Creek Independent School District*, 690 F.2d 470 (5th Cir. 1982)
- *Illinois v. Andreas*, 463 U.S. 765 (1983)
- *Jones v. Latexo Independent School District,* 499 F. Supp. 223, 236 (E.D.Tex.1980)
- *Katz v United States*, 389 U.S. 487 (1967)
- *Merrett v. Moore*, 58 F.3d 1547 (11th Cir. 1995)
- *Pennsylvania v. Labron,* 518 U.S. 938 (1996)
- *Robbins v. California*, 435 U.S. 420 (1981)
- *Terry v. United States*, 392 U.S. 1 (1968)
- *United States v. Aldaz*, 921 F.2d 227 (9th Cir. 1990)
- *United States v. Ayarza*, 874 F.2d 647 (9th Cir. 1989)
- *United States v. Barbee*, 968 F.2d 1026 (10th Cir. 1992)
- *Unites States v. Baro*, 15 F.3d. 563 (6th Cir. 1994)
- *United States v. Beale*, 736 F.2d. 1289 (9th Cir. 1984)
- *United States v. Bloomfield*, 40 F.3d 910 (8th Cir. 1994)
- *United States v. Buchanon*, 72 F.3d. 1217 (6th Cir. 1995)
- *United States v. Butler,* 904 F.2d 1482 (10th Cir. 1990)
- *United States v. Cagle*, 849 F.2d 924 (5th Cir. 1988)
- *United States v. Chadwick*, 433 U.S. 1 (1977)
- *United States v. Colyer*, 878 F.2d 469 (D.C. Cir. 1989)
- *United States v. Frost*, 999 F.2d 737 (3rd Cir. 1993), cert. denied 114 S. Ct. 573 (1993)
- *United States v. Goldstein*, 635 F.2d 356 (5th Cir. 1981)
- *United States v. Graham,* 982 F.2d. 273 (8th Cir. 1992)
- *United States v. Hogan*, 25 F.3d 690 (8th Cir. 1994)
- *United States v. Holloman*, 113 F.3d 192 (11th Cir. 1997)
- *United States v. Jacobsen,* 466 U.S. 109 (1984)
- *United States v. Mendenhall*, 446 U.S. 544 (1980)

- *United States v. Monsisvais*, 907 F2d 987 (10th Cir. 1990)
- *United States v. Morales-Zamora*, 914 F.2d 200 (10th Cir. 1990)
- *United States v. Place*, 462 U.S. 696 (1983)
- *United States v. Sharpe*, 470 U.S. 675 (1985)
- *United States v. Sterling*, 909 F.2d. 1078 (7th Cir. 1990)
- *United States v. Van Leeuwen*, 397 U.S. 249 (1970)
- *United States v. Whitehead*, 849 F.2d 849 (4th Cir. 1988)
- *Whren v. United States*, 517 U.S. 806 (1996)

6

Policing the Internet

Legal Issues on the Information Superhighway

Robert W. Taylor

Deanne Morgan

INTRODUCTION

The Internet has grown tremendously in the last several years. Originally developed to facilitate military communications, the Internet is now a worldwide network of computer systems, with users from all walks of life, both public and private. The 1990s, in particular, have seen explosive Internet growth, especially with the advent and widespread use of the World Wide Web. InterGOV International (1998) estimated that in 1998 there were 85 million web users (200,000 new users per day), up from 12 million users in 1997 (34,000 new users per day). It predicted that there would be 900 million users (1,726,000 new users per day) in 2000. We are in the midst of what will undoubtedly be labeled the "Information Age" or "Information Revolution," and are rapidly moving toward a virtual society, where many of the fundamental needs of Americans, from banking to entertainment, can be met through the Internet. Unfortunately, individuals wishing to steal credit card numbers or distribute child pornography can exploit the same medium that allows one to order flowers online for Mother's Day.

The challenges confronting police in the investigation and prevention of Internet and other computer-based crime are somewhat unusual. Outdated laws designed to address traditional property crimes (e.g., fraud, burglary, and theft) pose significant statutory limitations when applied to the computer environment because physical intrusion and the taking of tangible property are not elements of most computer crime activity. Further, most computer crimes (and especially Internet crimes) do not have traditional geographical boundaries. Police agencies are often forced to investigate such crimes in cooperation with other agencies having different geographical and legal responsibilities. Such cross-jurisdictional investigations have always posed significant investigative problems as officers and agents are forced to work together in an administrative environment that rewards individual success through arrest and conviction rather than cooperation. Adding to this dilemma, individual investigators often find themselves working with unfamiliar laws and competing for limited resources. Then too, most local police administrators are not aware of the magnitude of the problem. Their attention is focused on traditional crime, particularly violent crime, in the belief that computer crimes are "someone else's problem" and well beyond their financial and investigative capabilities. Lack of awareness results in lack of attention.

As a result, most police agencies have very few computer-literate investigators to conduct these complex investigations; and as Internet use continues to increase, the total number of computer crime incidents escalates exponentially. For instance, the total number of cybercrime cases more than doubled from 1998 to 1999, and estimates of unreported computer crime in 2000 are staggering (Uniform Crime Reports, 2000). The Internet poses other significant issues for the investigator of cybercrime. Specifically, the debate on Internet regulation continues to pit conservatives against civil libertarians, with police often caught in the middle. Hence, the legal implications of computer investigations must be discussed in light of several key factors: (1) understanding the nature of cybercrime; (2) constitutional issues; (3) investigative issues; (4) international issues; and (5) the practical limitations on such investigations.

THE NATURE OF CYBERCRIME

At a basic level, cybercrimes fall into one of three categories: (1) crimes where computers (or the data stored on computers) are the target, (2) crimes where the computer is merely a tool, typically replacing or augmenting non-computer technology or methods, and (3) crimes committed as a result of access to or use of the Internet. The first category of computer crimes includes denial-of-service attacks, unauthorized access to computer data, and other activities where the computer is the target. Such offenses include theft of intellectual property (e.g., an idea, invention, business method, unique name, or chemical formula), theft of marketing information (e.g., customer and price information), and blackmail based on information obtained from data files (e.g., insurance or personnel information).

Examples of the second type of crime, where the computer is merely a tool or instrument of the activity, include the drug dealer or madam who keeps a computerized database of contacts, and the bookie who tallies his "vig" from the weekend sports bet. Another common practice using computers as a means rather than an end involves the manipulation of existing computer programs and processes. Converting legitimate processes to illegitimate processes, including fraudulent use of bank accounts, automated teller machine (ATM) manipulation, credit card number theft, and telecommunications fraud, represent this second major category of cybercrime.

The last type of cybercrime activity is focused on the Internet, particularly its communication and distributive capabilities. These types of crime include terrorists who use e-mail to plan their next bombing, sexual predators who "cyberstalk" their next victim, and drug traffickers who launder money through on-line foreign accounts. More recently, viruses sent through the Internet have been focused more on vandalism than personal gain. These types of activities are aimed at stopping or denying service of major e-commerce sites. For instance, sending enormous IP (Internet Protocol) packets from multiple computers on the Internet requesting information from a single web site often results in that site "crashing," or becoming too overworked to answer any requests at all. The attacks on Yahoo, Ebay, E-Trade, and Amazon in February 2000 were examples of denial-of-service attacks. With widespread use of the Internet, these types of offenses have significantly increased, placing a unique demand on police investigators.

Viruses

The most compelling, and the most formidable from an investigative and legal perspective, is the proliferation of viruses. These relatively small (in length) programs are inserted into a standard computer program or the computer's operating system, causing printing errors, annoying messages, system failures, collapsed files, extended run times, and, in the most serious cases, deletion of data.

A virus has two objectives: propagation and destruction. Viruses are usually created by a malicious computer programmer with the intent to cause electronic confusion. These programs are often designed to be "invisible" or "opaque," meaning that they are extremely difficult, if not impossible, for the average user to detect. The computer appears normal during the propagation stage, but meanwhile the virus is reproducing or copying itself into other programs or onto storage devices (e.g., hard drives, tapes, CD-ROMs). During the destructive stage, the virus program is awakened by either direct intervention or some form of trigger, such as a certain date or keystroke. The virus often shows itself by producing a message or some other form of symbology, such as the infamous "Gotcha" or bouncing ping-pong ball which grows as it travels across the screen (Salle, 1988). Both the Melissa Virus and the "I Love You" worm manifested destructive data code. Other viruses produce messages without destroying data, as exemplified by the "Universal Message of Peace" virus that infected CompuServe. These types of viruses should not be confused with web site destruction, which alters existing home pages as recently happened to the FBI and Department of Justice web sites (Taylor, 2000). From an investigative point, these viruses are often mistaken as denial-of-service attacks (as previously mentioned). The untrained police investigator must understand the differences to apply the most relevant legal violation.

Media and the Law

The media are largely responsible for shaping the American public's perception of computer and Internet crime. Headlines such as "Internet Child Porn Ring Busted" (1998) grab the public's attention, and seem to be increasingly found in the news. Whether reflective of a genuine increase or widespread incidence of such events, or merely reported for their sensational value, such stories create and foster the perception among the American public that there are serious problems in the on-line world. These problems, as reported by the media, frequently involve issues that create immediate negative emotional responses in the general public (e.g., child pornography). Desiring to "do something" to end these problems, legislators, supported by various segments of the population, urge that the Internet be "regulated" or "policed" in terms of both traditional computer crime (e.g., unauthorized access to or manipulation of data) and content.

The United States and most other countries already have laws in place that address traditional computer crime issues, such as computer intrusions and the unauthorized manipulation of data (*United Nations Manual on the Prevention and Control of Computer-Related Crime,* 2001). As a result, much of the current call for Internet regulation deals with regulating the content of the Internet in some manner. The United States, among other nations, has passed or attempted to pass a variety of laws containing Internet-regulation provisions.

Computer crime and Internet-regulation legislation are not without their problems, however. On the one hand, there is a desire to protect individuals and society from exploitation and harm, whether it is child pornography, credit card fraud, denial-of-service attacks, or protecting information that is of importance to national security. On the other hand, there is a need to protect the constitutional and human rights of all members of society, including the rights to free speech or freedom of expression, and to privacy.

The need to balance these two seemingly contradictory goals is further complicated by the international nature of the Internet, with its mix of jurisdictions, social norms, and regulation or lack of regulation. These competing needs and complicating issues must be taken into consideration in any discussion of regulating or policing the Internet or of computer crime legislation in general.

In 1997, while declaring the Communications Decency Act unconstitutional, the Supreme Court ruled that "the Internet is entitled to 'the highest protection from governmental intrusion'" [*Reno v. ACLU* (1997)]. The Court in *Reno* noted that the Internet was a "unique medium" and comparable to a "vast library" immediately available to people all over the world [*Reno v. ACLU* (1997)]. While *Reno* set forth a broad and sweeping policy statement regarding the Internet, the decision falls short of identifying the complexity of applying the First Amendment to specific cases involving the Internet.

While there is an absolute need to safeguard constitutional and human rights, there is also the competing need to safeguard society from criminal activity. Thus, any Internet regulatory policy (which directly influences police investigations of computer crime) must strike a clear and acceptable balance between the two, especially when the policy is an attempt to regulate Internet content.

CONSTITUTIONAL ISSUES

The legal issues arising in the debate over Internet regulation continue to surround two major areas of discussion: rights to a pure speech arena, and freedom from governmental intrusion—privacy.

Pure Speech Arena

The Internet has been described as a "pure speech arena" because "all discussions and exchanges of information on the Internet are speech" (Berman, 1995, p. 3). As such, it is argued, that the Internet deserves the protection of the First Amendment of the U.S. Constitution, and any attempts to regulate the content of the Internet infringe on such protection. Beginning with *Schenck v. United States* (1919), the U.S. Supreme Court has evaluated the constitutionality of speech based on some form of activity resulting from the material under review (Weissblum, 2000). According to the Court, the First Amendment does not protect speech if it creates a "clear and present danger" of imminent lawless action, thereby establishing the first test as a means of determining protection. Since 1919, the Court has decided two other cases, *Brandenburg v. Ohio* (1969) and *Hess v. Indiana* (1973), that, together with *Schenck,* culminate in what is commonly referred to as the "speech plus doctrine."

In *Brandenburg,* a leader of the Ku Klux Klan made statements about Jews and African Americans at two separate public meetings that resulted in his being arrested under an Ohio criminal syndicalism statute for advocating violence as a means of political reform. The case hinged more on the constitutionality of the statute than the constitutional protection of Brandenburg's words. The Court explained that "some action or evidence of action beyond mere words must exist to justify a criminal prosecution of political advocacy activity," such that the speech must be intended to produce "imminent lawless action and must be likely to incite or produce such action" [*Brandenburg v. Ohio* (1969)]. Accordingly, the Brandenburg test appears to protect most speech on the Internet, because the production of imminent action is highly unlikely (Sunstein, 1996).

In *Hess v. Indiana* (1973), the *Brandenburg* test was further refined. The Supreme Court held in this case that speech must be "directed or intended toward the goal of producing imminent lawless conduct" and must be "likely to produce imminent illegal conduct" [*Hess v. Indiana* (1973)]. Hence, the speech must be directed to a specific audience and carry a specific message of imminent illegal conduct. Words alone cannot incite specific activity when placed on a web site for general observation or access. The speech must be directed to an individual with a specific criminal goal in mind.

The tests set forth in *Brandenburg* and *Hess* have been applied to other forms of media as well. Specifically, the Supreme Court recently ruled in a variety of entertainment cases (music, television, movies) that the publishers did not intend for viewers or listeners to commit acts of violence, and that musical recordings and broadcasts of specific pictures were not directed to specific audiences (Weissblum, 2000). Based on these rulings, it can be argued that much of the speech on the Internet is protected under the First Amendment.

Hate Speech and Bomb-Making Instructions   The tragic events in Littleton, Colorado, involving the murder of twelve Columbine High School students and a teacher by two fellow students, generated intense discussion concerning hate on the Internet. The two perpetrators of the Columbine killings (Eric Harris and Dylan Klebold) were found to be frequent visitors to a number of hate web sites that facilitated expressions of bigotry and explanations of bomb-making. In fact, evidence existed that Harris and Klebold obtained their bomb-making information from web sites. While concerns over on-line extremism were not new in 1999, the Columbine attack raised debate focused on regulating dangerous and violent instructions (specifically relating to poisons, drugs, weapons, and bomb-making) that could be used by criminals and terrorists alike. The claim that such instructions commonly found on the World Wide Web pose a specific threat and potential criminal-aiding and -abetting liability (for web site publishers and ISPs) most likely would not be upheld. Such information is freely available to almost anyone. Further, it is a specific individual who uses the instructions to make the crime occur, not the message content itself. Thus, because the directed requirement established in *Hess* is not satisfied, web site publishers (and by logical extension ISPs) offering instructions on everything from bomb-making to environmental sabotage will likely receive First Amendment protection.

Berman (1995) further addressed the issue of terroristic activity on the Internet and constitutional rights, arguing that, among other items, the publication of bomb-making instructions on the Internet should not be regulated. Berman (1995, p. 7) concludes that "our first amendment traditions and long-standing policing policy teach that criminal sanctions are only appropriate for 'speech plus' some criminal or likely violent actions." Quoting Judge Dalzell's *Reno v. ACLU* decision, Mota (1998, p. 12) argues that "the Constitution forbids the government from silencing speakers because of their particular message," with exceptions for obscenity and child pornography. Adults, however, do have a First Amendment right to indecency, and "the Government may only regulate indecent speech for a compelling reason, and [then only] in the least restrictive manner." Mota (1998, p. 13) further echoes the sentiment of the Supreme Court in *Reno* that, being a new communication medium, "the Internet should be afforded the *most* protection from government regulation." Certainly, the Supreme Court has made it very clear for police investigators that mere words cannot formulate justification for arrest and/or prosecution, no matter how reprehensible these words may be.

Hate speech, again, clearly falls within this protection. The first hate site on the World Wide Web was launched by white supremacist Stephen Donald (Don) Black in 1995: *Stormfront.* In addition, the Anti-Defamation League (1999) reported on various underground bulletin boards and computerized networks focusing on paramilitary hate groups as early as January 1985. Once again, the question is whether overt hate on-line should be protected from governmental regulation as part of the free speech arena. While no additional cases have been presented before the Supreme Court, the logical extension from previous case history suggests that in the United States, such speech is protected and guaranteed under the First Amendment; again, no matter how reprehensible the content may be. The same is true for hate sites that market directly to the young, such as the World Church of the Creator, which has established a number of web sites targeting teens (Anti-Defamation League, 1999). These sites often combine their messages of hate and bigotry with darker sides of the youth pop-culture found in Gothic music, black clothing, spikes, tattoos, and nihilism.

Pornography   Similar constitutional rulings also support protection of pornographic material on the Internet, except when directed toward children. A review of the legislation brought before the 1998 Congress finds several House and Senate bills dealing with free speech on the Internet: including H.R. 3783, the Child Online Protection Act, which required that those who sell or transfer material on the Internet that is harmful to minors restrict access to adults, and H.R. 3177, the Child Protection Act, which required mandatory filtering of Internet content for schools and libraries that receive federal funding (Center for Democracy and Technology, 1998). A Virginia law similar to the Child Protection Act, that required libraries to install software filters so that children accessing the Internet through their computers would not be exposed to obscene material, was struck down as unconstitutional in the fall of 1998. The Child Online Protection Act was also declared unconstitutional in November 1998.

Privacy Rights

In an attempt to safeguard both the integrity of investigations and the privacy rights of individuals and organizations, the U.S. Attorney General's Computer Crime Unit published a monograph titled *Searching and Seizing Computers: Federal Guidelines*. These guidelines provide police personnel with policy and practical guidance for conducting searches of computer systems. The document recognizes the need for technical expertise in conducting searches, especially to protect data that may constitute protected speech or be protected by various privacy acts, commingled information, and stored electronic communications (White & Charney, 1995). Despite these guidelines, Craine (1996) argues that there is a case law disparity between traditional and computer searches and seizures because "general searches and seizures, which are normally forbidden under traditional circumstances, have been permitted for searches and seizures of computers and computer-related equipment." Craine (1996) further contends that "administrative expediency turns a blind eye to Constitutionally-granted rights when technology that judges and police officers do not understand enters the equation." The argument that ignorance of computers in the criminal justice system is one of the primary causes of computer-related constitutional violations is furthered by Icove, Seger, and VonStorch (1995), who argue that "because so few judges and juries are familiar with computer crime and evidence, the defense is in a good position to challenge such evidence on all fronts."

The Electronic Frontier Foundation, the Electronic Privacy Information Center, and Computer Professionals for Social Responsibility have identified areas of specific concern regarding constitutional protections and computer users (Craine, 1996). One of the first areas of concern deals with the issuance of no-knock warrants for cases involving computers. These warrants are issued out of the fear that data will be destroyed, a valid concern, but one that can easily be abused (see also Hemmens's discussion in Chapter 2). Craine (1996) cites concern that these fears "often act as a sort of blanket probable cause for searches and seizures of any computer equipment" and are "based entirely in computer illiteracy." While no-knock warrants are "extremely intrusive" (Craine, 1996), they are at times necessary, such as "when a computer will be used for illegal purposes at the time of the search." The Department of Justice Search and Seizure Guidelines "indicate that showing more than the mere fact that evidence can be destroyed will be necessary to obtain a no-knock warrant" (Craine, 1996), although Craine argues that it has yet to be seen whether the Guidelines will be followed through into practice.

Another area of concern with regard to the search and seizure of computers pertains to the search of "bulletin board systems, media, and electronic mail" (Craine, 1996). These are particularly applicable to First Amendment protections because they are often used for personal communication or are temporary communications (Craine, 1996).

Finally, the most serious concern of computer privacy advocates is the general search and seizure of computers and computer equipment. Particular concern is focused on the seizure of entire hard drives and all the disks of small and medium-sized businesses, actions which can be crippling to their ability to continue business operations Craine, 1996). Craine (1996) argues that "law enforcement officials are quick to overlook the fact that other alternatives exist to wholesale searches and seizures of computer hardware and software." While some of this "overlooking" is undoubtedly due to ignorance on the part of investigators, there is also a possibility that investigators will take advantage of these unprotected areas to conduct searches based on less than probable cause.

INVESTIGATION ISSUES

Investigative issues revolve around two new practices available to police. These are surveillance of Internet communications and application of the FBI's Carnivore program.

Surveillance

Surveillance of Internet-based communications through wiretapping or eavesdropping can be a powerful tool in criminal investigations. However, such acts constitute "a very severe intrusion into the civil liberties of the person whose communications have been surveyed" because "tapping telecommunication systems and eavesdropping on computers is, generally, a permanent and clandestine intrusion" (*United Nations Manual on the Prevention and Control of Computer-Related Crime,* 2001). Such methods are in contrast to the traditional "powers of entry, search and seizure [which] usually constitute a single, 'visible' interference with civil liberties" (*United Nations Manual on the Prevention and Control of Computer-Related Crime,* 2001).

While laws exist to provide police with traditional wiretaps and other forms of surveillance, computers and the Internet present new challenges (Barrett, 1997). Currently, police agencies are able to intercept criminal wire and electronic communications (including Internet communications) under authority derived from Title III of the Omnibus Crime Control and Safe Streets Act of 1968 and portions of the Electronic Communications Privacy Act of 1986. Such police actions are conducted pursuant to an application presented to a judge who issues a court order for the collection of evidence. Important in this discussion is that criminal electronic surveillance laws focus on gathering specific evidence for a specific case and do not provide methodologies for random surveillance of the general public or intelligence gathering.

Isolating and intercepting the electronic communications of a single user on the Internet is a monumental task, especially when real-time intercepts are required. Many computer network providers are technically incapable of providing police officials with such intercepts. Berman (1995) argues that we must "treat proposals to expand surveillance authority with great caution." The 1986 Electronic Communication Privacy Act contains provisions that extend legal protection and powers of wiretapping to electronic communication. In 1992, the FBI proposed changing federal wiretapping law to "require all public and private networks to have a built-in capability for intercepting a criminal suspect's communications" (Betts, 1992; Schwartz, 1995). While the FBI argued that it "needs the built-in wiretapping capability so it can conduct court-ordered intercepts regardless of the technology involved," the ACLU argued that such legislation "might encourage overly broad government surveillance" (Betts, 1992). Civil liberties organizations question the legality of providing "the FBI with built-in intercept capability across the board before any crime is committed or a court order is obtained" (Betts, 1992). Despite these objections, in 1994, the U.S. Congress passed the Digital Telephony Act, "which requires future telecommunications systems to be accessible to wiretaps" (Sussman, 1995), thus allowing police "to keep pace with emerging communication technology" (Schwartz, 1995).

Carnivore

Certainly, nothing has merged the issues of government surveillance and individual privacy more poignantly than a new Internet and data interception program developed by the FBI called "Carnivore." Developed as a specialized network analyzer or "sniffer" program designed to work on a personal computer under Microsoft Windows, Carnivore raises the ire of many civil libertarians. Essentially, Carnivore analyzes portions of selected network packets, and copies them to a separate file for further analysis by the FBI. These packets are defined by specific filters set within the program, which conform to a court order. The filter set can be extremely fine, and comply with applications developed from Title III interception orders, pen register court orders, trap and trace court orders, and so on. As Kerr (2000) points out, however,

> The problem of discriminating between users' messages on the Internet is a complex one. However, this is exactly what Carnivore does. It does not search through the contents of every message and collect those that contain certain key words like "bomb" or "drugs." It selects messages based on criteria expressly set out in the court order, for example, messages transmitted to or from a particular account or to or from a particular user. If the device is placed at some point on the network where it cannot discriminate messages as set out in the court order, it simply lets all such messages pass by unrecorded.

It is this latter part of discriminating between messages that provokes such strong reactions. For Carnivore to work, it must first "read" every message passing over the network, those from suspect accounts named in the court order *and* those of others. Never before has the FBI had the authority or the capability to capture *all* of the communications passing through a network. According to the ACLU:

> Carnivore permits access to the email of every customer of an ISP and email of every person who communicates with them. Carnivore is roughly equivalent to a wiretap capable of accessing the contents of the conversations of all of the phone company's customers, with the "assurance" that the FBI will record only conversations of the specified target. . . . If you accept the FBI's arguments in favor of Carnivore, you reject the Fourth Amendment, which is built on the premise that law enforcement cannot be trusted with carte blanche authority when it conducts a search. (Steinhardt, 2000)

While Carnivore continues to be used by the FBI, a university team of computer scientists will conduct an independent review and issue a public report on its findings. Civil libertarians believe that this report will be the basis for a public outcry demanding legislation that eliminates or severely limits the use of Carnivore.

INTERNATIONAL ISSUES

The international nature of the Internet makes investigating Internet crime and implementing Internet-regulation policies at best complicated and at worst impossible. The *United*

Nations Manual on the Prevention and Control of Computer-Related Crime identifies one of the most significant problems when dealing with computer crime, including Internet crime: "Laws, criminal justice systems and international cooperation have not kept pace with technological change. Only a few countries have adequate laws to address the problem, and of these, not one has resolved all of the legal, enforcement and prevention problems." At the very least, to address Internet crime effectively, international cooperation is required. As set forth in the *United Nations Manual on the Prevention and Control of Computer-Related Crime* (2001), there are seven main obstacles to international cooperation in the investigation of computer crime, and they all can be readily applied to Internet crime:

1. The lack of global consensus on what types of conduct should constitute a computer-related crime.
2. The lack of global consensus on the legal definition of criminal conduct.
3. The lack of expertise on the part of police, prosecutors, and the courts in this field.
4. The inadequacy of legal powers for investigation and access to computer systems, including the inapplicability of seizure powers to intangibles such as computerized data.
5. The lack of harmonization between the different national procedural laws concerning the investigation of computer-related crimes.
6. The transnational character of many computer crimes.
7. The lack of extradition and mutual assistance treaties and of synchronized law enforcement mechanisms that would permit international cooperation, or the inability of existing treaties to take into account the dynamics and special requirements of computer-crime investigation.

One of the primary issues arising from the international scope of the Internet is the lack of harmonization of national computer crime laws and policies. The United Nations and the Council of Europe, together with other international bodies, are spearheading efforts to harmonize national computer laws, especially with regard to the alteration of computer data and computer espionage (*United Nations Manual on the Prevention and Control of Computer-Related Crime,* 2001). While the alteration of computer data and computer espionage are likely to be recognized on their face as criminal activities in most countries, the diverse social norms found throughout the world make identifying what other activities constitute criminal activity very difficult. This is particularly true when addressing the issue of regulating Internet content. An individual can sit at a computer in Dallas, Texas and download child pornography that is placed on a server located in Asia. While creating, distributing, or possessing the material is illegal in the United States, it may be legal in the country where the server is located. Likewise, literature promoting hatred against an identifiable group may be classified as "hate literature" and be illegal in Canada, and yet be protected under the First Amendment in the United States, where, while it may be objectionable to some, it is legal. While a nation has the right to enforce its laws and policies within its own borders, it may not have the right or the ability to enforce its laws extraterritorially. This principle is expressed in the following policy:

The primacy of the principle of territoriality is generally accepted in the sphere of criminal jurisdiction. The principle is based on mutual respect of sovereign equality between States and is linked with the principle of non-intervention in the affairs and exclusive domain of other States. Even in the exceptional event that a country might apply extraterritorial jurisdiction for the sake of protecting its own vital interests, the primacy of the extraterritorial principle is not altered. (*United Nations Manual on the Prevention and Control of Computer-Related Crime,* 2001).

In addressing the regulatory context of telecommunications-related crime, including some Internet-based crimes, Grabosky and Smith (1997) argue that "the pursuit of a strict regulatory agenda is, in most cases, not feasible because of the limited capacity of the state."

Finally, Barrett (1997) raises an interesting issue: international differences in laws can be used to benefit police investigating crimes on the Internet, just as they can be taken advantage of by the criminals. Criminal procedures, including rules regarding evidence and search and seizure laws, vary widely from country to country. What is not permissible in one nation may be permissible in another, thus allowing police to gather information that they may not otherwise normally be allowed to gather. Understanding these legal loopholes may allow police investigators to solve complex Internet crimes by narrowing the source of the action and identifying the criminal actors responsible for their dissemination. Even if prosecution is not possible (in the United States) due to the legality of seized evidence, police investigators can obtain significant intelligence on new criminal enterprises and techniques active on the Internet.

PRACTICAL LIMITATIONS

One of the fundamental areas that creates practical limitations for police investigations is insufficient training of individuals and organizations involved in the criminal justice and legislative systems. Police agencies employ few people who are sufficiently trained and experienced in computer technology, so the training of more personnel in this area is required. The *United Nations Manual on the Prevention and Control of Computer-Related Crime* argues that appropriate training would "impart a thorough understanding in five areas":

1. The difference between a civil and a criminal wrong.
2. The technology.
3. Proper means of obtaining and preserving evidence and of presenting it before the courts.
4. The intricacies of the international nature of the problem.
5. The rights and privileges of the accused and the victim.

One organization that conducts computer training for police personnel is SEARCH. This organization has trained over 6,000 police officers since the inception of its training program in 1990 (Radcliff, 1998). More recently, the National White Collar Crime Center has started training police investigators. New courses in digital forensics focus on teaching investigators the intricacies of locating, identifying, and securing electronic data, legally, as evidence in criminal cases. The need for computer training for police officers is further reinforced by Icove, Seger, and VonStorch (1995), who argue that "investigators will also need to become comfortable enough with computers to provide protection during investigations. Agents of the law must strive to avoid damage to the property, livelihood, and rights of bystanders and suspect users of computers in an investigation."

CONCLUSION

The American public and legislators are increasingly calling for regulation of the Internet. Serious constitutional concerns arise, however, when the issue of Internet regulation is discussed. These concerns deal primarily with free speech and privacy issues, and are strongest when looking at Internet content regulation. While there is a clear need for Internet regulation to protect society against the more traditional computer crimes, such as data manipulation and computer intrusions, that are carried out through or against the Internet, the need to protect society against the content of Internet communications is less clear.

In addition to constitutional issues, serious investigative issues arise. These include surveillance concerns, pertaining both to the ability of police to conduct surveillance and to the constitutionality of such surveillance. International issues compound the investigative difficulties. Traditional computer crime causes definable harm and is identified as criminal activity in most countries. Differing laws, however, make Internet content less easily identifiable as criminal. To complicate matters even further, varied criminal procedure rules combine with a lack of jurisdictional cooperation to make investigating any Internet crime difficult. Practical limitations, especially those revolving around the computer training of police personnel, further hamper the ability to regulate the Internet in practice. Hence, it appears that regulation and subsequent police activities related to the Internet present enormous technological and legal difficulties. Alternatives to formal regulation may rest in the goodwill of Internet Service Providers to voluntarily remove objectionable web sites (offering on-line pornography and hate) from their servers. Then too, each individual can exercise the right of personal choice by not visiting such sites or eliminating them through computer software filters.

Icove, Seger, and VonStorch (1995) argue that "the challenge to law enforcement with computing is basically the same as with any new technology: keeping a delicate balance between society's needs and individual rights." Police personnel must develop new techniques to investigate computer and Internet crime. At the same time, as they are protecting society from being victimized by criminals, police personnel must strive to prevent the curtailment of the constitutional rights of citizens, including the rights to free speech and privacy (Icove, Seger, & VonStorch, 1995). Thus, police must strive not to just be the enforcement tools of the legislative body, but also to uphold the rights of the citizenry that they are charged to both serve and protect. Police personnel and agencies must also inform legislators about the feasibility of enforcing proposed legislation. They must encourage laws that will facilitate the successful completion of their job, provided that such legislation also protects the rights of the citizenry.

Regardless of the current legal issues associated with computer crimes investigations, one thing is certain—things will change. Police must understand the current legal requirements and ramifications of computer crime investigations, and must begin to look

UNIFORM CRIME REPORTS. 2000. Washington, DC: United States Department of Justice, Federal Bureau of Investigation.

UNITED NATIONS. 2001. *United Nations Manual on the prevention and control of computer-related crime: International review of criminal policy*. [On-line]. Available: http://www.ifs.univie.ac.at/~pr2gq1/rev4344.html

WEISSBLUM, L. 2000. Incitement to violence on the World Wide Web: Can web publishers seek First Amendment refuge? *Telecommunications Technical Law Review, 35*. Available: http://www.mttlr.org/volsix/weisslbum.html

WHITE, A., & CHARNEY, S. 1995. Search and seizure of computers: Key legal and practical issues. *SEARCH Technical Bulletin* [On-line]. Available: http://www.securitymanagement.com/library/000177.html

Cases Cited

- *Brandenburg v. Ohio*, 395 U.S. 444 (1969)
- *Hess v. Indiana*, 414 U.S. 105, 109 (1973)
- *Reno v. ACLU*, 251 U.S. 844, 849 (1997)
- *Schenck v. United States,* 249 U.S. 47, 52 (1919)

beyond their current jurisdiction in understanding those laws. It is certain, however, that the laws will change; they must if the law is to keep up with changes in technology Therefore, police officers must learn to quickly adapt to changes in the law and to changes in technology if they are to be able to continue policing the Internet.

REFERENCES

ANTI-DEFAMATION LEAGUE. 1999. Poisoning the web: Hatred online. *Corrections Today, 61* (5), 102.

BACARD, A. 1995. *The computer privacy handbook*. Berkeley, CA: Peachpit Press.

BARRETT, N. 1997. *Digital crime: Policing the cybernation*. London: Kogan Page.

BERMAN, J. 1995. *Testimony before the Senate Judiciary Committee Subcommittee on Terrorism, Technology, and Government*. [On-line]. Available: www.cdt.org/policy/terrorism/internet_bomb.test.html [11 September 1998].

BETTS, M. 1992. FBI seeks to tap all net services. *ComputerWorld, The Newspaper of Information Systems Management, 26* (23), 2–4.

CENTER FOR DEMOCRACY AND TECHNOLOGY. 1998. *Legislation affecting the Internet: Free speech* [On-line]. Available: www.cdt.org/legislation/freespeech.html [11 September 1998].

CRAINE, P. K. 1996. *Search warrants in Cyberspace: The Fourth Amendment meets the twenty-first century* [On-line]. Available: http://www.smu.edu/~csr/sum96a2.htm

GRABOSKY, P. N., & SMITH, R. G. 1997. Telecommunications and crime: Regulatory dilemmas. *Law & Policy, 19* (3), 317–341.

ICOVE, D., SEGER, K., & VANSTORCH, W. 1995. *Computer crime: A crimefighter's handbook*. Sebastopol, CA: O'Reilly & Associates.

INTERGOV INTERNATIONAL. 1998. *Latest web statistics* [On-line]. Available: http://www.intergov.org/public_administration/information/latest_web_stats.html.

INTERNET CHILD PORN RING BUSTED. 1998. *Wired news* [On-line]. Available: www.wired.com/news/news/politics/story/15908.html [05 November 1998].

KERR, D. M. 2000. Internet and data interception capabilities developed by the FBI. Statement for the Record before the U.S. House of Representatives, Committee on the Judiciary, Washington, DC.

MOTA, S. A. 1998. Neither dead nor forgotten: The past, present, and future of the Communications Decency Act in light of *Reno v. ACLU. Computer Law Review and Technology Journal*. Winter, pp. 1–22.

RADCLIFF, D. 1998. Cybercop boot camp takes a byte out of computer crime. *CNN Interactive* [On-line]. Available: cnn.com/TECH/computing/9809/09/cybercop.idg/index.html [10 September 1998].

SALLE, R. 1988. Virus threat bytes computer users. *Houston Chronicle,* August 22 (8) p. 6B.

SCHWARTZ, D. A. 1995. The digital telephony legislation of 1994: Law enforcement hitches a ride on the information superhighway. *Criminal Law Bulletin, 31*(3), 195–210.

STEINHARDT, B. 2000. The Fourth Amendment and Carnivore. Statement for the Record before the U.S. House of Representatives, Committee on the Judiciary, Washington, DC.

SUNSTEIN, C. R. 1996. *Constitutional caution*. University of Chicago Legal Forum, 361, 366.

SUSSMAN, V. 1995. Cops want more power to fight cybercriminals. As their techno-battle escalates, what will happen to American traditions of privacy and property? *U.S. News and World Report* [On-line]. Available: www.well.com/user/kfarrand/usnews1.htm [30 November 1998].

TAYLOR, R. W. 2000. Computer crime. In *Criminal Investigation,* (7th ed.). C. R. Swanson, L. Territo, and N. Chamelin (Eds.), New York: McGraw-Hill, pp. 511–536.

7

Police Agency Responses to Changes in the Legal Environment

Michael Buerger

❖

INTRODUCTION

For an occupation that styles itself as "law enforcement," the American police over time have had a curious relationship to the law. American society and government have given the police multiple functions, including order maintenance, crime prevention, and the guarantee of constitutional rights for all citizens. Responsible for both substantive and procedural law, the police have attempted to define their role solely in terms of the enforcement of substantive criminal law, often to the exclusion of the procedural. At times, they have simply ignored their mandate to ensure citizen compliance with the law, most notably during the civil rights movement, but occasionally with regard to other laws. Nominally servants of the law, the police have traditionally defended others interests as well, from the vested interests of the political machines of the nineteenth century to the normative social order of segregationist America. Though it is difficult to draw definitive conclusions about the police in America because of the fragmentation that results from a long tradition of local control (Walker, 1992, p. 4), as well as the distinct differences between rural and urban policing, some broad representations may be made.

In general, the police define their role in society by a self-bestowed image as "crime-fighters." The police subculture often promotes itself as a society of Jedi knights endowed with special powers beyond mortal ken and answerable only to their own counsel. Fundamental change of any kind comes slowly, and often only after the police—individually or collectively (as entire agencies or as individuals "betrayed" by their superiors)—attempt by various means to prevent, to postpone, or to pervert that change. Paradoxically, once the change has taken root, the innate professionalism of the police responds, incorporating the change into formal policy and training, then more slowly into accepted practice. The most important thing to understand is that police response to changes in the legal environment is a slow-moving process, not an overnight event.

Four types of change in the legal environment require adaptations by police agencies: (1) radical redefinition of the substantive criminal law (an extremely rare event) or a shift in the political climate that places new emphasis on a previously ignored area, (2) sweeping procedural law changes at the national or state level, (3) lesser and incremental procedural changes that refine already established powers and limitations, and (4) the impact of civil judgments. These are not mutually exclusive categories, of course, as the examples below demonstrate: civil litigation often follows legislative and political changes, especially where the police response to new obligations is slow or inadequate.

Police reactions to changes in the law and the legal environment fall into tactical and strategic categories. Although the literature on organizations links tactics to strategies, the historical police response to legal changes has been bifurcated. Procedural changes were inspired by tactical responses, and the overall strategy of crime suppression remained the same. Strategic change in response to changes in the legal environment came only with radical redefinition of the substantive law or rules of liability.

In addition, there are two different dimensions of change, positive and negative. For the purposes of this chapter, positive changes are those that increase police power and authority; negative changes are those that restrict it, or require fundamental changes in police operations.[1] While the formal organizational response is the same for both, responses at the individual, workgroup, and "police culture" level can take many different forms, compounding the difficulty of ensuring compliance with negative changes.

In this chapter, the due process revolution will be discussed as a period of sweeping procedural changes. The general reactions to this revolution also serve the complementary category of refinement, since the fundamentals are the same, differing primarily in scope and degree of impact. The issue of the changing response to domestic violence is examined to demonstrate the impact of civil judgments, although the issue is also attended by changes in the political climate and in procedural law. Though a case might be made for examining the impact of *Tennessee v. Garner*, Walker and Fridell (1992, p. 101) found that 70 percent of their sample of police departments "did not have to revise their deadly force policies following *Garner* [because they] had previously adopted policies in accordance with, or more restrictive than, the Supreme Court rule." The change in police policies was already well underway before the *Garner* ruling, making it less illustrative than the impact of *Thurman v. Torrington* (1984). The issue of radical redefinition of the substantive criminal law is speculative, but will be treated through a hypothetical example of the repeal of prohibitions against recreational drug use and possession. A final speculative example, the possibility of enhanced personal liability for misconduct and error, rounds out the chapter.

THE LEGAL ENVIRONMENT OF POLICING

Changes in the law result in changes in the rules of the police work environment, and the formal organizational responses to such changes are simple and nearly universal. They are

---

[1]The analogy at the organizational level is the need to defend the chief's authority and control of the organization, central to the police establishment's resistance to civilian review.

not the focus of this chapter, though, because police decision-making at the street level is driven more by moral precepts than legal ones. It is one of life's ironies that the law often is seen as an obstacle to the law enforcers' ability to achieve justice. To examine the police response to legal change is also to examine the interplay of legal, societal, and organizations goals with those of the individual and the workgroup.

Reiss (1971) most cogently articulates the need of police officers to establish their authority as an instrument of control and peace-making (1971), and his observations are echoed by all of the major scholars of the police: Westley (1970), Skolnick (1966), Niederhoffer (1967), and Klockars (1985), among many others. The issues of authority, and of respect and deference, which stem from it, exist concurrently with the legalities of any given situation. Often the issues are more important than the legalities for the individual officer.

Those who study the police have long observed that legal precepts alone (such as the probable cause standard) do not drive police decision-making in making arrests. In one of the first systematic studies of police behavior, Reiss found

> a high probability that an officer will not make an arrest when he satisfies probable cause. Our observations of citizen initiated encounters with the police, for example, show that officers decided not to make arrests of one or more suspects for 43 percent of all felonies and 52 percent of all misdemeanors judged by observers as situations where an arrest could have been made on probable cause. Something other than probable cause is required, then, for the police to make an arrest.
>
> For the police, that something else is a *moral belief* that the law should be enforced and the violation sanctioned by the criminal-justice system . . . . Overall, an officer not only satisfies probable cause but also concludes after his careful observation that *the suspect is guilty and an arrest is therefore just.* (Reiss, 1971, pp. 134–135; italics in original)

Black's (1980) study added other elements to the decision-making equation, including, among others, the social status and social distance of the participants, the role of the complainant (including status, preference, and deference to the officer), and the seriousness of the offense. Each of these contributes to the fabric of that essentially moral decision.

Reuss-Ianni (1983) distilled the issue further, proposing that the street-cop culture was "a commonly shared ethos [that] unified the department through a code of shared understandings and conventions of behavior binding on everyone . . . the values of loyalty, privilege, and the importance of keeping department business inside the department." This monolithic "clubhouse" culture, she asserted, had been eroded by the social and political changes of the late twentieth century, creating a new "management cop" culture that worked from different understandings and imperatives: "greater emphasis on accountability and productivity—on management processes and products that could be quantified and measured in a cost-effective equation" (1983, p. 2). Where the top command in the old culture would protect the lower-ranking members, the new management cops were responsible for holding subordinates accountable for a broader range of behavior and responsibilities, including some, relating to the treatment (and employment) of women and minorities, that directly contravened the old understandings of street-cop culture. As a result, "What once was a family is now a factory" (1983, p. 4).

Reuss-Ianni (1983, p. 3) cautioned that the "nostalgic interpretation of the good old days may or may not be an accurate interpretation of the past, but street cops believe police work should be organized and carried out that way today". Although drawing upon only one city (New York City), and not universally applauded, her observations accord sufficiently with those of other scholars of the police to serve as a useful talking point. When we talk about police response to changes in the law, it is necessary to specify about which police we speak: an abstract occupational entity, a specific organization, the order-takers or order-givers within an organization, or the broad commonality referred to as the police subculture.

If the police were merely "snappy operatives working under the command of bureaucrats-in-uniform" (Bittner, 1970, p. 53),[2] this chapter would be a short one. A simple statement that "the police command issues new directives to accommodate the new changes, and the officers internalize the new orders and change their behavior accordingly" would suffice to tell the tale. In reality, of course, it does not suffice, for many reasons. Even in cases of positive change, the devil is in the details. Legal dicta and statutory language tend to be broad and sweeping, and cannot address the myriad specific fact patterns against which they will be applied. At the line and workgroup level, each change in the law creates not a new mandate, but a new variable to be assessed and either capitalized upon or neutralized in the setting of the existing corporate-culture definition of good work. The degree of acceptance that the changes enjoy depends upon many factors, including the state of relations between management and workers (upon which hinges the moral authority of the change orders themselves).

Walker (1999, p. 197) speaks of "the myth of full enforcement," an acknowledgment that the police cannot and do not enforce all laws equally and fully, but in discretionary fashion that stems from individual officers' "intuitive grasp of situational exigencies" (Bittner, 1970, p. 46). Despite some superficial similarities, there is a broad range of personalities who do police work, and they are often more conservative than the proponents of social change or governmental restraint who foster the changes in the police working environment. In yet another example of the "herding cats" metaphor, it is the task of police administrators to restrain and guide the full spectrum of individual responses into a reasonably coherent and consistent range of responses that can be said to reflect the stated policy of the agency.

THE FORMAL ORGANIZATIONAL RESPONSE

In almost all cases of change, the first step is to issue (or alter) operational directives to reflect the new legal standard. Larger urban departments (those with their own legal advisory staff) may issue advisory updates on their own; others will defer to the county or state's attorney to interpret the court ruling and assist in preparing any necessary operational guidelines for compliance (e.g., Duffy, 1995). Walker and Fridell (1992) summarize the complex relationship of the "classic professional" model, statutory change, political pressure, court-initiated change, and changes in civil liability that impels the formal organizational responses.

Beyond the paper exercise of establishing or changing policy, however, there are substantial issues of training, supervision, monitoring, and evaluation. At the end of the

---

[2]Described more colorfully by Klockars (1991, p. 420) as "cogs in a quasi-military machine who do what they are told out of a mix of fear, loyalty, routine, and detailed specification of duties."

day, a police agency's policy is not what is written on a sheet of paper in a binder, but what its officers are actually doing on the street. Both individually and collectively, police officers have the capacity to ignore, subvert, and twist both the logic and the application of the law to suit their own interpretations of justice.

The foregoing is not intended to suggest that the American police are lawless, because, with only rare exceptions, they are not. It is rather to recognize the complexity of work on the street, and to acknowledge the craft with which police officers apply themselves to the larger picture of the ends to which their various efforts are devoted: peace, order, and some measure of domestic tranquility through law observance.

There are four basic categories of organizational response to adverse legal changes, two of them legitimate, and two illegitimate. They are not mutually exclusive categories, as the material below should demonstrate. Police responses evolve over time (though it is true that some require a longer time than others), and what may begin as a foot-dragging avoidance reaction may become a legitimate adaptation once the spleen has been vented. Unfortunately, as discussed below, the opposite may also occur, as initial good-faith attempts to adapt to the new requirements lead to disillusionment or an unchecked creativity that becomes calcified in bad-faith brutalities.

Illegitimate Responses: Avoidance and Monkey-wrenching

Avoidance   Avoidance, or a *de minimus* response—the organizational equivalent of individual foot-dragging—constitutes the most convenient form of resistance to change: simply refusing to acknowledge it, and doing nothing. It requires almost no expenditure of resources beyond a change of vocabulary. Consciously or subliminally, all police officers and executives know that several factors insulate them from any possible repercussions for noncompliance: (1) full enforcement is a myth, and there is "wiggle room" in all but the most public of cases; (2) the low-visibility nature of the endeavor makes it extremely unlikely that any official version of events will be successfully challenged (the Holliday videotape of the beating of Rodney King is the rare exception that proves the rule); (3) if the noncompliance is discovered and pressed, the police actions are generally insulated by prosecutorial decisions: dropping the charge almost always ends the challenge.

Avoidance can be an individual or an agency response, or both. The success of individual resistance is obviously enhanced if the parent agency is similarly unconcerned with adapting to the change; individual resistance within generally compliant agencies is dependent upon the efficacy of supervision and the skill of the individual in masking the resistance. Agency success at avoidance is dependent upon the prevailing political climate and the presence or absence of members of the bar willing to push the issue in either civil or criminal venues. The recent revelations about the response of the New Jersey State Police to the decision in *New Jersey v. Soto* (1996) on racial profiling suggest both individual and organizational resistance: at the least, simple avoidance, but ranging to the possibility of outright defiance at worst (see, e.g., Barstow and Kocieniewski, 2000).

Monkey-wrenching   Somewhat higher on the scale of resistance is active suborning, and the invention of ways to circumvent the new rules. Sutton's "Getting Around the Fourth Amendment" (1986) is instructive in this regard, detailing a variety of means for officers to throw off the yoke of court-imposed rules: getting "consent," going "judge-shopping" for a sympathetic magistrate who will issue any warrant without examining the elements of probable cause too closely (or at all), and so on.

Comparable systems exist for thwarting Fifth Amendment due process restrictions, although they tend to be more subtle and individually based. There is no need for judge-shopping, since, unlike the need to obtain a warrant prior to a search, reviews of Fifth Amendment actions are retrospective. Fifth Amendment situations are much closer to Sutton's consent category, in that the primary question is whether or not the statement was made voluntarily.[3] This is not to say that the grace period will last forever: the British police are now required to videotape all interrogations, and the French have just moved to adopt the same restriction (Bremner, 2000). If public confidence in police veracity is further eroded, the United States police might see some comparable regulations imposed in this country, or in individual states. This question is visited below, in the review of the due process revolution.

Where procedural requirements are bypassed, they tend to be supported by the local political and criminal justice systems. Though the Mollen Commission's assertion that police routinely engage in "testilying" has been the focus of a great deal of the media attention (and of police ire), the more important part of the observation is that where it exists, testilying is tacitly accepted by other components of the system and by society as a lesser evil in the "holy war" against drugs and other threats to society (McNamara, 1996; Turow, 2000). Some of it is thought to be minor, only a matter of filling in the blanks of memory when surprised by questions from defense counsel. According to the theory, prosecutors and judges reluctantly have come to expect and tolerate it, so long as it does not become egregious and threaten the trial's main focus of assuring a just and proper finding based on the material facts (for a cogent summary, see Dershowitz, 1998; for an opposing view on the tolerance of perjury generally, see Glaberson, 1998; see also Pascarella, below in Chapter 10). The degree and scope of police perjury will continue to be debated as local scandals erupt (such as the Ramparts CRASH imbroglio, which—at the time of this writing—has resulted in the overturn of more than eighty felony convictions [Associated Press, 2000]).

Legitimate Responses: Distinguishing and Lobbying

Exasperation and grumbling aside, most police professionals immediately adapt their enforcement style to incorporate any new requirements. Though the public is constantly reminded of the exceptions to the rule, good-faith compliance with the law is the norm in police agencies across the nation. This is not to say that the response is that of the "snappy bureaucrat," because it is not. There is a difference between adaptation and acquiescence,

---

[3]Someone once observed that the *Miranda* warning had lost almost all of its original purpose, as it had melded into the iconography of American film and television entertainment, becoming merely a formal confirmation that the individual is, indeed, under arrest. In its June, 2000 decision in *Dickerson v. United States*, however, the Supreme Court forcefully affirmed 7–2 that the *Miranda* warning is in fact a constitutional requirement: "*Miranda* and its progeny in this Court govern the admissibility of statements made during custodial interrogation in both state and federal courts," and "*Miranda*, being a constitutional decision of this Court, may not be in effect overruled by an Act of Congress."

and to adapt does not require changing completely. In varying degrees, according to ability and interest, individual officers will study and absorb the new set of rules—some by listening only to the shorter version that is presented at roll call, others by seeking the full text of the statute or court opinion (when it is published) and studying it in detail—and begin the process of distinguishing, determining just how much of their operational style must change. Sometimes, when the outcome of the precedent case seems egregious, the police, individually or collectively, will seek alternative means (usually through the legislative process) to effect the correction of what they perceive to be a miscarriage of justice.

Distinguishing   Not every effort to overcome a legal change is outright chicanery. Legal decisions tend to be fairly narrowly defined, and good cops—trying to carry out their mandate (as they perceive it) despite the adverse rules—will push to find the elements that distinguish their immediate case from the precedent. They will work the gray areas, adhering to the new precepts but trying to find some element of the fact pattern that "requires" them to give greater weight and observance to another rule of law instead of the new rule. In most cases, this is good police work, something we hope all officers would do, as long as it is guided by a sense of fairness and respect for established precedent.

In a smaller number of cases, fueled by wrongful motives or passions, it is possible for well-intended actions to cross the line of legitimacy. This can create the kind of problems observed in the O. J. Simpson murder trial, the New York State Police fingerprint and the Philadelphia 39th District scandals, the Washington Heights corruption investigated by the Mollen Commission, and—in the extreme—the LAPD Ramparts CRASH scandal. None of those problems appears to have been a specific reaction to an adverse legal change; however they represent a more general disillusionment with the efficacy of the criminal justice system, and an abdication of professional responsibilities. Delattre (1996), followed by Crank and Caldero (2000), described this aspect of police culture as "the corruption of Noble Cause"; a set of moral blinders justifying the means of unlawful actions on the street, even brutality, and perjury in the courtroom in the pursuit of the righteous end of putting crooks in jail.

Lobbying   Though individual officers, and occasionally entire workgroups, may rend their garments and gnash their teeth over adverse court decisions, declaring that it is now impossible to do X or to enforce Y, these are largely symbolic statements that are prelude to active lobbying for changes in the law. Increasingly, police chiefs, police unions and other associations, and police officers individually are participating in the political process of lawmaking, bringing their professional expertise and moral authority to bear on pending statutory changes, or lobbying for such changes. The most public example in recent years is the high-profile support of gun control laws by police chiefs and national police union leaders.

That such lobbying is not always realistic is irrelevant: police officers are aware that in the system of checks and balances, legislative action can overcome disadvantageous court decisions (in some cases). Even if a particular legal gambit fails, there are collateral benefits to be gained from aggressive lobbying, especially concerning contracts and state-level interventions to thwart internal managerial controls.

One example is the Patrolmen's Benevolent Association's lobbying of the New York State Legislature "to change the way [New York City] settles contract impasses with its police officers" (Levy, 1996; Belluck, 1996; see also "A Bad Bill"), thus undercutting the Giuliani administration's 1996 attempt to control the city budget. Another is the recent petition of the Los Angeles Police Protective League (LAPPL) to be a party to the post-Ramparts CRASH negotiations between the city of Los Angeles and the U.S. Department of Justice (Newton & Daunt, 2000). The most egregious recent example of monkey-wrenching-by-lobbying occurred not in the United States but in Canada, where a police union under fire for a variety of reasons (see Canadian Sources 1) mounted Operation True Blue, an aggressive fund-raising effort in support of politicians sympathetic to the union, as a means to thwart administrative and political control (see Canadian Sources 2).

THE DUE PROCESS REVOLUTION

Within living memory, the only period of sweeping change has been that of the 1960s, when series of restrictions placed upon police operations created the illusion that the police were "handcuffed" by silly rules, criminals were "let off on technicalities," and effective punishments were overturned by "bleeding-heart liberals" in favor of "a slap on the wrist." Nowhere was the consternation of the police more evident than in the aftermath of the court decisions that seemed to turn the normative criminal justice system on its head: *Mapp v. Ohio* (1961) imposed the exclusionary rule on state courts; *Gideon v. Wainwright* (1963) mandated publicly compensated lawyers for indigent defendants; *In re: Gault* (1967) granted juvenile defendants the same due process rights as adults, *Escobedo v. Illinois* (1964) established that suspects' Fifth Amendment right to counsel was activated as soon as they became the focus of criminal investigation, and *Miranda v. Arizona* (1966) imposed upon police the duty to advise suspects of their Fifth and Sixth Amendment rights before custodial interrogations.

None of these Supreme Court decisions, which we now call collectively the due process revolution (Walker, 1992, p. 20), forced a wholesale revision of the police mission. They imposed a series of "do" and "don't do" requirements on the officers as individual agents, and some greater impetus on their organizations to provide training, oversight, and accountability; but the focus of the police response to crime was unchanged. That was not the impression of the times, though: the *Mapp* and *Miranda* decisions in particular were derided as heinous abrogations of the public trust that "turned criminals loose on technicalities," "handcuffed the police," and "gave criminals more rights than law-abiding citizens" (these shibboleths remain standards in the "tough on crime" lexicon to this day, despite the enormous enhancement of police powers under the Rehnquist Court). The thirty-five-year persistence of this urban legend in the police culture suggests that a review of the factual basis for it is in order.

In 1970, Oaks undertook a comprehensive review of the evidence that the exclusionary rule was deterring police misconduct. Reviewing the hypothetical alternatives to the exclusionary rule, Oaks asserted that

> In adopting the exclusionary rule for federal courts the *Weeks* Court indulged two assumptions: (1) that exclusion of evidence would discourage illegal behavior, and (2) that there was no feasible alternative for controlling such behavior. Subsequent Supreme Court opinions

have vacillated between conceding ignorance of these essential facts and simply asserting them. None has tendered anything remotely approaching evidence. (Oaks, 1970, p. 672)

Although he noted that the Supreme Court's rationale for the rule included the nominative justification of protecting judicial integrity (i.e., shielding the courts from being party to police misconduct), Oaks observed that when the Court declined to apply the exclusionary rule retroactively, it effectively vitiated that portion of the justification. His argument proceeded from the assumption that the exclusionary rule's only purpose was the practical one, to deter police misconduct.

Reviewing and dismissing criminal prosecution, state torts, Section 1983 actions, and departmental discipline as ineffective, Oaks summarized the available evidence relating to the exclusionary rule. The first study summarized was a thirty-eight-city survey on police training conducted by Supreme Court Justice Murphy. It indicated more "extensive" training in search and seizure in those states that already had an exclusionary rule, and "negligible" in those without one in 1949.[4] Oaks also reported on a post-*Mapp* survey conducted by Nagel in 1963, which examined 250 respondents' opinions on changes in "adherence to legality in searches," police education on legal searches, and "police effectiveness in searches." Like Justice Murphy, Nagel compared states that already had an exclusionary rule with those upon which *Mapp* imposed the rule. In both categories, more respondents felt there had been an increase in police adherence to search rules (57 percent in existing-rule states, 75 percent in imposed-rule states, compared to 9 percent and 4 percent, respectively, who saw a decline in legality) and police educational efforts (77 percent and 87 percent). Only 26 percent of existing-rule respondents considered that police search effectiveness had increased, compared to 9 percent who thought it declined; in imposed-rule states, only 17 percent saw increased effectiveness, and 43 percent were of the opinion that search effectiveness had declined. It is difficult to gauge the propriety of the responses without a more objective criterion as a reference point, but the opinions are telling: though promoting the appearance of compliance, a substantial proportion of the respondents in both groups essentially lobbied against the rule as the cause of diminished police effectiveness. (Whether the "no difference" respondents truly felt there had been no change, or knew they could get around the change surreptitiously, is a matter of conjecture.)

To examine the actual application of the exclusionary rule, Oaks updated a 1950 study of motions to suppress in the Chicago Municipal Court (Comment, 1952) with comparable 1969 figures. Reviewing 6,649 gambling, narcotics, and weapons charges (5,848, or 88 percent, of which were gambling-related), Oaks noted that "in no case was a conviction secured after the suppression of evidence" (1970, p. 683), primarily because the physical evidence of contraband constituted the sole basis for the charge. Oaks considered the motions to suppress "dispositive" of the case. In 1950, 98 percent of all motions were granted, and were dispositive of 69 percent of all cases before the court. In 1969, motions to suppress were filed in 5 percent of all gambling offenses, and dispositive in 45 percent; one-third of all narcotics cases and just under one-quarter of all weapons offenses were

---

[4]The findings arise from a weak methodology. Oaks noted that twenty-two of the thirty-eight cities responded to the survey, but Murphy reported results for only eleven. No operational definitions for "extensive" or "negligible" were provided in the Oaks text.

disposed of by suppression of evidence. Oaks concluded that these numbers were "considerably higher than would be necessary if the Chicago police were really serious about observing the search and seizure rules" (1970, p. 686).[5]

Comparing motions to suppress in the Chicago Municipal Court with those of the District of Columbia Court of General Sessions in 1965, Oaks noted the difference in courtroom culture: motions in 81 percent of Chicago gambling felonies but only 12 percent in DC; motions in 24 and 33 percent, respectively, of weapons and narcotics felony cases in Chicago, but only 1 and 4 percent in DC; and dispositive of all cases in Chicago, but in only half the cases in DC. Across the range of District of Columbia cases, fewer motions to suppress were filed, and a much lower percentage succeeded in those cases where the evidence was not dispositive.

In the District of Columbia, prosecutors reviewed all cases before presentation in court; in Chicago, they did not. Oaks attributed the difference in motion and suppression rates to this prosecutorial screening, which "no-papered" 10 percent of all cases. "No papering" meant declining to prosecute for various reasons, including the vulnerability of the evidence to suppression.

Drawing upon Cincinnati, Ohio, arrest figures from 1956 to 1967, Oaks noted that fluctuations in property recovery appeared to be driven by factors other than the exclusionary rule (1970, p. 693). Declines in seizures of gambling materials for evidence paralleled a substantial decline in the number of gambling raids conducted. Typically, such declines are driven by political or budgetary considerations, not court decisions. Further, Oaks concluded that the declines in gambling cases began two years before the *Mapp* decision (1970, p. 691). Weapons and narcotics seizures from 1960 to 1962 were unchanged, both for confiscation and for evidentiary purposes, nor did the recovery of stolen property decline as a result of the exclusionary rule (though it need not have: since the exclusionary rule only applies to cases in prosecution, officers could well have continued to "find it necessary to violate search and seizure rules in order to . . . [recover] stolen property" [1970, p. 692] because property recovery is not necessarily linked to arrest or prosecution). One of two conclusions presents itself: either the police activity in Cincinnati had always been lawful, or the exclusionary rule presented no real constraint on business as usual.

A Columbia Law School study (Comment, 1968) showed a precipitous decline in misdemeanor arrests by the NYPD Narcotics Bureau, from 1,468 in the six months before *Mapp* to 726 in the six months following it. Oaks noted that this might "give some evidence of illegality, but the evidence is inconclusive" (1970, p. 697), because in the same time period, Uniform Division narcotics arrests increased 4 percent, and Plainclothes Detail arrests increased by 23 percent.

A telling clue to the police adaptation lies in the reasons for the arrests given by narcotics officers in their reports. A 32 percent decrease in "hidden on person" arrests (and drops of 22 and 20 percent for the other two divisions) was matched by a corresponding increase in "dropsie" and "visible in hand" testimony supporting the arrests (28 percent

---

[5]However, in the wake of Operation Greylord and other revelations about corruption in the Cook County court system, other explanations might explain the data observed by Oaks; that is, it may not have been police misfeasance that was at work, but judicial malfeasance.

pre-*Mapp* to 40 percent post-*Mapp* [1970, pp. 698–699]). Oaks noted that "Kuh and Younger reached the same conclusion, that after the *Mapp* case there was an increase in police perjury designed to legalize an arrest and thus avoid the effect of the exclusionary rule" (1970, p. 699; Kuh, 1962; Younger, 1967). Absent some independent evidence of a wholesale change in street-level drug sale practices contemporaneous with *Mapp*, the most likely explanation is that the police merely altered their official explanations to present the verisimilitude of conformance to law, while not altering their actual practices at all.

The reason for this may be found in Oaks's citation of the observational work of LaFave (1965) in the pre-*Mapp* 1950s, and the post-*Mapp* observations of Skolnick (1966). Oaks quoted LaFave's observations that many departments were ignorant of search and seizure rules, and that in any case "the exclusionary rule is not a deterrent to improper police practices in situations where police have no desire to prosecute and convict the person who is arrested" (1970, p. 701, citing LaFave, 1965, p. 488). Skolnick asserted that because police officers' allegiance was to organizational rather than judicial norms, "the policeman fabricates probable cause [and] as a tactical matter . . . the demands of apprehension require violation of procedural rules in the name of the higher justification of reducing criminality" (Skolnick, 1966, pp. 215 and 228).

Examining the implementation of the *Miranda* rule in the District of Columbia, Medalie, Zeitz, and Alexander (1968) drew upon three sources of information about requests for attorneys: police logs, interviews with arrestees, and the Volunteer Attorney Reports of contacts from the Precinct Representation Project. They conducted a pre- and post-*Miranda* comparison of defendants' use of the free service, and the related behaviors of District police officers under General Order No. 9-C, which formally required compliance with the *Miranda* decision's requirements. Post-*Miranda* warnings of some kind (at least one of the four primary components) rose from 50 percent to 75 percent of the cases according to defendants interviewed. However, while warnings about the right to silence and right to counsel doubled, they still constituted only slightly more than half of all cases in which the warning should have been applied. Some 62 percent of the post-*Miranda* group claimed that they had been interrogated without being given any warnings at all.[6] Notice of the availability of an attorney was even less frequent.

Because the *Miranda* rules specifically apply to police custodial interrogation— "incommunicado interrogation of individuals in a police-dominated atmosphere, resulting in self-incriminating statements without full warnings of constitutional rights," in the language of the Court (1968, p. 1368)—Medalie et al. noted that the realities of actual police practice blur the clear lines of the court decision:

> Half the defendants reported not being given the silence warning, somewhat less than two-thirds reported not being given the station-house counsel warning, and over two-thirds as not being given all four *Miranda* warnings. Half the defendants said they had been interrogated by the police and even half of those requesting counsel maintained they had been interrogated before the attorneys arrived. (1968, p. 1394)

---

[6]The actual N is small, however, only eighteen arrestees. The authors did note the various limitations of their data sources, but those issues are not recapitulated here in the interest of space.

The authors contrasted their findings (which were based upon retrospective interviews with defendants) with those of the Reiss and Black participant observation study of field interrogations:

> During the observation period, the *Miranda* warning rarely was given to suspects in field settings. A citizen was apprised of at least one of the rights specified in the *Miranda* decision in 3 percent of all police encounters with suspects. In only three cases were all four rights warnings mentioned in *Miranda* used in the warning. (1968, p. 1368)

Interviews with defendants revealed that while some defendants considered the police explanation helpful, "a number were cynical about the procedure, and believed the warnings to be 'merely a formality'" and that "the police 'didn't seem to care whether we understood or not'" (1968, p. 1374). More significantly, the research team's questions about the meaning of the warnings' components revealed a wide, mostly inaccurate, range of interpretations of the right to an attorney (1968, p. 1375). Additional inquiry into why defendants spoke to police despite having heard their rights revealed multiple motives: some hoped for leniency, but many were distrustful of the police and feared a trick (1968, p. 1380).

At the conclusion of his historical section, Oaks conceded that the evidence he cited was insufficient to prove or disprove the efficacy of the exclusionary rule. In his summation of the evidence available in 1970, however, he noted two trends that are most likely indicative of police responses to changes in the legal environment, and which capture the trends noted in the Washington *Miranda* study. First, where the rules existed, there was evidence that training and directives to conform to the new standards increased.[7] Second, there was a parallel (and often countervailing) movement among line-level practitioners to redefine their practices—without actually changing them—to (in Skolnick's words) "appear to be obeying the letter of procedural law, while often disregarding its spirit . . . the working philosophy of the police has the end justifying the means" (Oaks, 1970, p. 700; Skolnick, 1966, p. 228). Similar observations can be made about police resistance to community policing reforms, asserting that "Zero Tolerance" is true community policing, and it is not unreasonable to expect a comparable effort in reaction to any new changes in the substantive or procedural law.

The due process revolution presents the only contemporary "natural laboratory" for looking at police response to a large-scale, radical change in the legal environment. Oaks's work has been cited extensively here because it is largely known to the general reader today, and the details bear upon actions and techniques rather than attitudes expressed in survey research. The studies he examined demonstrated the range of agency and individual responses. Both Justice Murphy's approach and the Nagel study employed rudimentary quasi-experimental designs, comparing cities or states with an exclusionary rule against those without one. Murphy's dependent variable was the level of training in search and seizure, an organizational responsibility. Nagel assessed "expert opinion" about police obedience to the new *Mapp* rules, and the effectiveness of the searches, tapping into the supervisory and oversight levels in cursory fashion. The Chicago and District of Columbia comparisons are difficult to assess because they represent different time

---

[7]The evidence is scant in that era, but there is certainly more pronounced evidence in the post-LEAA years.

periods in Chicago, and different courtroom cultures between the two cities. The Cincinnati figures are based upon assumptions that certain other measures would be affected by new curbs on police powers to search; assumptions that the other evidence suggests might not be well grounded. The Columbia study of NYPD narcotics arrests demonstrates an illegitimate form of adaptation, probable falsification of official reports (abetted if necessary by perjury), to mask the fact that police conduct continued as before. The evidence points to a clear case of "tell the judges what they want to hear," and the scale of it suggests at least passive collusion by the police organization and the courts.

Oaks's retrospective look incorporated research that was done within the first several years after the *Mapp* decision, and Medalie et al. published their article one year after the *Miranda* decision was delivered. Nevertheless, their results are comparable to those found elsewhere (see, e.g., Walker's [1999, p. 275] discussion of the impact of Supreme Court decisions). The responses to the change remain instructive about how comparable changes would be received today, with a mix of good- and bad-faith adaptations. Monkey-wrenching and avoidance slowly give way to acceptable practices over the long run.

It is reasonable to expect that resistance and monkey-wrenching (and all other efforts to bend the new rule to make it conform to accepted practice) would be highest in the initial, post-change period, when the contrast between the old accepted standard and the new would be most acutely felt by those who had internalized the former as The One True Way of doing police work. Those already in service would be most likely to ignore the rules and procedures promulgated by the agency as part of organizational compliance, offering sham compliance as a veil over business-as-usual practices.

The police have the ability to learn from the refinements of subsequent cases. The number of exceptions to the Warren Court rules that have arisen have changed the landscape of Fourth and Fifth Amendment protections almost as radically as the due process revolution. The inevitable discovery exception (*Nix v. Williams*), the plain feel doctrine (*Minnesota v. Dickerson*), and the public safety exception to *Miranda* (*New York v. Quarles*), among others, have either restored a proper balance or chipped away at individual liberties (depending upon one's perspective). One of the arguments against the preservation of the *Miranda* warning requirements had been that of its ineffectiveness, particularly in light of the police exploitation of the collateral use doctrine (established in *Harris v. New York*). Investigating the erosion of *Miranda* over the years, Hoffman (1998a) noted that

> In California, many police departments . . . seem to have sanctioned [the practice of interrogating suspects even after they ask to talk with an attorney]. In bulletins, interrogation law seminars and training videos, officers have been told that if they continue their interrogation even though a suspect has invoked Miranda, they have little to lose and much to gain.

This practice stemmed from the *Harris v. New York* decision, which permitted the use of statements that would ordinarily be inadmissible as direct evidence to impeach the suspect's testimony or other statements. Ancillary purposes include impeaching the subject's deceitful testimony at trial and obtaining leads: other information about crimes or offenders that could be corroborated and subsequently acted upon independently. As many earlier commentators noted, only in extraordinary circumstances does the exclusionary rule reach intrusions of these kinds. The collateral use doctrine in Fifth Amendment cases constitutes the equivalent of the "don't shoot nobody; don't kill nobody; just get the . . . [drugs] off the street" approach in Fourth Amendment cases (Sutton 1986 [1991, p. 439]). At the time it reaffirmed *Miranda*, however, the U.S. Supreme Court had a specific word for the Los Angeles and Santa Monica police departments: No.

> The high court turned down the departments' request to review a [Ninth Circuit Court] ruling that barred their long-standing but now-discontinued practice of continuing to question suspects even after those suspects had invoked constitutional rights to remain silent or to consult with lawyers. (Daunt, 2000)

The Ninth Circuit's ruling is not binding on other courts, but it provides a precedent that will be invoked by defendants. While the police still have an incentive for pursuing collateral use interrogations, their work is presented to the courts by prosecutors, who take their cues from the bench. Should the acceptance of collateral use recede in the courtroom, it will have a pronounced ripple effect in police practice as soon the police have something to lose.

The real impetus for change should be expected in succeeding generations of hires, as new trainees are exposed first to the formal training that incorporates the new rules, then to the "listen kid, forget all that [stuff] you learned in the academy" socialization process. Though powerful pressures from old-timers to ignore the new rules will persist (in some quarters they persist to this day, almost forty years after the court decisions), each new generation of officers learns them as "the rules," not "the new rules." The rules define the job, and the desire to do the job right means abiding by the rules (though as Sutton [1986 (1991)] points out, compliance is not a single point but a continuum of actions). The tension between the Court-defined expectations and the workgroup normative "crime-fighting" expectations probably will never vanish fully, particularly as the Supreme Court continues to repeal or narrow the earlier restrictions on police powers. As long as the current Court is perceived as being pro-police, there is an incentive for police officers to continue to push at the boundaries of due process.

The pendulum has swung back toward an expanded set of police powers in the last quarter-century, but with the important distinction that those powers exist within a framework of the rule of law. Though collateral use exceptions remain worrisome, the net effect is that of a smarter police community, no longer acting as a law unto itself (notwithstanding the vivid—and still important—exceptions to that rule), and for the most part staying within the Court-prescribed limits even while testing the limits with creative police work. As older *refuseniks* are replaced by generations that internalize the rules before the objections, we can expect the gap between the two to narrow and remain for the most part manageable, and tolerable.

DOMESTIC VIOLENCE

In the modern era, the closest we have seen to a new strategic course in police operations is the response to new legal mandates for the handling of domestic violence cases. The change in domestic violence laws actually expanded police powers of arrest, which victims' advocates considered a positive step, and which in almost any other area would be viewed as positive by the police as well. However, this change simultaneously placed a substantially greater burden on police agencies, and limited officer autonomy in important ways. Consequently, many police officers regard the change as negative, despite the public approval of their new charge and their agencies' formal declarations of support.

Initially, the domestic violence initiative was a political movement (see, e.g., Buzawa & Buzawa, 1992; Caulfield & Wonders, 1993; Daniels, 1997; Dobash and Dobash, 1979). It aimed to eradicate a dominant philosophical viewpoint that bifurcated the application of substantive assault law: the assumption that violence within intimate or familial relationships was a private matter and not the concern of the state. An important footnote in this regard, however, is the reminder that it was never the case that *no* family violence ever resulted in legal or extra-legal sanction from the police. Felony-level violence usually was treated as such, and some misdemeanor violence as well, though the latter was largely dependent upon circumstances and individual officer inclinations.

From the police perspective, however, domestic violence was perceived as a problem that was intransigent, and basically beyond the purview of the police power (see, e.g., Westley, 1970, p. 60; Wilson, 1968, p. 132). From the police perspective, the primary difficulty lay with the victim: if she did not actively interfere with the police arrest of her assailant (Westley, 1970, p. 60), she was likely to request that assault charges be dropped and her husband or boyfriend released from jail, refuse to testify against him in court, or simply fail to appear in court; thus passively causing the dismissal of the case.

As police officers interpreted the totality of these circumstances, few victims wanted a formal justice system response; most merely wanted the violence to end. Police practice consisted of restoring order, either leaving both parties at the scene (the "counseling" response) or sending one or the other party from the residence for the night (the "send" option), and leaving with a warning that if they had to come back, "somebody would be going to jail." The arrest option was used in egregious cases, or when the assault was continued in the presence of the officers, or in rare cases when the victim was adamant about the arrest and took immediate steps, such as making a citizen's arrest or going to swear out a warrant. In addition to those actions, and in cases where the offender was no longer present at the scene, the police advised the victim of the steps she needed to take to use other criminal justice system options (go to the courthouse, swear out a warrant, take it to the police station, testify at hearings and at the trial, etc.), and to seek additional support from family, friends, or social service agencies. If the victim would not cooperate with the police or the criminal justice system, it was taken as further proof of the illegitimacy of the complaint (and of the police role in handling such "family matters").

The requirements of the law aided and abetted the old police response. The law forbade police officers to arrest for misdemeanors that occurred outside their presence, and most domestic assaults were concluded by the time the police arrived on the scene. Without active victim participation, there was no legal action the police *could* take in many cases. When challenged by women's advocates about their failure to treat familial or intimate violence on an equal footing with stranger assault, the police responded that their hands were tied, as the law did not allow them to take the actions demanded by the advocates.

This part of the procedural law changed with the new domestic violence legislation. Advocates acknowledged the police objection and lobbied for legislation that would remove the obstacle on the grounds that the special and continuing nature of domestic violence required the additional leverage that a credible threat of arrest and punishment would theoretically create. They gave to the police a new power that enabled—and often mandated—officers to make arrests based upon probable cause (the felony standard) in cases of misdemeanor-level domestic violence. The arrest power usually was limited to a set time following the initial offense (four hours in the jurisdictions where the author has worked).

It was never the case, however, that the American police, as a group, were straining at the leash, eager to be turned loose to round up domestic batterers. The legal argument of "there's nothing we can do" was merely a convenient excuse. The police objection was based upon an assessment of victim behavior: if the victim was unwilling to participate in the criminal justice process, an arrest was not just. Police attitude was dictated by the cumulative weight of the individual behaviors observed, not by the law. When the law changed, the underlying behavior did not, and thus the police attitude was largely unchanged.

Many police officers also express a moral objection to probable cause requirements that are based solely on the victim's perceptions. They feel that a victim's fear alone is simply not enough to justify an arrest. It is based not in actual conduct, but in a perception of future conduct—"I'm afraid of what he *might* do," a threshold of probable cause not accepted in other areas of the criminal law[8]—and seems to open the door for victims to illegitimately use the police as a tool for relationship management (Reiss, 1989; Mace, 1997).

This is not to say that officers across the nation stonewalled the discharge of their new duties, because many of them did not. In some ways, an arrest and removal of the offender was a much simpler resolution than counseling, though it involved more time. Moreover, for a time the Minneapolis Domestic Violence Experiment (Sherman & Berk, 1984) gave credence to the advocates' views that arrests would reduce future violence in the relationships. By extension, this promised to reduce police responses to repeat incidents involving the couples, and to free officers from the onerous task of continually intervening in what appeared to be unresolvable conflicts. The controversies that arose in the wake of the Minneapolis Experiment, however, led to the National Institute of Justice's Spousal Abuse Replication Project (SARP). This initiative attempted to replicate the Minneapolis results in six cities across the nation, each with a different racial and ethnic population mix. When the results were published, the certainty about the efficacy of arrest for domestic violence was significantly diminished (the results are most cogently summarized in Sherman, 1992).

On an individual basis, many police officers resisted the change in the law even as their comrades attempted to enforce it in good faith. When departmental directives required arrest in all domestic violence cases where probable cause existed, the simplest form of resistance was to handle the incident in time-tested fashion (i.e., without an arrest), and radio in (or file a report) officially redefining the event as an argument, no violence involved, and hence no arrest required. Even more blatant was the practice of clearing a call as GOA, "Gone On Arrival," indicating either that there was no suspect at the scene or no complainant with whom

---

[8]Except in the realm of preventive detention, a concept that seems to enjoy the favor of the police when applied to gang members and others whose conduct is seen as being directly related to "real police work."

to speak, even in cases where both parties were present.[9] Police scholars are well aware of the difficulties of direct supervision of patrol officer responses: the organizational tendency to rely upon the responding officers' account of an incident is predicated upon the necessary assumption that all members of the agency are "snappy bureaucrats." (There are severe repercussions for the agency if the reverse is true, and officers are routinely treated as though they are dishonest, incompetent, or moronic.) Even the most flagrant disregard for policy can be beatified by "creative report writing": unless challenged with credible evidence—a rare event—the creative version of event becomes official truth, part of the agency's annual report, and often another datum point in a social science study of police behavior.

The decision in *Thurman v. Torrington* represents one of the rare events. Although a case involving felony-level violence rather than a misdemeanor, and though it stopped short of imposing direct consequences on individual officers, it changed the landscape of the police response to domestic violence. The multi-million-dollar judgment grabbed the attention of municipal risk management officers and police executives, providing a spur to organizational change and altering both supervision and internal accountability. The overall message was: no longer can the new rules for police response to domestic violence incidents be ignored or passively resisted with impunity. Officer misconduct brought the administrative response under the microscope, and created a new climate of direct accountability for police malfeasance. The financial risks are too great to permit the municipality or the administration to ignore officers' improper responses.

Canny administrators couch the new ground rules in terms meaningful to the street-level officer: any money the city or town pays in civil judgments is money we cannot use for new hires, new cruisers, better radio equipment, or training. Less adept organizations reemphasize the new rules by intensification of the heavy-handed command-and-control techniques associated with the police version of quasi-military organizations. Among the control techniques (all of which are defined by officers as punitive) are new directives that require a comprehensive report to be filed in all domestic cases regardless of whether violence was present. This removes incentives to reclassify a violent event into a no-paper one, and may increase the likelihood of arrest. Other requirements may direct supervisors to respond to every domestic call and file an independent report. This is a third-party tactic (Buerger & Mazerolle, 1998) that capitalizes on the shift supervisors' moral authority with their subordinates. The greater burden upon the supervisors creates an incentive for them to direct officers under their command to "play it straight" on domestics, which is predicated upon an expectation that street officers will be more responsive to pressures from their immediate workgroup than those of central administration. In addition, systematic recontact of victims by internal affairs or by supervisors from other shifts to validate the content of officers' reports eliminates (or at least decreases the risk of) trying to "rug" a call through creative report writing.[10] Finally, most departments, regardless of their

---

[9]Some of the battered women's advocates' greatest ire has been directed at officers who cruise past the residence without stopping, and call in a GOA clearance ("Gone if no one flagged down the cruiser"). The evidence of this is largely anecdotal, but the author has encountered it in two separate jurisdictions, each time linked to a specific dispatched event. While not necessarily typical police behavior, it is egregious enough to overshadow the quieter good work being done by other officers in the department.

[10]"Rug" as in "to sweep under the rug," by obscuring the fact that the proper technique was not employed.

place along the continuum of response, have been subjected to additional (often state-mandated) yearly in-service training in domestic violence.

At both extremes, and all the variations along the continuum between them, the officers in the department will likely complain bitterly that the research-derived instruction of the mandatory in-service training they must endure has the sole purpose of shifting legal liability from the agency onto them (Buerger, 1998).[11] The complaint stems from the still-unresolved affront to their moral sense,[12] and a deeply held belief that arrest does not prevent or deter future violence. Most draw from the cumulative weight of their own experience, and the vicarious experience of their peers, which teaches a different lesson, to wit: despite repeated arrests, neither batterers nor victims change their behavior, and the police keep going back to their domestic squabbles and fights with monotonous regularity. When training instruction and experience are in conflict, street cops put their faith in experience.

There are two flaws in the police experience, of course. Any negative feelings they may have about the police role in domestic violence—whether derived from personal experience or bestowed by socialization—are reinforced by selection bias: officers see the intervention's failures frequently, and the successes almost never. Furthermore, the purported information conveyed by the "war story socialization process" is both primarily anecdotal and devoid of external validity, save that it was said by another cop.

Concurrent with this is a second moral belief, that when victims have no intention of participating in the criminal justice process, an arrest is not just, and mandatory arrests are both a burden and a waste of system resources. Some officers also express a deep resentment at being the instrument of someone else's politically correct ideas about how to handle domestic violence. In the field, this resentment can give rise to a form of monkey-wrenching, the double arrest.

Dual arrests are a quick, efficient way to avoid the complexities of determining who the aggressor was, terminate the call as quickly as possible, and turn the victims' advocates own efforts against them ("counting coup" on the moral plane, as it were). By applying to the batterers the new evidentiary standard intended to protect victims (accepting at face value he said/she said mutual accusations of assault), the police easily reach probable cause to arrest both the batterer and the victim. Any evidence or admission of self-defense by the victim is turned on its head, becoming probable cause to arrest the victim for domestic violence because she lifted a hand to ward off injury or to defend herself. From the standpoint of the victim's advocates, this is an outrage: the victim's supposed rescuers turn into another instrument of her oppression, giving moral and legal support to her tormentor.

While there are times when a double arrest is appropriate, the phenomenon (where it occurs) seems to be a new reaction to external pressures by advocates to increase the police arrest response. At this point, though, the extent of the double arrest tactic is defined primarily by anecdotal evidence, backed by some local figures. It is still in need of documentation: where it occurs, it may well be the result of individual and small-group decision-making, and would not be likely to appear as a gross trend in agency-level statistics.

---

[11]A viewpoint not without foundation, as the nation saw during the trial of LAPD officers Powell, Brisenio, Wind, and Koon, where a primary focus of the trial was whether the officers' beating of Rodney King was or was not "within policy" of the Los Angeles Police Department.

[12]I am indebted to Stephen D. Mastrofski for his earlier observations about this phenomenon.

Women's advocates have other perspectives on victim reluctance to go forward with criminal prosecution, of course. Along with a parallel string of anecdotal evidence of callous police behavior, advocates cite economic and emotional dependency, the various obstacles to participation created (sometimes inadvertently) by the criminal justice system, and the threat of or actual violence by the batterer to dissuade the victim from testifying against him in criminal proceedings (for a review of early materials, see Frieze & Browne, 1989).

To thwart batterers' attempts to intimidate their victims into withdrawing from the criminal justice process, some jurisdictions have instituted victimless prosecution. Instead of placing the burden for prosecuting the case on the shoulders of the victims, the state prosecutes the case on the strength of the police officers' investigation, even if the victim refuses to testify. The theory behind the policy is that if the victim has no control over the prosecution, there is no incentive for the batterer to engage in further violence (in fact, the batterer risks additional penalties). The strength of the case is the evidence collected by the officers at the time of the initial call, and sometimes in its aftermath if the agency has a followup protocol. The officers testify to the statements made by the victim and any witnesses, and to the bruises or other evidence of injury. They also provide ancillary evidence, such as photographs of injuries or the physical condition of the home, that is indicative of a violent struggle.

One interesting aspect of victimless prosecution (at this point merely the author's theory rather than an empirically demonstrated fact) is the way it accomplishes what women's advocates had long sought: a police investigation that places domestic violence on the same footing as stranger violence. When there is an expectation that the victim will carry the burden of prosecution, all responding officers need do is file a bare-bones arrest report. Working within a victimless prosecution system, officers must thoroughly document the case in anticipation of the victim's withdrawal. The result is possibly a more thorough investigation and report, conceivably greater prosecution—both in quantum and effectiveness—and potentially a much larger deterrent effect than the more victim-centered traditional approach where few cases are actually prosecuted (however, this remains a testable proposition). It can also be a deterrent to double-arrest monkey-wrenching.

Victimless prosecution is a decision and a commitment made by the prosecutor's office in conjunction with the police agencies it serves. Such a commitment to the process (external to the police agency) gives domestic violence much greater symbolic importance than all in-service training exhortations combined. It places a greater responsibility on the responding officers ("Don't just make an arrest; do an investigation"), and changes the situation for victim and batterer as well. We do not yet know the long-term impact of victimless prosecution: whether it deters future violence or creates a "backfire effect" similar to that found by Sherman and his colleagues in Milwaukee (Sherman, 1992, p. 18 and Appendix 2); whether it empowers victims or discourages them from calling for police assistance in times of future need; or whether the additional burden on court resources translates into a sustainable social gain. These are all areas for future study.

AN ARMISTICE IN THE WAR ON DRUGS

The legal prohibition against recreational, or perhaps more accurately, non-medicinal, use of drugs has been as close as the police have had to an internal strategic focus. Where the new domestic violence procedures were externally imposed, the war on drugs has been the organizing theme of choice for police over the last fifteen to twenty years. The all-out suppression of drugs was hailed as a necessary crime-prevention technique: illegal drugs were demonized as the driving force behind then-spiraling rates of violent crime, and of property crime victimization as well.

Drug suppression provided the grist for many of the Fourth Amendment cases that gradually restored police search powers, and the eradication of street-level drug retailing was hailed as an integral component of quality-of-life community policing. The growth of PPUs—police paramilitary units (Kraska & Kappeler, 1997 [1999]; Egan, 1999; Cassidy, 1998; Kahn & Dowdy, 1998; Kaszuba, 1993)—was a reaction to the increased violence that attended the spread of the crack cocaine trade, and quickly became the epitome of "real police work." Fortified crack houses and armed resistance to search warrant raids provided the rationale for an escalation of weaponry and "overwhelming force" intervention techniques.

Proponents of drug prohibition have long pointed to the social costs of drug addiction as the reason for maintaining a suppression policy. Though they acknowledge that the war on drugs has not reduced those costs, they assert that the suppression policy has held the line, and prevented the problem from getting worse. Lift the ban, they say, and the floodgates will open and overwhelm us all.

Proponents of the alternative policy of dealing with drug use and addiction as a medical problem acknowledge that there will be social costs associated with lifting the prohibition. They deny that the war on drugs has held the line, though, arguing that it has actually increased the social cost by surrendering the markets to elements willing to use violence to keep costs (and thus profits) high. Medical-model advocates assert that legalization will stem the drain on the body politic (corruption), the drain on the public fisc, and the hypocritical corruption of the nation's spirit, all without notably increasing the ancillary social costs as claimed by prohibition supporters. The control and taxation of recreational drugs—treating drug use on the same footing as its predecessor pariahs, alcohol and gambling—will not completely eliminate the black market, but it will substantially diminish it and curtail the violence associated with illicit drug markets and turf wars. It could also make better use of the nation's tax dollars expended on the futile war, and the immense profits now flowing into the pockets of the drug cartels.

Should the medical model prevail in the social debate, the American police establishment likely will face a series of dislocations that are more spiritual than substantive. The changes in search and seizure powers will not be repealed. By-incident threats to officer safety represented by individuals on bad drug trips will remain, and may possibly be exacerbated. Certainly the need for SWAT-type teams will continue, because hostage and barricaded-suspect situations arise from circumstances other than drug use. Other changes are largely a matter for speculation, dependent as they are upon the form and scope of decriminalization or legalization, and the equally speculative responses of the public (users and non-users alike) to the new drug-available environment.

If we imagine a worst-case scenario, in which there are no criminal penalties for the possession, sale, or use of even the worst of the drugs (PCP, heroin, methamphetamines, etc.) how would the police role change? The reactive role would not: the police would still have the responsibility for dealing with the criminal acts resulting from or attendant upon drug abuse. It is unlikely that legalization would end all drug-related burglaries, for instance, even with cheaper prices resulting from licit operations: the dysfunctions that result from severe drug abuse would deprive some addicts of regular employment, thus diminishing their income as it does now, and leading them to use criminal means to obtain funds to purchase even government-controlled substances (as some now must to buy alcohol).

Of course, serving officers would have to endure the crow banquet for many years to come, as those who have been drug-suppression targets taunt former enforcers with their new quasi-legitimacy (just as officers in states that eliminated motorcycle helmet laws have had to endure the ride of the first helmet-free day, when hundreds—or at least scores—of bikers made a determined effort to count coup by riding helmetless, slowly and deliberately, past police headquarters, substations, and any motor units in sight). Since drug charges have often served as a tangible substitute for the more erratic behaviors that lead to stop-and-frisk contacts, we could very well see a rise in disorderly conduct arrests and other behavior-related charges in the short term— at least until the street life comes to understand the redefined rules governing respect.

More importantly, the arrest option on the street would change. Legalization of the substances will not eliminate noxious drug-related conduct on the street, and it potentially could increase the police workload in other areas: citizen fear of the behavior of drug users will not subside, and may well increase. Arrest would still be a viable tactic for illegal behaviors stemming from drug use, but the proactive use of drug charges to put a run on the criminal element would be eliminated (although presumably the Bureau of Alcohol, Tobacco, and Firearms would retain a tax-related jurisdiction over all controlled substances). Drug-sniffing dogs and "hits" on traffic stops would be a thing of the past, and we could anticipate a reduction in foot- and vehicle chases.[13]

Whether or not the problem of DWB ("Driving While Black, or Brown," being detained on the basis of a suspicion created by one's race rather than one's behavior) would abate is a matter of speculation. Absent the need to search vehicles for contraband, the incentive for the drug courier profiling of the current prohibitionist environment should all but vanish. The use of aggressive vehicle stops for uncovering other criminal activity would remain, as in the firearms interdiction projects of the early 1990s (Sherman & Rogan, 1995; Sherman, Shaw, & Rogan, 1995; Sherman & Bridgeforth, 1994), which suggests that complaints of "You stopped me because I am Black/Hispanic/Latino/Asian" would continue as well.

Whether the elite status of anti-drug units and PPUs would diminish is unclear. Hypothetically, antidrug resources would be redirected by agencies, leaving the traditional venues of detective work and PPUs as the primary status postings. It is likely that whatever the police role in the medical response to drugs, it would be low-status, dumped onto

---

[13]Chases would not be eliminated, however. In Alpert and Fridell's 1992 treatise on deadly force, only the California Highway Patrol study mentioned evading drug charges as a reason for initiating flight from police, bundling an unknown number of drug charges in with driving under the influence charges to total 19 percent of the reasons for flight in that study. In fact, the recent racial profiling cases in Maryland and New Jersey are predicated in large part upon the fact that persons carrying drugs stop for the police rather than flee from them. Most of the studies reviewed by Alpert and Fridell (1992) listed general motor vehicle offenses as the most likely reason for flight (more than half in most studies), followed by criminal activity, with DUI and reckless operation a distant third.

patrol operations (as the low-status "drunk wagon" is now). Requiring a more active police role in initiating medical and therapeutic protocols will entail substantial investments
in training, supervision, and quite possibly recruitment (as many serving police officers
define themselves, in part, as "not a social worker," and the new protocols would likely
push very hard against that definition).

ENHANCED ACCOUNTABILITY

Perhaps the most radical change in the legal atmosphere that could be imagined is a new
era of accountability for officer misconduct. It is unlikely that such a change would result
from court action, as *stare decisis* provides a firm anchor for existing doctrines insulating
individual agents of the state from suit. If a change occurs—and there is no certainty that
it will, only hints—it will probably come from legislative action, and it will almost certainly be initiated by city government or taxpayers groups galled by excessive tax burdens
created by police misconduct. It will take an egregious case to alter the current protective
landscape, a case on the order of the Los Angeles Ramparts CRASH scandal currently
under investigation, in which early estimates are that the county of Los Angeles will need
one-quarter of every new dollar to satisfy pending judgments and related investigation ex-
penses, calculated to be $11.4 million and rising (Riccardi, 2000).

The cost to individual municipalities for police conduct can be staggering. A few
examples include:

- A $6 million award against Boynton Beach in the 1987 shooting of Betty Will-
  ingham ("Woman Shot" 1998).
- A $10 million lawsuit against the city of Long Beach, New York, for the 1967
  beating of David Pearl (Schemo, 1999).
- A total of $40.6 million was paid in 1999 by New York City to settle 739 law-
  suits (among them a $2.55 million settlement in the 1994 Anthony Baez choking
  death case, and $2.75 million to settle a 1996 Greenwich Village beating case), a
  substantial increase over 1995's figures of $23.9 million for 379 lawsuits (Flynn,
  1999).
- A settlement of $3 million for illegal strip searches conducted in three New
  Hampshire county jails between 1990 and 1993 (Flynn, 1999).

Lawsuits are usually settled in advance of trial without an admission of guilt (e.g., Flynn,
1999), often with a financial payment even when no misconduct occurred, because the
cost and risk of defending the suit far outweigh the cost of settlement. Nevertheless, suspicion remains that many lawsuits could be averted entirely if the conduct of the officer or
the initial response of the agency to the complaint were better.

None of the cases of the due process revolution addressed issues of individual officer accountability, directed as they were toward the officers' role as agents of the state.
Oaks's critique of the exclusionary rule's effectiveness included the observation that

> A criminal prosecution of one person is at least an indirect and awkward forum for inquiring
> into the behavior of some other person, a police officer, with a view to punishing him or cre-
> ating some deterrent against similar conduct in the future. In addition, there is something

anomalous if not downright distasteful in the spectacle of a judicial officer engaged in what Chief Justice Burger has sternly characterized as the "suppression of truth in the search for truth." (Oaks, 1970, p. 743)

Oaks called for the abolition of the exclusionary rule, but only after it had been "replaced by an effective tort remedy against the offending officer or his employer [to] provide a viable remedy with attendant deterrent effect upon the police whether the injured party was prosecuted or not" (Oaks 1970, p. 756).[14] Oaks dismissed the current tort remedies as ineffective:

> since the measure of damages is not related to the enormity of the wrong committed by the defendant (police officer). Instead, the damages are determined by the injury suffered by the plaintiff, and that injury [for Fourth Amendment violations] often cannot be measured in economic terms. This defect could of course be remedied by changes in the cause of action and the measure of damages. (Oaks, 1970, p. 718)

Other known weaknesses in the use of civil torts and criminal charges against police officers include jury reluctance (stemming from both the hero image of the police and the inherent bias against "a plaintiff who was an accused or convicted criminal" [Oaks, 1970, p. 673]), general limits on individual officers' ability to pay civil judgments (more an issue in the 1960s than today, though it remains salient in many poor rural jurisdictions), and the range of sovereign and qualified immunities recognized by the courts. None of the due process cases, moreover, anticipated such behavior as the shooting and subsequent frame-up of Javier Francisco Ovando by Ramparts CRASH officers, the shooting death of Patrick Dorismond in New York, or the Abner Louima case.

Traditionally, the courts have protected individual agents of the state against errors committed as a function of their public duty, separating egregious acts into the realm of criminal prosecution, state tort law, and Section 1983 actions under the Civil Rights Act of 1871 (for a summary, see Kappeler, 1997). Since the evolution of the modern quasi-doctrine of "deep pockets"—filing suit against the entity most able to pay large sums of money—most police lawsuits center on the doctrine of *respondent superior*, holding the employing agency responsible for the misdeeds of its subordinates. In theory, this approach is proper both to the maintenance of public order and as a spur to agencies to properly hire, train, instruct, and supervise their personnel.

In reality, however, the task of directing and controlling a police agency is complicated by a network of federal and state employment laws, civil service requirements, and arbitration (Armstrong, 2000a; 2000b). In cases where civil service or independent arbitration vindicates individual officers' property interests in their jobs despite outrageous on-the-job conduct, the notion of quasi-military command-and-control of police agencies is exposed as fraudulent. Where the police union is perceived to be more powerful than the agency's command structure, there is little incentive for officers to heed training or exhortation for professional conduct

Authorities at all levels have traditionally been reluctant to hold police officers directly accountable for judgments of misconduct. One possible reason is that "Officers

---

[14]Police officers have also called for the abolition of the exclusionary rule, in different venues and for different reasons, though few (if any) are on record as offering an effective remedy as an alternative.

who faced the threat of expensive lawsuits might opt to avoid doing their jobs. Unless officers have to get involved, they figure why should they risk their house and their savings?" (Newton, 2000). This sentiment is well rehearsed among police officers, and waved like a bloody shirt whenever the issue of accountability is raised. Though on balance it is more likely to be more a rhetorical device that an actual one—most police officers do their jobs in spite of the foreboding negatives, whether threat of violence or threat of lawsuit—there are occasions when police service is eroded by fear of economic reprisal (See also chapter 4). For example, in the middle of the I-95 racial-profiling brouhaha, "arrests by New Jersey State Police were down 42 percent in September [1999] from the same period [in 1998]" (Arrests, 2000).

Even though the legal landscape is changing—for instance, many officers now purchase private indemnities against lawsuits—there has been no systematic revision of the balance between individual and corporate liability for misconduct. Overall, rogue officers remain well shielded by their agencies' policies, by their unions, and (where they exist) by the political systems of arbitration (Armstrong, 2000b). Part of their cover is the ability to manipulate the fears of honest, professional police officers that any change in the current state of protection will inevitably threaten even their financial security.

This argument has considerable weight, because police disciplinary and sanctioning practices have traditionally been something of a bludgeon, both internally and as matters of law. As the financial crisis created by police error and misconduct grows, however, it is possible for either the police or the civil authorities to institute a different level of control. Among the potential options:

- Requiring that officers maintain their own malpractice insurance policies, as physicians now do, on a par with POST Board licensing as a condition for employment. This would insert a powerful and independent new element—the insurance companies—into the dynamic, operating purely on a financial basis: if an insurance company canceled an officer's insurance for excessive claims, the officer would be ineligible for employment, without any action by the employer.
- Replacing the current presumptions of academy-to-retirement employment with three- to five-year contracts with presumptive renewal clauses subject to conditions related to misconduct and malfeasance complaints. This already exists at the level of chief of police in many jurisdictions, and is a feasible corporate response to the current rates of employee defections as well as a tool for handling consistently problematic officers (Wilson & Gregory, 2000; Lee, 2000; Ford, 2000).
- Expanding the review powers given to civilian review boards.
- Revision of the civil service to more appropriately reflect the state of employment conditions in the early twenty-first century, rather than the late nineteenth and the twentieth century, and amending current rules and practices governing not only hiring, but promotion and assignment.

Sevareid's law holds that "the chief cause of problems is solutions," and none of the potential solutions outlined above is foolproof. None is beyond monkey-wrenching or co-optation. These are potential outcomes for discussion in other venues. All of them, however, have the potential for imposing or stimulating agency and departmental changes in recruiting, training, supervision, and rewards that result in improved police service to the nation's communities.

CONCLUSION

We have a common-sense expectation that the law enforcers will themselves follow the law; but the issue of police response to changes in the law is more complex than this simple dictum. At the organizational level, the responses are fairly straightforward: the issuance of departmental orders (or amendment of existing ones) to incorporate the new requirements, and the administration of an appropriate training program to inform all employees of the new requirements and their practical implications. Beyond the formal organizational response, however, the process is much less simple, depending upon how far the new rules stray from the police culture's normative expectations. The historical record suggests that positive changes are eagerly accommodated, and the major managerial challenge is to set and define the outer limits of acceptable application of the new rules for use of force, searches, interrogations, or whatever area is affected. History also suggests that individual, group, and occasionally organization responses to negative changes will be slow, attended if not defined by foot-dragging, monkey-wrenching, and overt (usually fruitless) politicking to reverse the change. Where external oversight or control of the police is marginal, outright avoidance is possible. Under conditions of weak scrutiny, monkey-wrenching may take the form of linguistic changes to make it appear that the police are in compliance, even though actual practice remains unchanged. Such changes may also be attended by tacit and even overt complicity on the part of those charged with overseeing police operations.

Those who would foster change in police activities through changes in the law would be well advised to regard formal changes in policy as merely the first step, not as evidence of a job well done. Implementing formal changes requires a combination of continuous review, training that provides not only a statement of the law but also a moral framework justifying or validating the change, reinforcement of positive responses, and vigilance against monkey-wrenching and foot-dragging. It is wise to recall that police are both intellectually and morally committed to the rules and the sense of order under which they work, and they will diligently seek to protect and preserve that order wherever possible. Change occurs slowly, over time, but must be constantly nurtured and nourished until "the new rules" are simply accepted as "the rules."

REFERENCES

A bad bill on police. 1997. *New York Times*, A22. July 23.

ARMSTRONG, D. 2000a. Second chance for bad cops: Chiefs say civil service thwarts discipline. Globe spotlight conduct unbecoming series, Part 1. *Boston Sunday Globe*, A1, A22–A23. May 21.

ARMSTRONG, D. 2000b. Civil service panel criticized as unprofessional, pro-union. Globe spotlight conduct unbecoming series, Part 2. *Boston Globe*, A1, A8–A9. May 22.

Arrests by New Jersey troopers show another drop in September. 2000. *New York Times*, A22 (YNE ed.). October 22.

BARSTOW, D., & KOCIENIEWSKI. D. 2000. Records show New Jersey police knew of racial profiling in '96. *New York Times*. October 12.

BELLUCK, P. 1996. The street cop in pin stripes: Wielding political power of New York's police union. *New York Times*, B1, B4. March 6.

BITTNER, E. 1970. *The functions of police in modern society: A review of background factors, current practices, and possible role models*. Crime and Delinquency Issues. National Clearinghouse for Mental Health Information. Chevy Chase, MD: National Institute of Mental Health.

BLACK, D. 1980. *The manners and customs of the police*. New York: Academic Press.

BREMNER, C. 2000. Police angry at plan to record interviews. *Times* (London), March 31.

BUERGER, M. E. 1998. Police training as a Pentecost: Using tools singularly ill-suited to the purpose of reform. *Police Quarterly, 1* (1), 27–63.

BUERGER, M. E., & MAZEROLLE, L. GREEN 1998. Third-party policing: A theoretical analysis of an emerging trend. *Justice Quarterly, 15* (2), 302–327.

BUZAWA, E. S., & BUZAWA C. G. (Eds.). 1992. *Domestic violence: The changing criminal justice response*. Westport, CT: Auburn House.

CASSIDY, P. 1998. Police take a military turn: Counter to other image as neighborhood peacekeepers. *Boston Sunday Globe*, C1, C2. January 11.

CAULFIELD, S., & WONDERS, N. 1993. Personal and political violence against women and the role of the state. In K. D. TUNNELL (Ed.) *Political Crime in Contemporary America*. New York: Garland.

Comment. 1968. Effect of *Mapp v. Ohio* on search-and-seizure practices in narcotics cases. *Columbia Law Journal & Social Problems, 4,* 87, 92.

CRANK, J. P., & CALDERO, M. A. 2000. *Police ethics: The corruption of a noble cause*. Cincinnati: Anderson.

DANIELS, C. R. (Ed.). 1997. *Feminists negotiate the state: The politics of domestic violence*. Latham, MD: University Press of America.

DAUNT, T. 2000. High court rebuffs LAPD, Santa Monica. *Los Angeles Times*, June 27. http://www.latimes.com/communities/news/los_angeles_metro/20000627/t000060706.html

DELATTRE, E. J. 1996. *Character and cops: Ethics in policing*. (3rd ed.). Washington, DC: AEI Press.

DERSHOWITZ, A. M. 1998. Testimony before the House of Representatives judiciary committee. December 1. http://www.house.gov/judiciary/ 101308.html

DOBASH, R. E., & DOBASH, R. P. 1979. *Violence against wives: A case against patriarchy*. New York: Free Press.

DUFFY, J. J. 1995. *Domestic violence: Police response guidelines*. Jersey City, NJ: Hudson County (NJ) Prosecutor's Office. February 27.

EGAN, T. 1999. Soldiers of the drug war remain on duty. *New York Times, A1*, A16 (YNE ed.). March 1.

FLYNN, K. 1999. Record payouts in settlements of lawsuits against the New York City police are set for year. *New York Times*, A27 (YNE ed.). October 1.

FRIEZE, I. H., & BROWNE, A. 1989. Violence in marriage. In Lloyd Ohlin and Michael Tonry (Eds.), *Family violence, crime and justice: A review of research* (Vol. 11). Chicago: University of Chicago Press.

GLABERSON, W. 1998. In truth, even little lies are sometimes prosecuted. *New York Times*, A1, A14. November 17.

HOFFMAN, J. 1998a. Police tactics chipping away at suspects' rights. Questioning *Miranda*, Part 1. *New York Times*, 1, 35. March 29.

HOFFMAN, J. 1998b. Police refine methods so potent, even the innocent have confessed. Questioning *Miranda*, Part 2. *New York Times*, A1, A18. March 30.

KAHN, R., & DOWDY, Z. R. 1998. "Iron Fist" of policing; SWAT team use questioned. *Boston Globe*, A1, B12. May 11.

KAPPELER, V. E. 1997. *Critical issues in police civil liability* (2nd ed.). Prospect Heights, IL: Waveland Press.

KASZUBA, M. 1993. SWAT on the move: Despite lack of big crime wave, suburban teams are pro-liferating. *Star Tribune*, 1A, 12A. March 10.

KLOCKARS, C. B. 1985. *The idea of police*. Beverly Hills, CA: Sage.

KLOCKARS, C. B. 1991. The Dirty Harry problem. In C. B. Klockars and S. D. Mastrofski (Eds.), *Thinking about police: Contemporary readings* (2nd ed. pp. 413–423). New York: McGraw-Hill.

KRASKA, P. B., & KAPPELER, V. E. 1997 (1999). Militarizing American police: The rise and nor-malization of paramilitary units. *Social Problems, 44* (1). Reprinted in V. E. Kappeler (Ed.), *The police & society touchstone readings*, 2nd ed., pp. 463–479). Prospect Heights, IL: Waveland.

LaFAVE, W. 1965. *Arrest: The decision to take a suspect into custody*. Boston: Little, Brown.

LEVY, C. J. 1996. New York City police union pounds beat in state capitol. *New York Times*, A1, B5. February 6.

MACE, R. 1997. Personal communication.

McNAMARA, J. D. 1996. Why cops lie about drug evidence. *Philadelphia Inquirer*, A13. February 13.

MEDALIE, R. J., ZEITZ, L., & ALEXANDER, P. 1968. Custodial police interrogation in our nation's capital: The attempt to implement *Miranda. Michigan Law Review, 66*, 1347–1422.

NEWTON, J. 2000. Hahn's reviews mixed on handling police misconduct. *Los Angeles Times*. May 8. http://www.latimes.com/news/state/reports/rampart/ lat_rampart000508.htm

NEWTON, J., & DAUNT, T. 2000. City, U.S. begin talks on LAPD reform. *Los Angeles Times*. May 18. http://www.latimes.com/communities/news/los_angeles_metro/ 20000518/ t000046993.html

NIEDERHOFFER, A. 1967. *Behind the shield: The police in urban society*. Garden City, NY: Dou-bleday.

OAKS, D. H. 1970. Studying the exclusionary rule in search and seizure. *University of Chicago Law Review, 37*, 665–757.

REISS, A. J., Jr. 1971. *The police and the public*. New Haven: Yale University Press.

REISS, A. J., Jr. 1989. Personal communication.

REUSS-IANNI, E. 1983. *Two cultures of policing: Street cops and management cops*. New Brunswick, NJ: Transaction Books.

RICCARDI, N. 2000. Rampart scandal's cost to county rising fast. *Los Angeles Times*. May 11. http://www.latimes.com/news/state/reports/rampart/lat_rampart000511.htm

SCHEMO, D. J. 1999. Decades later, officer's confession gives redemption to beating victim. *New York Times*, A19 (YNE ed.). June 29.

SHERMAN, L. W. 1992. *Policing domestic violence: Experiments and dilemmas*. New York: Free Press.

SHERMAN, L. W., & BERK, R. A. 1984. The specific deterrent effects of arrest for domestic assault. *American Sociological Review, 49*, 261–272.

SHERMAN, L. W., & BRIDGEFORTH, C. A. 1994. *Getting guns off the streets, 1993: A survey of big-city police agencies*. Crime Control Reports No. 8. Washington, DC: Crime Control Insti-tute.

SHERMAN, L. A., & Rogan, D. P. 1995. Effects of gun seizures on gun violence: "Hot Spots" patrol in Kansas City. *Justice Quarterly, 12* (4), 673–693.

SHERMAN, L. A., SHAW, J. W., & ROGAN, D. P. 1995. *The Kansas City gun experiment*. NIJ Re-search in Brief. Washington, DC: National Institute of Justice.

SKOLNICK, J. H. 1966. *Justice without trial: Law enforcement in democratic society*. New York: John Wiley.

SUTTON, L. P. 1986. The Fourth Amendment in action: An empirical view of the search warrant process. *Criminal Law Review, 22,*(5), 405–429. Reprinted as "Getting Around the Fourth Amendment" in C. B. KLOCKARS & S. D. MASTROFSKI (Eds.), *Thinking about police: Contemporary readings* (2nd ed., pp. 433–446). New York: McGraw-Hill, 1991.

TUROW, S. 2000. Lying to get the bad guys. *New York Times* Op-Ed, Week in Review, 13. February 20.

WALKER, S. 1992. *The police in America: An introduction* (2nd ed.) New York: McGraw-Hill.

WALKER, S. 1999. *The police in America: An introduction* (3rd ed.). New York: McGraw-Hill.

WALKER, S., & FRIDELL, L. 1992. Forces of change in police policy: The impact of *Tennessee v. Garner. American Journal of Police, 11* (3), 97–112.

WESTLEY, W. A. 1970. *Violence and the police: A sociological study of law, custom, and morality.* Cambridge, MA: MIT Press.

WESTON, P. B., WELLS, K. M., & HERTOGHE, M. 1995. *Criminal evidence for police* (4th ed.). Englewood Cliffs, NJ: Prentice Hall.

WILSON, J. Q. 1968. *Varieties of police behavior: The management of law and order in eight communities.* Cambridge, MA: Harvard University Press.

WILSON, T., & GREGORY, T. 2000. Police search far and wide for new recruits. *Chicago Tribune,* April 7. http://www.chicagotribune.com/news/metro/chicago/article/0,2669,ART-44151,FF.html

Woman shot by police awarded $6 million. 1998. *New York Times,* 20. April 12.

YOUNGER, I. 1967. Constitutional protection on search and seizure dead. *Trial, 3* (41) (August–September). Quoted in F. Remington, D. Newman, E. Kimball, M. Melli, and H. Goldstein, *Criminal justice administration* (1969; no publisher, no city given).

Canadian Sources 1

DiMANNO, R. 2000. To swerve and protect. *Toronto Star.* March 10. http://thestar.ca/thestar/editorial/news/20000310NEW02_CI-DIMANNO10.html

DUNCANSON, J. 1998. Firearms unit's former boss fired. *Toronto Star,* December 12. http://www.thestar.com/thestar/editorial/news/ 981212NEW06_CI-GUNS12.html

DUNCANSON, J. 1999a. Strip searches set to be studied. *Toronto Star,* January 16. http://www2.thestar.com/thestar/editorial/news/ 990116NEW06c_CI-STRIP16.html

DUNCANSON, J. 1999b. Watchdog urged officer face charges. *Toronto Star,* May 27. http://www2.thestar.com/thestar/editorial/news/ 990527NEW01b_CI-SUIT27.html

DUNCANSON, J. 1999c. 13 guns missing, review finds. *Toronto Star,* June 26. http://www2.thestar.com/thestar/editorial/news/990626NEW10b_CI-GUNS26.html

DUNCANSON, J. & RANKIN, J. 2000. Five police charged in cash probe. *Toronto Star,* April 8. http://www.thestar.ca/thestar/editorial/news/20000408NEW01d_CI-COPS8.html

DUNCANSON, J. & RANKIN, J. 1999. Police brass slammed on discipline. *Toronto Star,* July 14. http://www2.thestar.com/thestar/editorial/news/ 990714NEW01_CI-FORCE14.html

RANKIN, J., & MILLER, C. 2000. Officer is held over bogus drug raids. *Toronto Star,* March 11. http://thestar.ca/thestar/editorial/news/ 20000311NEW01_CI-GUNS11.html

Canadian Sources 2

DeMARAAND, B., & BRAGG, R. 2000. Police union slammed by council; True blue campaign makes them see red. *Toronto Star,* January 28. http://www.thestar.ca/thestar/editorial/news/ 20000128NEW01_CI-COUNCIL28.html

DUNCANSON, J. 2000a. Drive not linked to force, chief says; Union head says fund campaign getting response. *Toronto Star,* January 23. http://www.thestar.com/editorial/news/20000123NEW04_CI-BLUE23.html

DUNCANSON, J. 2000b. Union may be untouchable—legally. *Toronto Star,* January 28. http://www.thestar.ca/thestar/editorial/news/ 20000128NEW18_NU-BLUE28.html

MOLONEY, P., & DEMARA, B. 2000. New bylaw bans true blue. *Toronto Star*, January 29. http://www.thestar.ca/thestar/editorial/ news/20000129NEW01_CI-BLUE.html

Open your wallet and toe that thin blue line. 2000. *Toronto Star*, January 22. http://www.thestar.ca/thestar/editorial/news/ 20000122NEW02_SLINGER.html

PARADKAR, B. 2000. True blue gets mixed reviews from officers: Many reluctant to voice opinion on union campaign. *Toronto Star*, January 28. http://www.thestar.ca/thestar/editorial/news/ 20000128NEW19_CI-MOOD28.html

QUINN, J. 2000. Back off or be sued, police union tells board: True blue continues but decals won't be traded for cash." *Toronto Star*, February 1. http://www.thestar.ca/thestar/editorial/news/ 20000201NEW01b_CI-BLUE1.html

Cases Cited

- *Escobedo v. Illinois*, 378 U.S. 478 (1964).
- *Dickerson v. United States,* 121 S.Ct. 183 (2000).
- *Gideon v. Wainwright*, 372 U.S. 335 (1963).
- *Harris v. New York*, 401 U.S. 222 (1971).
- *In re: Gault*, 387 U.S. 1 (1967).
- *Mapp v. Ohio*, 367 U.S. 643 (1961).
- *Minnesota v. Dickerson,* 508 U.S. 366 (1993).
- *Miranda v. Arizona*, 384 U.S., 436 (1966).
- *New Jersey v. Pedro Soto et al.* 734 A.2nd 350 (N.J. Super. Ct. Law Div. [1996]).
- *New York v. Quarles*, 467 U.S. 649 (1984)
- *Nix v. Williams*, 467 U.S. 431 (1984).
- *Tennessee v. Garner*, 471 U.S. 1 (1985).
- *Thurman v. City of Torrington*, 595 F. Supp. 1521 (D. Conn. 1984).

8

Privacy Rights of Police Officers

Dimensions of Employer Regulations

William P. Bloss

INTRODUCTION

In 1986 William Von Raab, commissioner of the U.S. Customs Service, implemented a compulsory police employee drug-testing program. The new policy mandated automatic urinalysis for police employees who worked in drug interdiction, carried firearms, or sought promotion in drug enforcement. Though the war on drugs had been ongoing for several years, never before had it involved the drug testing of police employees without suspicion or warrant. After the Supreme Court upheld the testing policy, a new direction emerged in police privacy rights. Subsequent cases began expanding employer authority to engage in search and testing in the police workplace. The result has been a modification of fundamental privacy principles that were established two centuries before.

Nowhere in the Bill of Rights is privacy expressly stated as an intrinsic right of citizens. Nonetheless, constitutional scholars assert that it is considered a fundamental right based on the intent of the Framers and numerous references throughout the amendments to the U.S. Constitution (Ducat, 1999; Warren & Brandeis, 1890). The notion of an individual right of privacy is deeply rooted in both English common law and American jurisprudence (Gerety, 1977; Glancy, 1979); hence, American courts acknowledge the existence of an individual privacy expectation and have rendered decisions establishing various privacy principles. Privacy rights generally come from court interpretations of aspects of the amendments to the U.S. Constitution (typically the First, Fourth, Fifth, and Fourteenth). The essence of these principles is to protect individuals from government intrusion into private domains.

135

The Supreme Court has commented in several cases on the importance of individual privacy rights [*Union Pacific Railway Co. v. Botsford* (1891); *Hebert v. Louisiana* (1926)]. However, the two most often cited references are Justice Brandeis's famous dissent in *Olmstead v. United States* (1928, 445), where he stated that "the right to be let alone is the right most valued by civilized men," and *Griswold v. Connecticut* (1965, 479), where the Court held that the Bill of Rights created a "zone of privacy" in which persons were protected from certain governmental intrusions.

Not only have the courts established fundamental privacy protections for citizens, but they have also extended dimensions of these rights to police officers in their capacity as public employees (Brancato & Polebaum, 1981; Cathcart, 1995; Aitchison, 1996; Bloss, 1996; Klotter, Kanovitz, & Kanovitz, 1999). However, police officers are distinguished as a *separate* class of public employees because of the authority and power entrusted to them [*Foley v. Connelie* (1978); *Bivens v. Six Unknown Named Agents* (1971)]. They continue to retain certain privacy protections, albeit different from those of private citizens [*Connick v. Meyers* (1983)]. As Justice Douglas noted in *Garrity v. New Jersey* (1967, 500), "We conclude that policemen, like teachers and lawyers, are not relegated to a watered-down version of constitutional rights."

Federal and state courts have dealt with police officer employee privacy rights in a host of areas. Though the privacy concept can be amorphous, cases have been litigated on issues that predominately stem from the First, Fourth, Fifth, and Fourteenth Amendments. Constitutional claims cover an extensive gamut of conduct, expression, association, discipline, and procedural employment issues (Aitchison, 1996; see generally Klotter et al., 1999; Bloss, 1996). Rather than deal with each of these privacy areas, this chapter addresses four police workplace privacy issues—workplace searches, drug testing, HIV/AIDS testing, and sexual conduct.

Constitutionally, testing stems from Fourth Amendment protections, whereas the regulation of employee sexual conduct emanates from the general privacy concept of the right to be let alone from governmental intrusion (Cooley, 1881; Warren & Brandeis, 1890; see Brandeis's dissent in [*Olmstead v. United States* (1928); *Griswold* (1960)]. Although a plethora of issues arise in the police employee-employer relationship (Aitchison, 1996), this chapter specifically focuses on individual privacy concerns of employees, rather than matters relating to the administration of the workplace (e.g., administrative misconduct, disciplinary actions, non-privacy issues). Specifically, the chapter examines the constitutional privacy aspects of intrusive searches, testing, and employer regulation of interpersonal relations. Each of these is a *cornerstone* protection area in privacy jurisprudence. The rights of police employees regarding employer intrusion and regulation are analyzed in the areas of the search of employee workplace belongings, employer authority to require drug and HIV/AIDS testing, and control of interpersonal sexual conduct.

EMPLOYER AUTHORITY TO REGULATE POLICE EMPLOYEE CONDUCT

In spite of the presence of certain privacy rights, police employees are subject to an array of employer regulations. In general, the courts have bestowed considerable authority upon police employers to govern various types of on- and off-duty conduct (Aitchison, 1996). For example, the courts have permitted police employers to regulate employee activities involving grooming [*Kelley v. Johnson* (1976)], residency [*Ahern v. Murphy* (1972)], disruptive speech [*Rankin v. McPherson* (1987)], and political candidacy [*Nikodem v. Pennsylvania State Police* (1982)]. Similarly, government employers have been permitted to engage in warrantless searches of employee workplaces [*O'Connor v. Ortega* (1987)], drug testing [*National Treasury Employees Union v. Von Raab* (1989)], polygraph testing [*Gardner v. Missouri State Highway Patrol* (1995)], and communicable disease testing [*Anonymous Fireman v. City of Willoughby* (1991)].

Emergence of Constitutional Privacy Standards

As noted in such landmark cases as *Griswold v. Connecticut* (1965), *Eisenstadt v. Baird* (1972), and *Roe v. Wade* (1973), individual privacy issues often entail governmental involvement in personal decision-making. Prompted by lawsuits brought by police employees, many traditional privacy matters have been applied to the workplace. As with many other legal doctrines, contemporary court interpretation of police officer employment privacy has its beginning in case precedent. Early privacy doctrine involving government intrusion was established in *Olmstead v. United States* (1928, 441), where the Supreme Court held that warrantless government electronic surveillance was not violative of Fourth Amendment provisions because there was no "trespass into a constitutionally protected area." Essentially, the *Olmstead* doctrine sought to protect *places,* not people, from governmental intrusion.

The Expectation of Privacy Standard   In *Katz v. United States* (1967), the Supreme Court supplanted the *Olmstead* principle with the expectation of privacy standard. The *Katz* privacy doctrine consists of a two-prong test with both a subjective and an objective requirement of reasonable expectation of privacy. The subjective requirement held that if a person knowingly exposes private matters to the public view, he or she renounces or diminishes the expectation of privacy. Additionally, the courts measure the validity of an individual's expectation of privacy claim by the reasonableness of the assertion. If an individual citizen strives to shield his or her private matters from public or police view and the assertion is deemed reasonable by the courts, the person is considered to have proclaimed an expectation of privacy that protects him or her from warrantless government intrusion. Hence, the *Katz* expectation of privacy doctrine has become the benchmark standard to determine whether a government warrantless search and seizure is reasonable in relation to privacy protection (Reamey, 1992). Although this standard has traditionally been applied in both privacy and search and seizure cases, the Supreme Court in recent years has subrogated the *Katz* expectation of privacy measure with a balancing of competing interests test in public employee privacy cases [*O'Connor v. Ortega* (1987)].

The Balancing of Competing Interest Test Standard   Historically, privacy jurisprudence has been shaped by the relationship between citizens and searches conducted by government agents. Until the last two decades, scant attention was devoted to the privacy relationship between the government and public employees. Moreover, police employees, and the scope of their individual privacy protection in the workplace, were largely overlooked. The situation changed dramatically with the Supreme Court's holding in *O'Connor v. Ortega* (1987). In *Ortega,* the Court modified the contours of public employees' expectation of privacy by asserting that they possessed a diminished expectation of privacy in the workplace. The result of the *Ortega* holding is that public employees, including police employees, retain less constitutional privacy protection in the workplace than others, notwithstanding the fact that private employers, unlike public employers, are not subject to Fourth Amendment warrant and probable cause requirements (Hoekstra, 1996). Not only did *Ortega* influence the status of the public employee workplace privacy expectation, but the decision also became the catalyst for revisions in the interpretation of the reasonableness standard in subsequent cases. One of the crucial principles that emerged from *Ortega* was that court determination of public employee workplace privacy protection was no longer based on an analysis of traditional precepts of the Fourth Amendment or its established exceptions. Rather, in the post-*Ortega* era, such a determination was based upon a balancing of competing interests test. This measure began supplanting the perennial reasonableness standard from which search and privacy interpretations were traditionally made. The balancing test weighs individual employee expectation of privacy elements against the legitimacy of government interests in maintaining an effective and efficient workplace [*O'Connor v. Ortega* (1987)]; [*National Treasury Employees Union v. Von Raab* (1989)].

Several commentators have observed that Fourth Amendment and constitutional privacy tenets have been eroded by the emergence of a panoply of exceptions (e.g., special needs, administrative search, stop and frisk) (Vaughn & del Carmen, 1993; Nuger, 1992). By adding the balancing of competing interests test standard as a substitute for the traditional reasonableness determination, the Supreme Court increased the effect of these exceptions on police employee privacy (Bloss, 1995). Although the *Ortega* decision provided the impetus for utilization of the new balancing test, several subsequent police employee court decisions have relied upon this doctrinal standard [see *National Treasury Employees Union v. Von Raab* (1989), and its progeny].

ANALYSIS OF POLICE EMPLOYEE WORKPLACE PRIVACY RIGHTS

At this point, the four core individual privacy topics in this chapter will be examined. Workplace search, drug testing, and HIV/AIDS testing are all employee regulatory areas that stem from Fourth Amendment protections. As noted, the courts no longer require employers to rely on probable cause or a search warrant to subject police employees to workplace search or testing. The creation of balancing tests supplanted these traditional protections, allowing police employers to engage in warrantless searches of employees in the workplace.

Employer Warrantless Search in the Police Workplace

As noted, in addition to the establishment of the balancing of competing interests test, the Supreme Court in *O'Connor v. Ortega* (1987) changed the contours of public employee workplace privacy by asserting that these employees have a diminished expectation of privacy. The Court reasoned that a lessened employee expectation was necessary to promote an efficient government agency.

Several factors contributed to the Supreme Court's changing perspective on the expectation of privacy and traditional Fourth Amendment warrant and probable cause requirements (Vaughn & del Carmen, 1997). Two exceptions to the Fourth Amendment that affected the Court's modification in the scope of search protection are the doctrines of administrative search [*Camara v. Municipal Court* (1967)] and special needs [*New Jersey v. T.L.O.* (1985)]. These standards provided the impetus for the Court to permit warrantless search and seizure without the presence of probable cause (Hanson, 1993; Larsen, 1987; Sundby, 1988; Searle, 1989).

Although the *Ortega* decision involved a public hospital workplace, it established the doctrine that later courts used to permit police employers to engage in warrantless searches of police employee work areas (Bloss, 1998). In the *Ortega* case, Ortega's office was searched during his administrative leave for alleged malfeasant procurement of state property. In *Ortega,* the Court permitted the search, holding that public employer warrantless workplace searches "for noninvestigatory, work-related purposes, as well as for investigations of work-related misconduct, should be judged by a standard of reasonableness under all circumstances [including] both the inception and scope of intrusion" [*O'Connor v. Ortega* (1989, 709–710)]. In supplanting traditional probable cause with a reasonableness standard, the Court's reasoning relied upon three principles—a balancing of competing interests test, special needs, and the nature of the government workplace. The Court held that when comparing individual employee privacy protection to the government's legitimate interest in the efficient operation of the agency, government needs were more substantial. This determination resulted in the diminution of employee expectation of privacy in the public workplace, and, enabled government employers to engage in regulatory nonprosecutorial workplace searches without a warrant or probable cause. Further, the Court held under a special needs justification that requiring employers to demonstrate probable cause and obtain a warrant for work-related searches as unrealistic and unnecessary.

Though the police workplace differs from the hospital setting in the *Ortega* case, lower courts have applied the same principles to employer warrantless searches in the police workplace. Between 1988 and 1996, lower federal and state courts decided ten cases involving employer warrantless search in the police workplace. These courts continued to rely on *Ortega* precepts, and each ruled that police employers are permitted to conduct warrantless work-related searches of police employee work areas (Bloss, 1998). As indicated in Table 8.1, in the presence of suspected work-related misconduct involving agency property or work areas, police employers are permitted to search offices, lockers, desks, briefcases, or issued vehicles (Bloss, 1998, p. 63).

Thus far, the overriding determination of the courts is that police employers are permitted to engage in warrantless workplace searches if they involve suspected work-related misconduct or government property. These courts utilized *Ortega* reasoning, finding that police employees have a diminished expectation of privacy in the workplace; and when relying on a balancing of competing interests test, government employers have legitimate interests in maintaining an effective workplace through such measures as warrantless search. The common denominator among these warrantless workplace search cases is that the searches may not include evidence obtained for criminal prosecution (Bloss, 1998). Barring such evidence, employers may conduct a variety of searches to control workplace misconduct. In an effort to unobtrusively control potential misconduct, the district court for Kansas in *Thompson v. Johnson County Community College* (1996) permitted the use of video surveillance in the employee locker area. Several courts allowed the employer to

TABLE 8.1 Lower Federal and State Court Cases Applying the *Ortega* Doctrine to Law Enforcement Workplace Search

Case	Employee Claim of Violated Right	Object of Search	Basis for Search Permissibility
Thompson v. Johnson County Community College 930 F. Supp. 501 (D. Kan. 1996)	Fourth Amendment and expectation of privacy	Locker area	Video surveillance permitted because work-related and controls employee misconduct
United States v. Taketa 923 F.2d 665 (9th Cir. 1991)	Fourth Amendment and expectation of privacy	Joint private office	Work-related purpose only, employee misconduct, nature of government workplace
Shields v. Burge 874 F.2d 1201 (7th Cir. 1989)	Fourth Amendment	Desk, briefcase, and vehicle	Strong government interest in controlling employee misconduct, government-issued property
Lowe v. City of Macon, Ga. 720 F. Supp. 994 (M.D. Ga. 1989)	Fourth Amendment and 42 U.S.C. §1983	Office, desk, and bag	Search for criminal evidence requires probable cause barring exigency, search for work-related employee misconduct based on reasonable suspicion
State v. Stoddard 909 S.W.2d 454 (Tenn. Cr. App. 1994)	Fourth Amendment and expectation of privacy	Vehicle and briefcase	Work-related misconduct, government-issued property, nature of government workplace
State v. Nelson 434 S.E.2d 697 (W.Va.1993)	Fourth Amendment	Desk	Inventory of government property
Moore v. Constantine 574 N.Y.S.2d 507 (Sup. 1991)	Fourth Amendment	Locker	Work-related employee misconduct, "special needs" of government workplace
Gamble v. State 552 A.2d 928 (Md. App. 1989)	Fourth Amendment	Vehicle	Government property
State v. Francisco 790 S.W.2d 543 (Tenn. Cr. App. 1989)	Fourth Amendment and expectation of privacy	Vehicle and briefcase	Work-related misconduct, government-issued property, presence of notice and regulation
People v. Duvall 428 N.W.2d 746 (Mich. App. 1988)	Fourth Amendment and expectation of privacy	Office and desk	Diminished expectation because shared desk with others, government-owned property

Source: Bloss (1998, pp. 63–64).

engage in a warrantless search of government-issued items, such as desks [*State v. Nelson* (1993); *Shields v. Burge* (1989); *People v. Duvall* (1988)] and vehicles [*State v. Stoddard* (1994); *Gamble v. State* (1989;) *State v. Francisco* (1989)]. Additionally, courts have allowed searches of offices [*Lowe v. City of Macon, Ga.* (1989); *U.S. v. Taketa* (1991)] and lockers [*Moore v. Constantine* (1991)] to control the workplace or if employee misconduct was suspected. These cases demonstrate the court's majority support for employer warrantless search in the police workplace. Unfettered employer regulation has been permitted in this privacy area because of a court interpretation that these employees have a diminished expectation of privacy in the government workplace.

Warrantless Drug Testing of Police

Adhering to the reasoning established in the *Ortega* decision, the Supreme Court applied these new privacy doctrines in a seminal warrantless drug-testing case in *National Treasury Employees Union v. Von Raab* (1989). The groundwork had been laid in *Ortega,* creating employer warrantless search authority based on the diminution of public employee privacy protection. In *Von Raab,* the Court further eroded police employee privacy rights, holding that neither the Fourth Amendment warrant requirement nor probable cause and its reasonable suspicion exception were necessary to compel police employees to submit to suspicionless workplace drug testing. In *Von Raab,* the Court held that to maintain an effective workplace, police employers could require employees to submit to warrantless and suspicionless drug testing. Where *Von Raab* deviated from conventional police employee drug-testing doctrine was that employers were no longer required to demonstrate "particularized reasonable suspicion" to justify compulsory drug testing [*City of Palm Bay v. Bauman (*1985); *Capua v. City of Plainfield (*1986); *Policemen's Benevolent Association of New Jersey v. Washington Township* (1987); see also Lewis, 1987].

In the *Von Raab* case, the Commissioner of the U.S. Customs Service implemented a compulsory employee drug-testing program that was challenged by the federal Treasury Department employees' union. The new policy established mandatory, warrantless, suspicionless drug testing for Customs employees involved in police work who satisfied specific criteria pertaining to assignment or promotion. Urinalysis testing was required of any employee who sought transfer or promotion into an assignment that involved interdiction of illegal drugs, carrying of firearms, or access to sensitive or classified materials. Under the compulsory program, Customs employees who tested positive for drugs were subject to dismissal without criminal prosecution.

The Supreme Court upheld the portion of the Customs Service program that required compulsory drug testing of employees involved in drug interdiction and the carrying of firearms. The Court reasoned that the testing program was a Fourth Amendment search, and thus was subject to a reasonableness requirement. Justice Kennedy, writing for the majority, held that the government has a "compelling interest in safeguarding borders and public safety," therefore the Customs Service's justification for the warrantless search outweighed individual privacy interests [*National Treasury Employees Union v. Von Raab* (1989, 680)]. In developing its reasoning, the Court cited the principles of special needs, diminished expectation of privacy, and the balancing of competing interests from *O'Connor v. Ortega* (1987) and *New Jersey v. T.L.O.* (1985).

Von Raab reaffirmed a diminished expectation of privacy perspective for police employees, stating that, "unlike most private citizens or government employees in general, employees involved in drug interdiction reasonably should expect effective inquiry into their fitness and probity" [*National Treasury Employees Union v. Von Raab* (1989, 672)]. In the aftermath of *Von Raab,* numerous lower federal and state courts have rendered decisions in police drug-testing cases. Between 1989 and 1997, twelve police employee drug cases were heard in lower federal courts, and fourteen cases were decided in state courts. Among these cases, almost two-thirds (62 percent) of the courts adopted the *Von Raab* suspicionless testing standard, while the remaining one-third continued to require that drug screening be based upon some type of reasonable suspicion. As indicated in Tables 8.2 and 8.3, these twenty-six cases can be divided between two types of drug-testing requirements—compulsory/mandatory and random. In rendering their decisions, the courts relied on five rationales in their decision-making—individualized suspicion, selected covered positions, medical fitness/post-accident, pre-employment/conditional, and systematic random testing (Bloss, 1996). The first four of these fall under compulsory or mandatory drug testing, whereas the last category stands procedurally on its own.

Compulsory or Mandatory Drug Testing   Compulsory/mandatory drug-testing policies or practices are those in which the police employer conditionally requires employee drug screening. These cases constituted 69 percent of the types litigated after *Von Raab,* and involve such conditions as suspicion-based testing, select job assignments, medical fitness or post-accident, and pre-employment or conditional testing.

Suspicion-Based Testing   The requirement of individualized or particularized reasonable suspicion acted as a demarcation point for several lower federal and state courts. Although *Von Raab* supplanted reasonable suspicion with a balancing of competing interests test and a special needs standard, several of the lower courts continued to adhere to the earlier reasonable suspicion requirement as an element of their decision [*Feliciano v. City of Cleveland* (1993); *Jackson v. Gates* (1992); *Ford v. Dowd* (1991); *Guiney v. Police Commissioner of Boston* (1991); *National Treasury Employees Union v. Bush* (1989); *Pike v. Gallagher* (1993); *Fraternal Order of Police, Miami Lodge 20 v. City of Miami* (1992); *Miller v. Vanderburgh County* (1993); *Rawlings v. Police Department of Jersey City, New Jersey* (1993); *The City and County of Denver v. Casados et al.,* (1993)].

In 1992, the Court of Appeals for the Ninth Circuit in *Jackson v. Gates* and the Supreme Court of Florida in *Fraternal Order of Police, Miami Lodge 20 v. City of Miami* held that suspicion of employee drug use was required to permit random testing programs. While in *National Treasury Employees Union v. Bush* (1989), the court found the testing permissible if based solely on reasonable suspicion, the Supreme Court of California in *Loder v. City of Glendale, et al.* (1997) ruled that currently employed city employees, including police officers, could only be subjected to compulsory urinalysis if based on individualized suspicion. Other courts mandated individualized suspicion in circumstances where the agency lacked any specific guidelines or procedures for employee drug testing [*Pike v. Gallagher* (1993); *Ford v. Dowd* (1991); *Miller v. Vanderburgh County* (1993); *Rawlings v. Police Department of Jersey City, New Jersey* (1993)]. In these cases, the courts either mandated a suspicion determination or considered it an alternative require-

TABLE 8.2 Lower Federal Court Cases Applying the *Von Raab* Doctrine to Police Drug Testing

Case	Employee Challenge	Type of Testing	Standard Required	Government Interest	Basis for Government Interest	Covered Positions
National Treasury Employees Union v. U.S. Customs Service 27 F.3d 623 (1994)	Constitutionality of drug-testing program	Random	No suspicion required	Compelling	Protection of Sensitive and confidential drug-interdiction information	Employees with access to sensitive computer databases involving drug interdiction
Feliciano v. City of Cleveland 988 F.2d 649 (1993)	42 U.S.C. § 1983 Validity of testing procedures	Compulsory	Reasonable suspicion and valid testing procedure	Legitimate	Prevention of officer drug use	All cadets
Jackson v. Gates 975 F.2d 648 (1992)	42 U.S.C. § 1983 and Fourth Amendment	Compulsory	Reasonable suspicion or systematic random	Special compelling	Special needs involving triggering event or pre-promotion	All officers
Ford v. Dowd 931 F.2d 1286 (1991)	42 U.S.C. § 1983 and Fourth Amendment	Compulsory	Reasonable suspicion or routine systematic random	Legitimate and compelling	Prevention of officer drug use	None stated
Penny v. Kennedy 915 F.2d 1065 (1990)	Drug-testing program	Compulsory	No particularized suspicion required	Compelling	Prevention of officer drug use and insuring officer fitness	All officers
National Treasury Employees Union v. Bush 891 F.2d 99 (1989)	Constitutionality of drug-testing program	Random	Reasonable suspicion for all officers and suspicionless random for officers in sensitive positions	None stated	None stated	Officers in sensitive positions

(continued)

143

TABLE 8.2 Lower Federal Court Cases Applying the *Von Raab* Doctrine to Police Drug Testing (continued)

Case	Employee Challenge	Type of Testing	Standard Required	Government Interest	Basis for Government Interest	Covered Positions
Guiney v. Roache 873 F. 2d 1557 (1989)	Fourth and Fourteenth Amendments	Random	No suspicion required of covered positions	Compelling	Prevention of officer drug use and public safety	Drug interdiction officers and carrying firearms
Harmon v. Thornburgh 878 F.2d 484 (1989)	Drug-testing program	Random	No suspicion required of covered positions	Legitimate	Protection of government interests in national security	Employees with "top secret" security clearances
Pike v. Gallagher 829 F. Supp. 1254 (1993)	42 U.S.C. § 1983, First, Fourth and Fourteenth Amendments	Compulsory	Systematic random or individualized reasonable suspicion	None specifically stated	Need to deter and detect officer drug use	None stated
National Treasury Employees Union v. U.S. Customs 829 F. Supp. 408 (1993)	Constitutionality of drug-testing program and Fourth Amendment	Random	No suspicion required of covered positions	Legitimate	Protection of sensitive information	Employees with access to sensitive computer databases involving drug interdiction
American Federation of Government Employees v. Derwinski 777 F. Supp. 1493 (1991)	Drug-testing program	Random	No suspicion required	Compelling	Nexus between job duties and drug risk, maintaining integrity of officers and workplace, public safety and sensitive information	Safety-sensitive positions

(continued)

TABLE 8.2 Lower Federal Court Cases Applying the *Von Raab* Doctrine to Police Drug Testing (continued)

Case	Employee Challenge	Type of Testing	Standard Required	Government Interest	Basis for Government Interest	Covered Positions
McKenna v. City of Philadelphia 771 F. Supp. 124 (1991)	42 U.S.C. § 1983 and Fourth Amendment	Compulsory	No suspicion required, determination of medical fitness for duty	Strong state	Administrative search exception, highly regulated industry, prevention of officer drug use, and ensure medical fitness	Officer post-injury reinstatement to duty
Brown v. City of Detroit 715 F. Supp. 832 (1989)	Drug-testing program	Random	No suspicion required	Legitimate	Special needs and public safety	Sworn personnel

ment if no departmental testing guidelines were in place. To avoid capriciousness, the Court of Appeals of Indiana directed the police department to establish specific drug-testing guidelines or procedures in the absence of warrant or probable cause [*Miller v. Vanderburgh County* (1993)].

Conversely, the New York Supreme Court Appellate Division in *Worrell v. Brown* (1991) ruled that suspicionless random testing, without notice, was permissible, reasoning that a positive drug test provided substantial evidence of misconduct, and therefore prior suspicion was unnecessary. The Court of Appeals for the Sixth Circuit in *Penny, et al. v. Kennedy, et al.* (1990) held that suspicionless mandatory drug urinalysis could be conducted on police employees based on a balancing of competing interests test, as outlined in *Von Raab*. Though the majority of courts interpreting the suspicion requirement chose to adopt *Von Raab* principles and permit suspicionless testing, some courts continued to insist upon the presence of suspicion to justify the warrantless drug test.

Select Job Assignments   In closely following *Von Raab,* some lower courts restricted employee eligibility for warrantless drug testing to officers involved in drug interdiction or who carried firearms [*Guiney v. Roache* (1989); *Brown v. City of Detroit* (1989); *The City and County of Denver v. Casados et al.* (1993)]. Other courts permitted the expansion of the covered position categories to sensitive or safety-related positions. As an example, the Court of Appeals for the District of Columbia in *National Treasury Employees Union v. U.S. Customs Service* (1994) held that it was reasonable for the Custom Service's warrantless suspicionless drug-testing policy to include employees with access to sensitive computer database information on agency drug-interdiction efforts [see also *National Treasury Employees Union v. U.S. Customs Service* (1993)]. In a related case, the same court in *Harmon v. Thornburgh* (1989) reasoned that random drug testing was permissible for employees with top-secret security clearances because of a legitimate government interest in protecting national security information. In 1991, the District Court for the Northern District of California in *American Federation of Government Employees v. Derwinski* (1991) permitted random drug testing of employees in "safety-sensitive" positions, where a nexus could be demonstrated between employee duties and the potential risks from drug impairment. Hence, in addition to the original provision of *Von Raab* covering drug interdiction and armed employees, other police employees can be covered by drug-testing requirements (e.g., public safety, safety-sensitive, access to drug interdiction intelligence).

Medical Fitness or Post-Accident   Drug testing of police employees has also been held permissible based on medical fitness or following an accident. Suspicionless mandatory drug testing has also been allowed if it is part of a reinstatement or physical examination to determine medical fitness for duty. The District Court for the Eastern District of Pennsylvania in *McKenna v. City of Philadelphia* (1991) held that mandatory drug testing as part of a medical screening for reinstatement to duty was permissible. Involving post-hospital drug testing, the Supreme Court, Appellate Division, of New York in *Gdanski v. New York City Transit Authority* (1990) found allowable the mandatory testing of officers following a hospital stay to determine medical fitness for duty. Post-accident drug testing was also found acceptable by the same court in *Barretto v. City of New York et al.* (1990).

In *Barretto,* the court reasoned that the agency was permitted to require mandatory drug testing of employees following an on-duty accident involving agency-issued vehicles. Medical fitness for duty regarding drug usage has also been supported in pre-employment or conditional drug testing requirements.

Pre-Employment or Conditional Testing   Some courts have found pre-employment or conditional employment mandatory drug testing acceptable. These programs typically provide police candidates and/or officers with notice of the required drug screening as a condition of employment. In *O'Connor v. Police Commissioner of Boston* (1990), the Supreme Judicial Court of Massachusetts authorized pre-employment, random, suspicion-less drug testing of police cadets. The court found that agency notice and employee consent acted to further lessen employee expectation of privacy, resulting in a proper pre-employment drug-testing requirement. Similarly, the Supreme Court of Hawaii in *Mc-Closkey v. Honolulu Police Department* (1990) ruled that the policy of random, mandatory, suspicionless drug testing as a condition of employment was allowable and valid in light of the government's compelling interest in a drug-free police workplace. The Court of Appeals of Maryland found in *City of Annapolis, et al. v. United Food and Commercial Workers, Local 400 et al.* (1989) that a mandatory, suspicionless drug-testing program of city police and firefighters, administered as part of a required annual physical examination, was not violative of Fourth Amendment protections. Hence, pre-employment and conditional drug testing of police candidates have been readily supported by some courts, and those programs that are mandatory or with notice result in less litigation than drug testing of veteran officers (Bloss, 1996).

Not all of the courts, however, ruled on compulsory cases. The remaining 31 percent of the cases stemmed from police employee challenges of random-type testing procedures. These courts advanced various rationales in deciding the permissibility of random drug testing by employers.

Systematic or Random Testing   Some courts held that systematic or standardized testing procedures were needed to minimize broad discretion and caprice by the employer. In those cases where random testing procedures were used as an alternative to individualized suspicion requirements, courts insisted that the procedures be uniform, systematic, or routine to reduce disparate treatment of employees subject to drug testing [*Delaraba v. Nassau County Police Department* (1994)]. Relying on a reasonableness standard, the Court of Appeals for the Sixth Circuit, in *Feliciano v. City of Cleveland* (1993), stressed the importance of either suspicion-based or previously established drug-testing procedures. In the same vein, in *Miller v. Vanderburgh County* (1993), the Indiana Court of Appeals for the First District held that, in spite of the permissibility of employee drug testing based on reasonable suspicion, the department lacked a "preconceived, legitimate drug screening policy" (p. 863) which is necessary for valid suspicionless testing. The court held that if the department engaged in random or compulsory drug testing in the absence of a formal systematic procedure, the testing would be overly capricious and therefore invalid.

In addition to the need for agencies to establish specific drug-testing procedures, some courts have found that agencies that utilize random testing procedures must ensure

TABLE 8.3 State Court Cases Applying the *Von Raab* Doctrine to Police Drug Testing

Case	Employee Challenge	Type of Testing	Standard Required	Government Interest	Basis for Government Interest	Covered Positions
Delaraba v. Nassau County Police Department 610 N.Y.S.2d 928 (1994)	Drug-testing program	Random	No reasonable suspicion required and systematic random not to exceed twelve tests annually	Substantial and compelling	Ensuring no officer drug use, public safety and confidence	Narcotic and scientific investigation officers
Sciortino v. Department of Police 643 So.2d 841 (1994)	Fifth and Fourteenth Amendments due process	Random	No suspicion required, due process right of independent confirmation testing and dismissal hearing confrontation	None stated	None stated	All officers
Miller v. Vanderburgh County 610 N.E.2d 858 (1993)	Fourth Amendment	Compulsory	Established testing procedures for suspicionless or reasonable suspicion required	Compelling	Detecting officer drug use, ensuring officer sobriety and public safety	All officers
Rawlings v. Police Department of Jersey City, N.J. 627 A.2d 602 (1993)	Fourth Amendment and Fifth Amendment self-incrimination	Compulsory	Reasonable suspicion required	Compelling	Special need to deter officer drug use and ensuring public safety	Officers in safety-sensitive positions
The City and County of Denver v. Casados 862 P.2d 908 (1993)	Drug-testing program and Fourth Amendment	Compulsory	Objectively established reasonable suspicion required	Compelling and legitimate	Prevention and detection of officer drug use	Officers involving public safety or security-sensitive positions

(continued)

TABLE 8.3   State Court Cases Applying the *Von Raab* Doctrine to Police Drug Testing

Case	Employee Challenge	Type of Testing	Standard Required	Government Interest	Basis for Government Interest	Covered Positions
Fraternal Order of Police, Miami v. City of Miami 609 So.2d 31 (1992)	Drug-testing program and unreasonable search and seizure	Random	Particularized reasonable suspicion required	None specifically stated	Public safety and integrity of department	Sworn officers
Worrel v. Brown 576 N.Y.S.2d 543 (1991)	Fourteenth Amendment due process	Random	No suspicion or prior notification required	None stated	None stated	All officers
Guiney v. Police Commissioner of Boston 582 N.E.2d 523 (1991)	Constitutionality of drug-testing program	Random	Reasonable suspicion required	Substantial	Presence of specific department drug problem or substantial public need	All officers
McCloskey v. Honolulu Police Department 799 P.2d 953 (1990)	Drug-testing program and right to privacy	Random/compulsory and condition of employment	No suspicion required	Compelling	Ensure officer and public safety, departmental effectiveness and integrity	All officers
O'Connor v. Police Commissioner of Boston 557 N.E.2d 1146 (1990)	Right to privacy and unreasonable search and seizure	Random/compulsory and condition of employment	No suspicion required	Compelling	Deterrence of officer drug use	All officers

(continued)

TABLE 8.3 State Court Cases Applying the *Von Raab* Doctrine to Police Drug Testing (continued)

Case	Employee Challenge	Type of Testing	Standard Required	Government Interest	Basis for Government Interest	Covered Positions
Gdanski v. New York City Transit Authority 561 N.Y.S.2d 51 (1990)	Drug-testing program and unreasonable search and seizure	Compulsory	No suspicion required, determination of medical fitness for duty	State's greater	Ensure medical fitness for duty	Officer post-hospitalization reinstatement for duty
Barretto v. City of New York 555 N.Y.S.2d 382 (1990)	Fourth Amendment	Compulsory	No suspicion required, post on-duty accident	Legitimate	Sensitive nature of police work, accident incident and public safety	Officers involved in on-duty accidents
City of Annapolis v. United Food 565 A.2d 672 (1989)	Drug-testing program	Compulsory	No suspicion required	Sufficient compelling	Prevention and deterrence of officer drug use, public safety and officer fitness	All police officers and firefighters

that the integrity of the random selection process be maintained. The Court of Appeals for the Ninth Circuit, in *Jackson v. Gates* (1992), found that selecting employees for urinalysis within a random screening procedure was violative of Fourth Amendment rights if compelling officers to submit to testing was missing randomness in the selection process. In *Ford v. Dowd* (1991, 1287), the Court of Appeals for the Eighth Circuit reasoned that drug-testing procedures that "[were] neither routinely or randomly applied" were unreasonable. Similarly, the District Court for New Mexico in *Pike v. Gallagher* (1993) found that drug-testing programs must be based either upon narrowly defined guidelines that provide a dimension of randomness or on individualized suspicion. The District Court for the Northern District of California in *American Federation of Government Employees v. Derwinski* (1991) went a step further, finding that elements of a random drug-testing program must include a "nexus" between designated employee duties and the potential risk of drug usage or impairment of employee function. In one case, *Sciortino v. Department of Police* (1994, 842), the Court of Appeals of Louisiana held that the denial of an officer's request to independently retest his positive urine sample or to question the laboratory technician conducting the testing resulted in the employee's being "deprived of fundamental fairness and due process in the way the case was prepared." The court suggested that the agency had developed an unreasonable and constitutionally violative testing procedure and found the officer's dismissal improper.

Summary of Drug-Testing Cases   In the nine years following the *Von Raab* decision, 62 percent of the lower federal and state courts adopted the suspicionless drug-testing standard enunciated by the Supreme Court. Nonetheless, several lower courts continued to adhere to variations of the earlier individualized suspicion requirement. Post–*Von Raab* precedent also reflects a diverse reasoning which permits random or compulsory drug testing of police employees. What can be gleaned from these lower court decisions is that, because of a lessened expectation of privacy in the police workplace and a balancing of competing interests test, police employers are permitted to utilize several types of employee drug-testing programs. Those drug-screening practices that are based upon individualized suspicion, involve employee consent, or follow employee notice present the least employee litigation risk and enhance the protection of employee privacy rights. However, as a result of the *Von Raab* permissibility of suspicionless drug testing of certain drug interdiction–related "covered positions," lower courts have supported suspicionless drug-testing programs which are pre-employment, systematic, procedurally specific, involve drug/safety-related positions, or relate to medical fitness.

The *Von Raab* decision established a bright-line rule allowing police employee suspicionless drug testing. By abandoning a warrant, probable cause, or individualized suspicion standard, the Supeme Court fostered considerable diversity in reasoning among the lower courts. Among the twenty six cases decided after *Von Raab,* variation exists in reasoning and interpretation, although a majority of the lower courts supported the fundamental principles of the *Von Raab* Court's holding. In spite of this support, *Von Raab* did leave some issues unresolved. The shortcomings observed by the Court of Appeals for the District of Columbia in *Harmon v. Thornburgh* (1989) poignantly sum up many of the concerns of scholars and lower courts when applying the doctrine. As the *Harmon* (1989, p. 488) court noted,

The *Von Raab* majority made no effort to articulate an analytical rule by which legitimate drug testing programs could be distinguished from illegitimate ones. It simply weighed individual privacy interests against the government's policy objectives, enumerating several factors that it deemed relevant in performing this balancing process. The Court did not, however, indicate whether it deemed the case a close one, in the sense that minor variations in the facts would have tipped the balance in the other direction. Nor did it indicate which [if any] of the relevant factors would be *essential* to the constitutional testing plan.

Although the *Von Raab* decision promoted a balancing of competing interests test and sanctioned suspicionless drug testing, it failed to provide the specific criteria for applying the balancing test to police employee drug-testing programs. Left to interpretation, the lower courts have expanded the doctrine to include additional covered positions and broader applications of permissible circumstances under which drug testing could be required of police employees. The lower courts now authorize both individualized suspicion and suspicionless drug testing of police employees from pre-employment candidates to veteran officers. The *Von Raab* provision that testing only apply to particular positions has been expanded by the lower courts to include a plethora of positions whereby employed officers can be subject to drug testing in the police workplace.

HIV/AIDS Testing of Police

With the considerable rise in the incidence of HIV, ARC, and AIDS among a cross-section of society, some public employers are seeking constitutionally permissible screening procedures to HIV-test employees. Unlike drug testing of police employees, HIV/AIDS testing involves several other Fourth Amendment, constitutional privacy, and employment discrimination issues in light of existing federal anti-discrimination legislation (Leonard, 1985; Melton, 1989; Hunter & Rubenstein, 1992; Banta, 1988). Although no specific Supreme Court doctrine exists involving public or police employer compulsory HIV/AIDS testing, several scholars suggest that the doctrine established in *The School Board of Nassau County, Florida v. Arline* (1987) provides the current constitutional basis for public employee communicable-disease testing (Jarvis, Closen, Hermann, & Leonard, 1996; Banta, 1988; Louis, 1988; Dreuil, 1988; Powell, White, & Robinson, 1987; Starr, 1988; Curran, 1990). In *Arline,* the Supreme Court interpreted the Rehabilitation Act of 1973 § 504 as it pertained to contagious disease and disability. Though the case did not involve compulsory public workplace disease testing, the lower courts have largely relied on the doctrine developed in *Arline* to interpret the permissibility of public and police employers to HIV/AIDS-test employees (Bloss, 1996).

In the *Arline* case, Gene Arline was terminated for lack of medical fitness after she tested positive twice for infectious tuberculosis. The Supreme Court agreed to hear Arline's appeal to determine whether contagious diseases qualified for handicap protection under the Rehabilitation Act of 1973. In *Arline,* the Court ruled that, within the meaning of the statute, if an individual was "otherwise qualified" to perform the duties of his or her position, the employer could not discriminate against the person solely because of a contagious disease that might have rendered him or her handicapped. The Court found that Arline was protected against discriminatory termination because the contagious tuberculosis qualified as a handicap, and she could not be dismissed if otherwise qualified for the position merely because of the "threat her tuberculosis posed to the health of others" (*Arline,* 1987, p. 282). The Court reasoned that it is impermissible for public employers to discriminate against handicapped employees because of the presence of presumed or perceived contagiousness, which may or may not otherwise impair the employee's ability to be otherwise qualified and perform the essential functions of the job. The Court asserted that a risk that a person "may pose a serious health threat to others" does not justify excluding all employees from coverage under the Act (*Arline,* 1987, p. 282).

Absent legal precedent, some scholars speculate that lower courts may extend *Arline*-type protections against discriminatory testing, exclusion, or termination to HIV infection. As Louis (1988, 198) noted, "A strict reading of the *Arline* decision, coupled with the similarities between AIDS and tuberculosis, leads one to conclude that AIDS victims are handicapped individuals and therefore will be protected from employment discrimination." Mello (1995) suggests that legislation following *Arline* codified the Court's tacit implication that HIV/AIDS-infected employees are considered handicapped, and thus protected from job discrimination under the Rehabilitation Act of 1973.

In 1988, Congress amended the Rehabilitation Act of 1973 with the Civil Rights Restoration Act (Act), whereby HIV-infected persons were covered under the Rehabilitation Act. Additional amendments to the act by Congress included provisions for the exclusion of individuals whose disease condition presented a "direct threat" to others, and that, following the *Arline* Court's holding, threat determinations should be based on medical interpretation (Jarvis et al., 1996). The employee or applicant must continue to be otherwise qualified for the position, as stated in the statute, and present no "direct [disease] threat" to others in the workplace. Such provisions of the act are only applicable to the federal government, federal contractors, and recipients of federal assistance. Because of the limited scope of the Rehabilitation Act and other statutes, Congress passed the Americans with Disabilities Act (ADA) in 1990 to provide broader anti-discrimination protection in both the public and private workplace for persons with disabilities. Although elements of the ADA could be interpreted to protect HIV-infected applicants or employees from discrimination, most claimants rely on the interpretation of the Rehabilitation Act's "handicapped" and "otherwise qualified" components in litigation alleging employer communicable-disease discrimination (Jarvis et al., 1996).

As with provisions of the Rehabilitation Act, the ADA does not protect applicants or employees who are not able to perform the essential functions of the job, and thus are not considered otherwise qualified. Hence, the HIV/AIDS disability is not protected from discrimination under the Rehabilitation Act or ADA statutes if the individual is not otherwise qualified or is unable to perform the essential functions required of the position (Jarvis et al., 1996). The Americans with Disabilities Act of 1990, Section 101 [8], defines *qualified* individuals as "an individual with a disability, who, with or without reasonable accommodation, can perform the essential functions of the employment position." Both the Rehabilitation Act and the ADA permit the use of medical examinations to determine the qualification of the individual in terms of ability to perform the essential functions of the job. As Aitchison (1996, p. 441) noted, "[under the ADA] an employer can compel an employee to undergo a medical examination if it has reason for doing so which is job related and consistent with business necessity." Both anti-discrimination laws prescribe that the qualification and essential function requirements be applicable to everyone, while the ADA specifically prohibits medical screening before a conditional job offer. The implication is that part of the permissible medical examination administered by agencies can include HIV/AIDS testing (Starr, 1988; Curran, 1990). In spite of the Rehabilitation Act of 1973, the Civil Rights Restoration Act of 1988 modifications, the *Arline* decision, and the ADA, the courts have yet to establish clear and specific doctrine on the permissibility of public employer compulsory HIV/AIDS testing.

In several cases before and after *Arline,* the courts have prohibited the exclusion of individuals with HIV/AIDS in the school and workplace. In *Thomas v. Atascadero Unified School District* (1986), the District Court for the Central District of California held that a child infected with AIDS was an otherwise qualified handicapped individual under § 504 and could not be excluded from school. The Court of Appeals for the Ninth Circuit, in *Chalk v. United States District Court Central District of California* (1988, 704), ruled that an AIDS-infected teacher could not be excluded from employment unless the employee could not disprove a "significant risk of communicating [the] infectious disease to others." Suggesting that the expansive protection of § 504 could be broadly applied to *all* contagious disease, the New Jersey Supreme Court, in *Board of Education v. Cooperman* (1987), held that the protection afforded in *Arline* could be generalized to apply to the exclusion of AIDS children from school.

Lower Federal Court Application of the *Arline* Doctrine to Police-Related HIV/AIDS Testing   Even though *Arline* is the prevailing Supreme Court standard in the area of interpretation of the Rehabilitation Act of 1973 § 504 and its application to contagious disease in the public workplace, lower courts have relied on a diversity of precedents in addressing issues involving the permissibility of compulsory communicable-disease testing in the police workplace. One of the first related federal court cases prior to *Arline, Local 1812, American Federation of Government Employees v. United States Department of State* (1987), addressed the issue of mandatory HIV/AIDS testing of Department of State Foreign Service employees. In *Local 1812,* the District Court for the District of Columbia held that the employees union had provided insufficient justification to obtain an order enjoining the Department of State from testing for HIV/AIDS as part of an employee medical fitness program under the Rehabilitation Act of 1973. The court found that the purpose of the Department's HIV/AIDS testing was to ensure medical fitness, and that the testing was "closely related to fitness for duty" (*Local 1812,* p. 53). The court reasoned that although HIV-infected persons are handicapped individuals under the Rehabilitation Act of 1973, the department "demonstrated serious grounds for concern" about the risk of assigning HIV carriers to foreign service (*Local 1812,* p. 54).

In a case directly related to public safety issues, *Anonymous Fireman v. City of Willoughby* (1991), the District Court for the Northern District of Ohio held that it was permissible for the fire department to require mandatory HIV/AIDS testing of firefighters/paramedics as part of an annual medical screening because of the medical high-risk nature of their work. The court reasoned that the city had a compelling governmental interest in providing a safe work environment and ensuring protection of the public, to support the mandatory, suspicionless, HIV/AIDS testing of firefighter and paramedic employees. In supporting the government's compelling interest in safety, the court found the mandatory testing program "rational and closely related to fitness for duty" (*Willoughby*, 1991, p. 416).

Closely following the reasoning of *Arline,* the District Court for the District of Columbia, in *Doe v. District of Columbia* (1992), held that the District of Columbia Fire Department could not exclude an applicant who was otherwise qualified based solely upon his HIV-positive condition. The court found that the asymptomatic HIV-positive applicant presented neither a "direct or significant threat" nor a "measurable risk" to other firefighters or the public and "was fully fit to serve as a fire fighter" (*Doe*, 1992, p. 569).

In *Tanberg v. Weld County Sheriff* (1992), the District Court for the District of Colorado held that a dismissed reserve deputy sheriff was entitled to compensatory damages under the Rehabilitation Act of 1973 but was required to demonstrate that he had been terminated solely because of his HIV-positive status and was otherwise qualified to perform the duties of deputy sheriff. Similarly, the District Court for the Northern District of Illinois, in *Doe v. City of Chicago* (1994), ruled that police applicants who were excluded from employment because they tested positive for HIV in pre-employment medical testing had a valid complaint and could proceed against the city. The court found that the applicant's claim would fall squarely under the provisions of the Rehabilitation Act of 1973.

The ability of police employers to compel applicants/employees to submit to HIV/AIDS testing is an unsettled area of the law. Under current doctrine, there are no specific HIV/AIDS-testing constitutional guidelines for agencies. As indicated in Table 8.4, among the few cases directly dealing with compulsory HIV/AIDS testing or the exclusion of applicants/employees discovered to be HIV-infected, about half of the courts permitted the testing or exclusion of the applicant/employee, while the other half found exclusion impermissible. Those courts that allowed the testing or exclusion of applicants/employees held that the agency had demonstrated a compelling interest in ensuring fitness for duty and/or evidence of a substantial risk to others [*Local 1812 American Federation of Government Employees v. U.S. Department of State* (1987)]; [*Anonymous Fireman v. City of Willoughby* (1991)]. In contrast, those courts that prohibited the exclusion of HIV-positive applicants/employees based their decisions on the level of direct threat presented and the fact that the individuals were otherwise qualified to perform the duties of the position [*Tanberg v. Weld County Sheriff* (1992)]; [*Doe v. District of Columbia* (1992)]; [*Doe v. City of Chicago* (1994)].

In the absence of lucid doctrine and substantial precedent, it is instructive to consider how the federal courts have addressed the ability of police employers to test, exclude, or dismiss applicants/employees involving other communicable and noncommunicable diseases in the workplace. As Table 8.5 indicates, the courts have largely based their decisions on the dimension of risk presented by the afflicted individuals and whether they were otherwise qualified for the position. Risk level was also influenced by the type and manageability of the disorder involved. Only the District Court for the Northern District of Ohio, in *Bombrys v. City of Toledo* (1993), involving an applicant with diabetes, required the police agency to render "reasonable accommodation" for the afflicted employee. All of the other courts found it unnecessary for the agency to make accommodations for the applicant/employee's disease or disorder as required by the Rehabilitation Act of 1973.

TABLE 8.4 Lower Federal Court Cases Interpreting Employee HIV/AIDS Testing or Exclusion

Case	Employee Challenge	Type of Disease	Testing or Exclusion Permissible	Basis for Employer Testing, Exclusion, or Accommodation
Local 1812, American Federation of Government Employees v. U.S. Department of State 662 F. Supp. 50 (1987)	Rehab Act of 1973; Fourth, Fifth Amendments	HIV/AIDS	Mandatory testing permissible	Testing permissible to ensure fitness for duty and because of risk of serious harm to employees and department's mission
Anonymous Fireman v. City of Willoughby 779 F. Supp. 402 (1991)	Privacy; Fourth, Ninth, Fourteenth Amendments	HIV/AIDS	Suspicionless mandatory testing permissible	Agency has "compelling interest" in fitness of "high-risk" employees and public safety
Tanberg v. Weld County Sheriff 787 F. Supp. 970 (1992)	Rehabilitation Act of 1973	HIV/AIDS	Exclusion not permissible	Employee permitted to bring action if it was "otherwise qualified" and was excluded "solely because of handicap"
Doe v. District of Columbia 796 F. Supp. 559 (1992)	Rehabilitation Act of 1973; 42 U.S.C. §1983	HIV/AIDS	Exclusion not permissible	Asymptomatic HIV applicant was "otherwise qualified" and posed no "direct threat" or "measurable risk"
Doe v. City of Chicago 883 F. Supp. 1126 (1994)	Rehabilitation Act of 1973; 42 U.S.C. §1983; Fourteenth Amendment (due process)	HIV/AIDS	Court rejected police department motion for dismissal	Excluded applicants were justified in seeking action against city

TABLE 8.5   Lower Federal Court Cases Interpreting Police Applicant/Employee Non-HIV Disease Testing

Case	Type of Disease	Testing or Exclusion Permissible	Basis for Employer Testing, Exclusion, or Accommodation
Davis v. Meese 692 F. Supp. 505 (1988)	Diabetes	Exclusion permissible for special agent position	Risk of being disabled by disease on duty; risk to public
Hogarth v. Thornburgh 833 F. Supp. 1077 (1993)	Manic-depressive disorder on medication	Dismissal permissible	Employee not "otherwise qualified" because of disease; unable to perform duties
Bombrys v. City of Toledo 849 F. Supp. 1210 (1993)	Diabetes	Exclusion not permissible	Enjoined department "blanket exclusion policy" of all diabetic applicants; department must consider applicants on case basis
Fedro v. Reno 21 F.3d 1391 (1994)	Hepatitis B	Not considered	Employer must make reasonable accommodations related to handicap, not create a new position or provide preferential treatment if employee is "otherwise qualified"
Lassiter v. Reno 885 F. Supp. 869 (1995)	Paranoid disorder on medication	Dismissal permissible	Employee not "otherwise qualified" because unable to perform essential functions of job; risk to employees and public

Employer Regulation of Police Employee Sexual Conduct

Privacy issues involving intimate relations and sexual conduct are some of the most vigorously litigated in the police workplace (Doss, 1990). As noted, one of the most important components of the individual privacy construct is the "right to be let alone" [*Cooley* (1881); *Olmstead v. United States* (1928)]. In his seminal analysis of privacy, Griswold (1960, p. 212) suggested, "The right to be let alone is the underlying theme of the Bill of Rights. It has continued to be the fertile soil for the cultivation of individual freedom." At the very threshold of the debate over the right to be let alone lies the right to make personal decisions about intimate associations between individuals.

Early Police Employee Sexual Conduct Doctrine   Although several courts have decided cases involving interpretations of state statutes [*Fout v. California State Personnel Board* (1982); *Borough of Darby v. Coleman* (1979); *Risner v. State Personnel Board of Review* (1978); *Battle v. Mulholland* (1971)], one of the most frequently cited early cases based on constitutional deprivation was *Major v. Hampton* (1976). The District Court for the Eastern District of Louisiana held that it was violative of the employee's due process rights for the Internal Revenue Service to dismiss an agent where his off-duty extramarital sexual conduct did not discredit the agency. In finding the employee's termination improper, the court ruled that to justify dismissal of an employee for allegedly unbecoming conduct, the employer must demonstrate that the employee's behavior "could rationally be considered likely to discredit the government" (*Major*, 1976, p. 71). In blocking the employee's firing, the court established a doctrine requiring police employers to demonstrate that the unbecoming conduct had a rational relationship to the effective functioning of the agency.

In a subsequent case, the court again supported the relationship between officer sexual conduct and effectiveness of agency operation when the District Court for the Middle District of North Carolina, in *Wilson v. Swing* (1978), upheld the dismissal of an officer involved in an off-duty extramarital affair. The court reasoned that the department's policy and dismissal action were not violative of the employee's privacy rights because the "adulterous conduct casts a poor light on the department as a whole and the morale and discipline of the Department which suffers as a result of community disapproval" (*Wilson*, 1978, p. 563). Further, the court rejected the employee's assertion that his First Amendment rights had been violated, holding that adultery is not a protected right.

The District Court for the Eastern District of Pennsylvania, in *Shuman v. City of Philadelphia* (1979), ruled that the department could not discipline an officer for failure to answer compulsory questions pertaining to off-duty cohabitation. In holding in favor of the employee, the court reasoned that the probing questions about the officer's off-duty sexual conduct bore no legitimate relationship to the effective operation of the agency. The court found that the department went "far beyond what might be justified in the exercise of the legitimate inquiry into the fitness and competency of its employees" (*Shuman*, 1979, p. 460).

These cases prior to 1980 represent the court's intent to establish a privacy doctrine mandating that the police agency demonstrate a *nexus,* or relationship, between departmental policy, disciplinary action, or regulation of police employee's sexual conduct and the effective operation of the agency. Hence, the doctrinal rule of the *nexus* between an employee's unbecoming sexual conduct and an effect on departmental efficacy has become a cornerstone of this type of police employee privacy jurisprudence.

Recent Lower Federal and State Police Employee Sexual Conduct Cases   Because of the nature of the constitutionally protected rights of police personnel regarding sexual conduct, most cases are litigated in the federal courts based on constitutional deprivations. Typically, claimants request protection of either a fundamental constitutional privacy right or a First Amendment privilege of expression or association (Bloss, 1997a). Because there is no single mandatory authority or bright-line rule governing the regulation of sexual conduct of police personnel, the lower federal courts have adopted several divergent standards. Some courts have permitted the dismissal, disciplining, or exclusion of applicants/employees based on sexual conduct, whereas others have prohibited the department from taking such actions. Division among courts often occurs because of the lack of Supreme Court guidance concerning the scope of privacy rights. As the Court of Appeals for the Ninth Circuit stated in *Fleisher v. City of Signal Hill* (1987, 1497), "the Supreme Court has not defined the outer limits of the right to privacy." Thus, the lower court will often base its interpretation of the dimensions of privacy protection and the permissibility of regulation on the individual merits and factual basis of the case.

As indicated in Table 8.6, the cases examined herein reveal that, between 1976 and 1996, 68 percent of the courts allowed the dismissal or disciplining of officers for improper sexual conduct, while 32 percent rejected dismissal, disciplining, or exclusion by departments. Of those courts permitting departmental action against employees for sexual misconduct, 67 percent dismissed officers engaged in improper sexual conduct, while 27 percent disciplined or demoted officers, and 1 percent conducted internal investigations into alleged sexual conduct. Also, 40 percent of the cases interpreted constitutional claims stemming from policies of conduct unbecoming an officer, 86 percent of the decisions relied primarily on analyses of constitutional privacy or freedom of association, and 14 percent involved other issues. These cases indicate that claimants frequently rely on both privacy and freedom of association protections (Bloss, 1997a).

Cases Supporting Police Employee Discipline for Sexual Misconduct   Specific doctrine began to emerge in the decisions in several federal cases in the 1980s. This acted to provide some precedent and direction for other courts to follow. Aside from incidents involving particularly egregious sexual misconduct (e.g., sexual conduct with a minor or on-duty sexual conduct with known prostitutes), the courts tended to base their decisions as to the permissibility of agency regulations on an assessment of the impact of the employee's conduct on the effective operation of the agency.

In three cases, the courts supported decisions to dismiss police employees who engaged in off-duty extramarital sexual relationships, ruling that the adulterous conduct was conduct unbecoming an officer [*Fabio v. Civil Service Commission of the City of Philadelphia* (1980); *Smith v. Price* (1980); *Suddarth v. Slane* (1982)]. Similarly, the Supreme Court of Texas, in *City of Sherman v. Henry* (1996), found discipline of the officer and denial of promotion supportable reasoning that off-duty adulterous sexual conduct is not a constitutionally protected privacy right that adversely affected the agency's operations.

The District Court for the Western District of New York, in *Baron v. Meloni* (1983), reasoned that the agency could dismiss an officer who engaged in intimate association with the wife of a reputed criminal. The District Court for the Western District of Michigan, in *Jackson v. Howell* (1982), found it was allowable for the agency to demote and temporarily suspend an officer who solicited and engaged in a sexual relationship with a crime complainant whom he approached during an investigation. Finally, in *Shawgo v. Spradlin* (1983), the agency was authorized by the Court of Appeals for the Fifth Circuit to demote and reassign officers who were dating and cohabitating because of agency concerns about "moral discipline and public image."

Supporting the disciplining of a police supervisor, the Colorado Court of Appeals held, in *Puzick v. City of Colorado Springs* (1983), that it was permissible to reprimand a

TABLE 8.6   Lower Federal and State Court Cases Involving Police Sexual Misconduct

Case	Employee Claim of Violated Right	Permissibility of Department Regulation	Basis for Department Regulation of Sexual Conduct
Major v. Hampton 413 F. Supp. 66 (1976)	Fifth Amendment Due Process Right to Privacy	Dismissal impermissible	Off-duty sexual conduct had no rational relationship to department's reputation
Wilson v. Swing 463 F. Supp. 555 (1978)	First, Fourth, Fifth, Sixth, Fourteenth Amendments; 42 U.S.C. § 1983	Dismissal permissible	Adulterous conduct has adverse affect on department's reputation
Shuman v. City of Philadelphia 470 F. Supp. 449 (1979)	First, Fourth, Fourteenth Amendments; 42 U.S.C. § 1983	Dismissal impermissible	Compulsory questions about off-duty adultery were improper, intrusive into protected "zone of privacy" and nonjob-related
Smith v. Price 616 F.2d 1371 (1980)	First Amendment right to privacy	Dismissal permissible	Extramarital sexual conduct is "unbecoming" and combined with other misconduct adversely affects department operations
Fabio v. Civil Service Commission 414 A.2d 82 (1980)	Fourteenth Amendment; statutory constitutionality	Dismissal permissible	Extramarital sexual conduct is "unbecoming"; adverse effect on department's operations
Suddarth v. Slane 539 F. Supp. 612 (1982)	42 U.S.C. § 1983; due process, equal protection, and association	Dismissal permissible	No First Amendment protection for off-duty adultery; adverse effect on department's reputation
Swope v. Bratton 541 F. Supp. 99 (1982)	First, Fifth, Fourteenth Amendments; 42 U.S.C. § 1983 & 1985	Dismissal impermissible	Off-duty cohabitation in "zone of privacy"; no adverse affect on department
Jackson v. Howell 577 F. Supp. 47 (1982)	First, Fourth, Ninth, and Fourteenth Amendments	Discipline permissible demotion	Unbecoming sexual conduct directly related to official duties

(*continued*)

TABLE 8.6   Lower Federal and State Court Cases Involving Police Sexual Misconduct (continued)

Case	Employee Claim of Violated Right	Permissibility of Department Regulation	Basis for Department Regulation of Sexual Conduct
Baron v. Meloni 556 F. Supp. 796 (1983)	First and Fourteenth Amendments; 42 U.S.C. § 1983	Dismissal permissible	No First Amendment protection for off-duty sexual conduct; conduct deleterious to department's operations
Briggs v. North Muskegon Police Department 563 F. Supp. 585 (1983)	42 U.S.C. § 1983	Dismissal impermissible	Cohabitation protected as privacy and association right; no adverse effect on department's operations
Thorne v. City of El Segundo 726 F.2d 459 (1983)	Title VII; 42 U.S.C. § 1983	Exclusion impermissible	Nonjob-related prior sexual conduct cannot exclude applicant
Shawgo v. Spradlin 701 F.2d 470 (1983)	42 U.S.C. § 1983; right to privacy	Discipline permissible demotion and reassignment	Department can regulate off-duty sexual conduct if "rational relation" to job performance is demonstrated
Puzick v. City of Colorado Springs 680 P.2d 1283 (1983)	First amendment privacy and association rights	Discipline permissible temporary suspension and removal from promotion list	Off-duty sexual conduct which is "unbecoming" is unprotected by First Amendment or "zone of privacy"
Wilson v. Taylor 733 F.2d 1539 (1984)	First and Fourteenth Amendments; 42 U.S.C. § 1983	Dismissal impermissible	Dating conduct protected as First Amendment association
Fugate v. Phoenix Civil Service Board 791 F.2d 736 (1986)	42 U.S.C. § 1983; right to privacy	Dismissal permissible	On-duty, open, notorious sexual conduct with prostitutes was "unbecoming conduct"

(continued)

161

TABLE 8.6 Lower Federal and State Court Cases Involving Police Sexual Misconduct (continued)

Case	Employee Claim of Violated Right	Permissibility of Department Regulation	Basis for Department Regulation of Sexual Conduct
Kukla v. Village of Antioch 647 F. Supp. 799 (1986)	First and Fourteenth Amendments due process, privacy, and association rights; 42 U.S.C. § 1983	Dismissal permissible	Off-duty fraternization and cohabitation has adverse effect on job performance and department's operations
Fleisher v. City of Signal Hill 829 F.2d 1491 (1987)	42 U.S.C. § 1983; privacy and association rights	Dismissal permissible	Illegal and immoral sexual conduct with a minor had deleterious effect on department morale, operations, reputation
Reuter v. Skipper 832 F. Supp. 1420 (1993)	42 U.S.C. § 1983; right to privacy	Dismissal impermissible	Policy unable to show state interest in department's safety and protection
Struck v. Hackett 668 A.2d 411 (1995)	Fifth and Fourteenth Amendments Due process right to privacy 42 U.S.C. § 1983 State Constitution	Dismissal permissible	First Amendment privacy right must be "clearly established" and none exists for dating conduct
City of Sherman v. Henry 928 S.W.2d 464 (1996)	Right to privacy under federal and state constitutions	Discipline permissible promotion denial	Off-duty, legal sexual conduct is not a protected privacy right; effect on department operations

supervisor who engaged in off-duty sexual conduct with a probationary officer. In *Kukla v. Village of Antioch* (1986), the District Court for the Northern District of Illinois found it allowable to dismiss an officer and dispatcher who were cohabitating and engaging in off-duty sexual conduct because of the possible deleterious effect on their job performance and the operations of the agency. The Court of Appeals for the Ninth Circuit supported the agency in *Fugate v. Phoenix Civil Service Board* (1986) in discharging officers who were involved in on-duty sexual conduct with known prostitutes because of the impact on the "general order of the department." Citing the need to protect agency reputation in *Fleisher v. City of Signal Hill* (1987), the Ninth Circuit court also held that the dismissal of a probationary officer for prior sexual conduct with a minor was allowable because of the illegal conduct. Rejecting an employee's claim of First Amendment protection, the Supreme Judicial Court of Maine, in *Struck v. Hackett* (1995), permitted the termination of a probationary deputy for dating and cohabitating with the Sheriff's secretary.

Those courts that permitted the exclusion, dismissal, or discipline of officers engaged in proscribed sexual conduct predominantly considered the presence and extent of any adverse impact on the agency's efficacy as a pivotal element in their reasoning.

Cases Rejecting Police Employee Discipline for Sexual Misconduct   Several courts rejected efforts to dismiss, exclude, or discipline employees based on sexual conduct. Not all of their decisions in favor of claimants were based on a protected privacy right. Some of the lower court rulings that denied efforts to sanction employees stemmed from challenges too vague or overbroad policies or violations of substantive or procedural due process, while other courts asserted that off-duty conduct was permissible because it had no deleterious effect on job performance or agency operations.

Refusing to support the employee's termination, the District Court for the Western District of Arkansas held in, *Swope v. Bratton* (1982), that the dismissal of an officer for off-duty sexual conduct that was not "notorious" and did not interfere with job performance was unjustified and violative of constitutional due process. Citing the absence of a requisite nexus between misconduct and adverse effect on job performance, the District Court for the Western District of Michigan, in *Briggs v. North Muskegon Police Department* (1983), ruled that it was improper to dismiss an officer for off-duty sexual conduct.

Regarding applicant selection, the Court of Appeals for the Ninth Circuit, in *Thorne v. City of El Segundo* (1983), found it impermissible to exclude an otherwise qualified applicant because of prior non-job-related sexual conduct. The court reasoned that these actions were violative of the applicant's privacy rights and freedom of association. The Court of Appeals for the Eleventh Circuit, in *Wilson v. Taylor* (1984), held that the agency could not dismiss an officer for having off-duty intimate associations with the daughter of a reputed criminal because that was an infringement on protected association rights. In *Reuter v. Skipper* (1993), the District Court for Oregon found that termination of a jailer was unwarranted because the agency was unable to demonstrate that the relationship between the employee and an ex-felon presented a specific risk to agency operational safety and protection. The court held that failure to show a rational connection between the employee association and a "substantial state interest" in safety rendered the policy unenforceable and the dismissal violative of privacy rights.

Similar to the predominant rationale of the courts supporting sanctions against employees, those courts that rejected regulation of employee sexual conduct often relied on the nexus between the employee conduct and the adverse impact on agency functioning. The failure of the agency to produce persuasive evidence of the negative effect of the employee conduct resulted in the court finding that agency regulation was violative of constitutional privacy protections.

Although the majority of claimants rely on an eclectic combination of constitutional grounds, the courts have emphasized certain categories of preferred principles in their interpretations. The preponderance of the courts based their analyses on the constitutional principles of privacy and association rights. Several other courts rested their interpretations on the principle of conduct unbecoming an officer. The unbecoming issue largely emerged from agency policy, which was subject to constitutional challenges mostly for statutory vagueness, overbreadth, or procedural/substantive due process violations.

Because lower federal and state courts are divided on the precise scope of the privacy rights and protections involving police employee sexual conduct, several doctrines and principles have emerged in this area of law. Many of the courts interpret the permissibility of agencies to regulate sexual conduct of employees as contingent upon the demonstration of a nexus between the behavior and on-job performance or an adverse effect on agency's operation, morale, or reputation.

Employer Regulation of Police Employee Homosexual Conduct   In addition to the regulation of heterosexual on/off-duty sexual behavior, homosexual conduct among police employees is an emerging area of litigation in sexual misconduct regulation. In this area of police employee privacy jurisprudence, court doctrine is unclear on the employer's authority to exclude or dismiss homosexual officers (Bloss, 1997b). As Table 8.7 indicates, several police cases have emerged recently, primarily in the federal courts, involving the hiring and continued employment of homosexuals. Since there is no specific Supreme Court doctrine governing sexual orientation in the public workplace, courts have turned to *Bowers v. Hardwick* (1986) for guidance. In *Bowers,* the Supreme Court held that Georgia's criminal sodomy statutes did not violate the fundamental privacy rights of homosexuals. In its ruling, the Court reasoned that homosexuality was not a fundamental right of privacy, and stated that "proscriptions against that [homosexual] conduct have ancient roots" (*Bowers*, 1986, p. 193). The Court recognized the right of individual states to prohibit various behaviors "based on notions of morality," noting that twenty-five states had continued to outlaw sodomy (*Bowers*, 1986, p. 197). Although some courts have not relied on *Bowers* reasoning in police employee cases, Manak (1986) asserts that the *Bowers* decision is tantamount to giving police agencies the authority to regulate homosexual employee conduct in a "relatively straightforward" way vis-à-vis state criminal sodomy statutes.

In light of the constitutional denial of particularized privacy rights to homosexuals, as reflected in precedent and asserted in *Bowers v. Hardwick* (1986), there currently exists little protective basis for claims of sexual orientation discrimination or exclusion by police applicants or employees (see generally Achtenberg, 1985). Even in the face of the *Bowers* decision, few of the lower courts relied on its doctrine directly in interpreting claims brought by police applicants or employees. Rather, the lower federal court decisions reflect a diversity of standards; yet a majority has held dismissal or exclusion of homosexuals permissible. Hence, notwithstanding other protections available to *all* police employees regarding constitutional and civil rights, privacy claims stemming from sexual orientation find little support in the current state of the law.

From 1979 to 1993, two-thirds of the federal courts found it permissible for police employers to exclude or dismiss employees for alleged homosexual conduct (Bloss, 1997b). Those employees who prevailed in preventing the agency from terminating them typically based their claim on procedural grounds more than on the employer's ability to regulate homosexual conduct. In two cases, the courts prohibited the police employer from excluding or terminating the allegedly homosexual employee, but relied on very different logic. In *Ashton v. Civiletti* (1979), the Court of Appeals for the District of Columbia Circuit held that questions involving homosexual preferences posed to an officer as part of an internal investigation, and his subsequent termination, were improper because they were not specific to the officer's official duties. The District Court for the Northern District of California, in *Buttino v. FBI* (1992), held that the special agent's security clearance revocation and termination were impermissible because they were violative of First Amendment speech and association protections. The court in *Buttino* reasoned that the agent was terminated solely because of his admission of homosexual conduct following an internal investigation. Such action by the agency was considered violative in the absence of a demonstration that the agent's homosexual conduct was "rationally related to a legitimate government interest" (*Buttino*, 1992, p. 306).

Aside from these two cases, the courts have permitted police employers to dismiss or exclude applicants/employees based on alleged homosexual activities. One of the earliest cases involved a civilian police employee who was excluded from employment consideration based on admitted homosexual conduct [*Childers v. Dallas Police Department* (1981)]. In *Childers,* the District Court for the Northern District of Texas reasoned that the homosexual applicant's exclusion was permissible because of the police department's greater interest in "protecting its public image" and promoting efficient operation through controlling the conduct of its employees (p. 142). Although the court acknowledged the applicant's First Amendment rights of speech and association, it found that the employer had a more compelling interest that outweighed those of the individual employee. Similarly, the District Court for the District of Kansas, in *Endsley v. Naes* (1987), held that the dismissal of a patrol deputy after rumors of her homosexuality was permissible and not violative of First Amendment rights of association. The court in *Endsley* found that the department had "sufficient" and "legitimate" justification for the employee's termination to "protect the public image and close working relationship with the officers and community" (*Childers,* 1981, p. 1033).

In another 1987 case, *Padula v. Webster,* the Court of Appeals for the District of Columbia Circuit found that the FBI's practice of excluding practicing homosexual applicants was not a violation of constitutional equal protection. In supporting the policy of the FBI, the court found that it was reasonable that the applicant's homosexual conduct could "adversely affect the agency's responsibilities" and that the agency could not be expected to hire "agents who engage in conduct criminalized in roughly one-half of the states" (p. 104). Following *Bowers* (1986), the court in *Padula* reasoned that homosexuals were not a protected class eligible for safeguards under constitutional equal protection, and therefore their employment could adversely affect the operation and responsibilities of the

**TABLE 8.7   Lower Federal Court Cases Interpreting Regulation of Police
Applicant/Employee Homosexual Conduct**

Case	Employee Claim of Violated Right	Permissibility of Dismissal or Exclusion	Basis for Dismissal or Exclusion
Ashton v. Civiletti 613 F.2d 923 (1979)	Fifth Amendment due process	Dismissal impermissible	Employee possessed property interest and agency must use proper procedural due process
Padula v. Webster 822 F.2d 97 (1987)	First, Fourth, Fifth, Fourteenth Amendments	Exclusion permissible	Homosexuality not an eligible suspect class and adverse effect on agency
Endsley v. Naes 673 F. Supp. 1032 (1987)	First Amendment association and 42 U.S.C. § 1983	Dismissal permissible	Protect public image and relationship with community and legitimate government interest
Todd v. Navarro 698 F. Supp. 871 (1988)	Fourteenth Amendment equal protection and 42 U.S.C. § 1983	Dismissal permissible	Rationally related to a legitimate government purpose and homosexuality not an eligible suspect class
Delahoussaye v. City of New Iberia 937 F.2d 144 (1991)	Fourteenth Amendment due process and equal protection	Exclusion permissible	Effect on departmental operations and public image
Buttino v. FBI 801 F. Supp. 298 (1992)	First Amendment speech and association Fifth Amendment due process	Dismissal impermissible	Violation of First Amendment speech and association rights

agency. In a similar vein, the District Court for the Southern District of Florida, in *Todd v. Navarro* (1988), ruled that it was allowable to terminate a lesbian deputy, finding that no violation of equal protection existed because homosexuals are not a constitutionally protected class. The court in *Todd* found that the department need only show that its dismissal actions were "rationally related to a legitimate purpose" (e.g., that of maintaining an effective and reputable police agency) (p. 875). The Court of Appeals for the Fifth Circuit, in *Delahoussaye v. City of New Iberia* (1991), held that the decision to not reinstate an officer based on allegations that he had engaged in homosexual conduct in public was allowable and not violative of Fourteenth Amendment due process and equal protection rights. The court found that the agency's actions were "rational," and that it was permissible for the agency to protect its effectiveness and public interest by excluding an officer whose actions were "prejudicial to departmental service and contrary to public interest" (*Padula*, 1987, p. 149).

Another recent case, involving the Central Intelligence Agency's dismissal of a "covert electronic technician" for admitted homosexual conduct, can be instructive. The Court of Appeals for the District of Columbia Circuit, in *Doe v. Gates* (1993), held that it was permissible for the CIA to terminate the homosexual employee because of a "potential threat to national security." The court ruled that the agency had a "legitimate government security interest" in light of the sensitivity of the position and its concern about the employee's "trustworthiness" after he hid information of his homosexuality (p. 1324).

Additional tacit guidance may be provided by the Supreme Court's *Romer v. Evans* (1996) decision. Here the Court held that a Colorado constitutional amendment prohibiting local government or ordinance from including "homosexual orientation, conduct, practices, or relationships" as protected under anti-discrimination laws was violative of the equal protection clause of the Fourteenth Amendment [*Romer* (1996, p. 1622)]. The Court stated that the amendment targeted a class of individuals, denying them the protection of anti-discrimination laws available to others, and "lack[ed] a rational relationship to legitimate State interests" [*Romer* (1996, p. 1626)]. The Court acknowledged the absence of precedent to support much of its holding, yet found that statutes that are status-based and treat persons such as homosexuals in an unequal manner are violative. The *Romer* decision did not directly affect the standing of *Bowers*, but may influence the ability to select particular "homosexual classes" of persons for inclusion or exclusion in the workplace in the future. As noted, no specific Supreme Court authority exists in the area of police employer exclusion or dismissal of homosexual applicants/employees. As evidenced by the modicum of consensus in the lower federal courts, however, police employers are permitted to regulate the presence of homosexual employees in the workplace.

CONCLUSION

Though the dimensions of employer regulatory authority depends on the area of police employee conduct, the courts have permitted increased employer regulation in recent years in privacy-related areas. Significant changes have occurred in police employee privacy rights due to court modification of traditional protective doctrines (i.e., warrant, probable cause, reasonable suspicion). In addition to the reformulation of long-standing Fourth Amendment provisions, the courts have established several doctrines (expectation of privacy, special needs, and balancing of competing interests) that have facilitated a new interpretation of police employee privacy in the workplace.

Following the Supreme Court's pivotal ruling in *Ortega* regarding the diminution of public employee expectation of privacy, police employers have gained increased regulatory power over their employees. In the police workplace, the previous constitutional litmus tests of Fourth Amendment and privacy have been supplanted by a balancing of competing interests test standard, where employer control is contingent upon the demonstration of a legitimate governmental interest that is more compelling than individual employee privacy rights.

Because of the amorphous nature of privacy jurisprudence, the extent and dimensions of police employer regulatory control in the future are uncertain. However, in light of several precedent-setting decisions in the 1980s [e.g., *New Jersey v. T.L.O.* (1985)]; *Bowers v. Hardwick* (1986); *O'Connor v. Ortega* (1987); *National Treasury Employees Union v. Von Raab* (1989)], the Supreme Court has redefined constitutional protections that affect the police workplace. As lower courts apply these standards and abandon traditional protections, individual employee privacy rights may continue to be diminished. At present, police employers have been given considerable authority to regulate on- and off-duty conduct of employees. Prospects for the continued diminution of police employee privacy rights vis-à-vis a lessened expectation of privacy in the workplace are clearly present. Future employee litigation will define the scope of employer regulatory powers. In the meantime, it is incumbent upon police employers to develop constitutionally valid regulatory policies and procedures that both maintain the effective operation of the agency and protect the privacy of their employees. At this point, police employees must continue to look to the courts to outline the dimensions of their privacy rights in the government workplace.

REFERENCES

ACHTENBERG, R. 1985. *Sexual orientation and the law*. San Francisco: Lawyers Guild Press.

AITCHISON, W. 1996. *The rights of police officers* (3rd ed.). Portland, OR: Labor Relations Press.

BANTA, W. 1988. *AIDS in the workplace*. Lexington, MA: Lexington Books.

BLOSS, W. 1995. Privacy rights of police officers: A constitutional analysis. In Nicky Ali Jackson (Ed.), *Contemporary issues in criminal justice: Shaping tomorrow's system* (pp. 135–157). New York: McGraw-Hill.

BLOSS, W. 1996. *Privacy issues involving law enforcement personnel: A constitutional analysis*. Unpublished doctoral dissertation. Sam Houston State University, Huntsville, Texas.

BLOSS, W. 1997a. Privacy rights of police officers: A constitutional analysis of agency regulation of employee sexual conduct. Unpublished paper. Presented at the annual meeting of the Southern Criminal Justice Association, Richmond, VA.

BLOSS, W. 1997b. Privacy rights of police officers: A constitutional analysis of compulsory workplace HIV/AIDS disease testing and lifestyle preference. Unpublished paper. Presented at the annual meeting of the Academy of Criminal Justice Sciences, Louisville, KY.

BLOSS, W. 1998. Warrantless search in the law enforcement workplace: Court interpretation of employer practices and employee privacy rights under the *Ortega* doctrine. *Police Quarterly, 1*(2), 51–69.

BRANCATO, G., & POLEBAUM, E. 1981. *The rights of police officers*, New York: Avon Books.

CATHCART, D. 1995. Privacy in the workplace: Emerging claims and defenses, C983 *ALI-ABA* 451.

COOLEY, T. 1881. *Torts* (2nd ed.). New York: Little, Brown.

CURRAN, C. 1990. Mandatory testing of public employees for the human immunodeficiency virus: The Fourth Amendment and medical reasonableness. *Columbia Law Review, 90,* 720–759.

DOSS, M. 1990. Police management: Sexual misconduct and the right to privacy. *Journal of Police Science and Administration, 17,* 194–204.

DREUIL, M. 1988. A contagious disease becomes a handicap: *The School Board of Nassau County, Florida v. Arline. Loyola Law Review, 34,* 224–243.

DUCAT, C. 1999. *Constitutional interpretation* (7th ed.). St. Paul, MN: West.

GERETY, T. 1977. Redefining privacy. *Harvard Civil Rights and Civil Liberties Law Review, 12,* 233–250.

GLANCY, D. 1979. Invention of the right to privacy. *Arizona Law Review, 21,* 1–27.

GRISWOLD, E. 1960. The right to be let alone. *Northwestern University Law Review, 55,* 216–228.

HANSON, H. 1993. The Fourth Amendment in the workplace: Are we really being reasonable? *Virginia Law Review, 79,* 205–227.

HOEKSTRA, D. 1996. Workplace searches: A legal overview. *Labor Law Journal, 47,* 127–138.

HUNTER, N., & RUBENSTEIN, W. 1992. *AIDS agenda: Emerging issues in civil rights.* New York: New Press.

JARVIS, R., CLOSEN, M., HERMANN, D., & LEONARD, A. 1996. *AIDS Law in a Nutshell* (2nd ed.). St. Paul, MN: West.

KLOTTER, J., KANOVITZ, J., & KANOVITZ, M. 1999. *Constitutional Law* (8th ed.). Cincinnati: Anderson.

LARSEN, K. 1987. Governmental intrusion into the public employee workplace: *O'Connor v. Ortega. Creighton Law Review, 21,* 409–421.

LEONARD, A. 1985. Employment discrimination against persons with AIDS. *University of Dayton Law Review, 10,* 681–703.

LEWIS, D. 1987. Drug testing in the workplace: Legal and policy implications for employers and employees. *Detroit Civil Liberties Review,* 699–721.

LOUIS, T. 1988. Civil rights—the *Arline* decision as applied to AIDS victims: Shield or sword. *Mississippi College Law Review, 9,* 181–201.

MANAK, J. 1986. An emerging liability issue for the law enforcement employer: Homosexual lifestyles and AIDS in the workplace. *Prosecutor, 7,* 7–15.

MELLO, J. 1995. *AIDS and the law of workplace discrimination,* Boulder, CO: Westview Press.

MELTON, V. 1989. Without probable cause: The constitutional ramifications of mandatory AIDS testing in the workplace. *University of Missouri, Kansas City Law Review, 57,* 863–897.

NUGER, K. 1992. The special needs rationale: Creating a chasm in Fourth Amendment analysis. *Santa Clara Law Review, 32,* 89–109.

POWELL, J.; WHITE, J.; & ROBINSON, R. 1987. Contagious disease in the workplace: *The School Board of Nassau County, Florida v. Arline. Labor Law Journal, 1987, (38)*11, 702–707.

REAMEY, G. 1992. When "special needs" meet probable cause: Denying the devil benefit of law. *Hastings Constitutional Law Quarterly, 19,* 295–316.

STARR, D. 1988. AIDS as a handicap? *Arline,* Tuberculosis and AIDS. *Toledo Law Review, 19,* 859–884.

SEARLE, L. 1989. The administrative search from *Dewey* to *Burger*: Dismantling the Fourth Amendment. *Hastings Constitutional Law Quarterly, 16,* 261–285.

SUNDBY, S. 1988. A return to the Fourth Amendment basics: Undoing the mischief of *Camara* and *Terry. Minnesota Law Review, 72,* 383–401.

VAUGHN, M., & DEL CARMEN, R. 1993. "Special needs" in criminal justice: An evolving exception to the Fourth Amendment warrant and probable cause requirements. *George Mason University Civil Rights Law Journal, 3,* 203–215.

VAUGHN, M., & DEL CARMEN, R. 1997. The Fourth Amendment as a tool of actuarial justice: The "special needs" exception to the warrant and probable cause requirements. *Crime and Delinquency, 43,* 78–101.

WARREN, S., & BRANDEIS, L. 1890. The right to privacy. *Harvard Law Review, 4,* 193–213.

Cases Cited

- *Ahern v. Murphy,* 457 F.2d 363 (7th Cir. 1972).
- *American Federation of Government Employees v. Derwinski,* 777 F. Supp. 1493 (N.D. Cal. 1991).
- *Anonymous Fireman v. City of Willoughby,* 779 F. Supp. 402 (N.D. Ohio 1991).

- *Ashton v. Civiletti*, 613 F.2d. 923 (1979).
- *Barretto v. City of New York, et al.*, 555 N.Y.S.2d 382 (A.D.2 Dept. 1990).
- *Baron v. Meloni*, 556 F. Supp. (W.D.N.Y. 1983).
- *Battle v. Mulholland*, 439 F.2d 321 (1971).
- *Bivens v. Six Unknown Named Agents*, 403 U.S. 388 (1971).
- *Board of Education v. Cooperman*, 523 A.2d 655 (1987).
- *Bombrys v. City of Toledo*, 849 F. Supp. 1210 (N.D. Ohio 1993).
- *Borough of Darby v. Coleman*, 407 A.2d 468 (1979).
- *Bowers v. Hardwick*, 478 U.S. 186 (1986).
- *Briggs v. North Muskegon Police Department*, 563 F. Supp. 585 (W.D. Mich. 1983).
- *Brown v. City of Detroit*, 715 F. Supp. 832 (E.D. Mich. 1989).
- *Buttino v. F.B.I.*, 801 F. Supp. 298 (N.D. Cal. 1992).
- *Camara v. Municipal Court*, 387 U.S. 523 (1967).
- *Capua v. City of Plainfield*, 643 F. Supp. 1507 (D.N.J. 1986).
- *Chalk v. United States District Court Central District of California*, 840 F.2d 701 (9th Cir. 1988).
- *Childers v. Dallas Police Department*, 513 F. Supp. 134 (N.D. Tex. 1981).
- *City of Annapolis, et al. v. United Food and Commercial Workers, Local 400, et al.* 565 A.2d672 (Md. 1989).
- *City of Palm Bay v. Bauman*, 475 So.2d 1322 (Fla. Dist. Ct. App. 1985).
- *City of Sherman v. Henry*, 928 S.W. 2d 464 (Tex. 1996).
- *Connick v. Myers*, 103 S. Ct. 1684 (1983).
- *Davis v. Meese*, 692 F. Supp. 505 (N.D. Ohio 1988).
- *Delahoussaye v. City of New Iberia*, 937 F.2d 144 (5th Cir. 1991).
- *Delaraba v. Nassau County Police Department*, 610 N.Y.S.2d 928 (Ct. App. 1994).
- *Doe v. City of Chicago*, 883 F. Supp. 1126 (N.D.Ill.1994).
- *Doe v. District of Columbia*, 796 F. Supp. 559 (D.D.Cir. 1992).
- *Doe v. Gates*, 981 F.2d 1316 (D.C. Cir. 1993).
- *Eisenstadt v. Baird*, 405 U.S. 438 (1972).
- *Endsley v. Naes*, 673 F. Supp. 1032 (D. Kan. 1987).
- *Fabio v. Civil Service Commission of the City of Philadelphia*, 414 A.2d 82 (Pa. Cmwlth. 1980).
- *Fedro v. Reno*, 21 F.3d 139 (7th Cir. 1994).
- *Feliciano v. City of Cleveland*, 988 F.2d 649 (6th Cir. 1993).
- *Fleisher v. City of Signal Hill*, 829 F.2d 1491 (9th Cir. 1987).
- *Foley v. Connelie*, 435 U.S. 291 (1978).
- *Ford v. Dowd*, 931 F.2d 1286 (8th Cir. 1991).
- *Fout v. California State Personnel Board*, 186 Cal. Rptr. 452 (App. 1982).
- *Fraternal Order of Police, Miami Lodge 20 v. City of Miami*, 609 So.2d 31 (Fla. 1992).
- *Fugate v. Phoenix Civil Service Board*, 791 F.2d 736 (9th Cir.1986).
- *Gamble v. State*, 552 A.2d 928 (Md. App. 1989).
- *Gardner v. Missouri State Highway Patrol Superintendent*, 901 S.W.2d 107 (Mo. App. W.D. 1995)
- *Garrity v. New Jersey*, 385 U.S. 493 (1967).

- *Gdanski v. New York City Transit Authority,* 561 N.Y.S.2d 51 (A.D.2 Dept. 1990).
- *Griswold v. Connecticut,* 381 U.S. 479 (1965).
- *Guiney v. Police Commissioner of Boston,* 582 N.E.2d 523 (Mass. 1991).
- *Guiney v. Roache,* 873 F.2d 1557 (1st Cir. 1989).
- *Harmon v. Thornburgh,* 878 F.2d 484 (D.C. Cir. 1989).
- *Hebert v. Louisiana,* 272 U.S. 312 (1926).
- *Hogarth v. Thornburgh* 833 F. Supp. 1077 (S.D.N.Y. 1993).
- *Jackson v. Gates,* 975 F.2d 648 (9th Cir. 1992).
- *Jackson v. Howell,* 577 F. Supp. 47 (W.D. Mich. 1982).
- *Katz v. United States,* 389 U.S. 347 (1967).
- *Kelley v. Johnson,* 425 U.S. 238 (1976).
- *Kukla v. Village of Antioch,* 647 F. Supp. 799 (N.D.Ill. 1986).
- *Lassiter v. Reno,* 885 F. Supp. 869 (E.D. Va. 1995).
- *Local 1812, American Federation of Government Employees v. United States Department of State,* 662 F. Supp. 50 (D.D.Cir. 1987).
- *Loder v. City of Glendale, et al.,* 927 P2d. 1200 (1997).
- *Lowe v. City of Macon, Georgia, et al.,* 720 F. Supp. 994 (M.D. Ga. 1989).
- *Major v. Hampton,* 413 F. Supp. 66 (E.D. La. 1976).
- *McCloskey v. Honolulu Police Department,* 799 P.2d 953 (Hawaii 1990).
- *McKenna v. City of Philadelphia,* 771 F. Supp. 124 (E.D. Pa. 1991).
- *Miller v. Vanderburgh County,* 610 N.E.2d 858 (Ind.App.1 Dist. 1993).
- *Moore v. Constantine,* 574 N.Y.S.2d 507 (Sup. 1991).
- *National Treasury Employees Union v. Bush,* 891 F.2d 99 (5th Cir. 1989).
- *National Treasury Employees Union v. United States Customs Service,* 829 F. Supp 408 (D.D.C. 1993).
- *National Treasury Employees Union v. United States Custom Service,* 27 F.3d 623 (D.C. Cir. 1994).
- *National Treasury Employees Union v. Von Raab,* 489 U.S. 656 (1989).
- *New Jersey v. T.L.O.,* 469 U.S. 325 (1985).
- *Nikodem v. Pennsylvania State Police,* 439 A.2d 1325 (Pa. Cmwlth. 1982).
- *O'Connor v. Ortega,* 480 U.S. 709 (1987).
- *O'Connor v. Police Commissioner of Boston,* 557 N.E.2d 1146 (Mass. 1990).
- *Olmstead v. United States,* 277 U.S. 438 (1928).
- *Padula v. Webster,* 822 F.2d 97 (D.C. Cir. 1987).
- *Penny, et al. v. Kennedy, et al.,* 915 F.2d 1065 (6th Cir. 1990).
- *People v. Duvall,* 428 N.W.2d 746 (Mich. App. 1988).
- *Pike v. Gallagher,* 829 F. Supp. 1254 (D.N.M. 1993).
- *Policemen's Benevolent Association of New Jersey v. Washington Township,* 672 F. Supp. 779 (D.N.J. 1987).
- *Puzick v. City of Colorado Springs,* 680 P.2d 1283 (Colo. App. 1983).
- *Rankin v. McPherson,* 483 U.S. 378 (1987).
- *Rawlings v. Police Department of Jersey City, New Jersey,* 627 A.2d 602 (N.J. 1993).
- *Reuter v. Skipper,* 832 F. Supp. (D. Or. 1993).
- *Risner v. State Personnel Board of Review,* 381 N.E.2d 346 (1978).
- *Roe v. Wade,* 410 U.S. 113 (1973).

- *Romer v. Evans*, 116 S. Ct. 1620 (1996).
- *Sciortino v. Department of Police*, 643 So.2d 841 (La. App. 4 Cir. 1994).
- *Shawgo v. Spradlin*, 701 F.2d 470 (5th Cir. 1983).
- *Shields v. Burge*, 874 F.2d 1201 (7th Cir. 1989).
- *Shuman v. City of Philadelphia,* 470 F. Supp. 449 (E.D. Pa. 1979).
- *Smith v. Price*, 616 F.2d 1371 (5th Cir. 1980).
- *State v. Francisco*, 790 S.W.2d 543 (Tenn. Cr. App. 1989).
- *State v. Nelson*, 434 S.E.2d 697 (W.Va. 1993).
- *State v. Stoddard*, 909 S.W.2d 454 (Tenn. Cr. App. 1994).
- *Struck v. Hackett*, 668 A.2d 411 (Me. 1995).
- *Suddarth v. Slane*, 539 F. Supp. 612 (W.D. Va. 1982).
- *Swope v. Bratton*, 541 F. Supp. 99 (W.D. Ark. 1982).
- *Tanberg v. Weld County Sheriff*, 787 F. Supp. 970 (D. Colo. 1992).
- *The City and County of Denver v. Casados, et al.*, 862 P.2d 908 (Colo. 1993).
- *The School Board of Nassau County, Florida v. Arline*, 480 U.S. 273 (1987).
- *Thompson v. Johnson County Community College,* 930 F. Supp. 501 (D. Kan. 1996).
- *Thorne v. City of El Segundo*, 726 F.2d 459 (9th Cir.1983).
- *Thomas v. Atascadero Unified School District,* 662 F. Supp. 376 (C.D. Cal. 1986).
- *Todd v. Navarro*, 698 F. Supp. 871 (S.D. Fla. 1988).
- *Union Pacific Railway Co. v. Botsford,* 141 U.S. 250 (1891).
- *U.S. v. Taketa*, 923 F.2d 665 (9th Cir. 1991).
- *Wilson v. Swing*, 463 F. Supp. 555 (M.D.N.C.1978)
- *Wilson v. Taylor*, 733 F.2d 1539 (11th Cir. 1984).
- *Worrell v. Brown*, 576 N.Y.S.2d 543 (A.D.1 Dept. 1991).

Statutes

- Americans with Disabilities Act 1990, *codified* 42 U.S.C.A. § 12101.
- Civil Action for Deprivation of Rights 1871, *codified* 42 U.S.C §1983.
- Civil Rights Restoration Act 1988, *codified* 20 U.S.C.A. § 1687.
- Rehabilitation Act of 1973, *codified* 29 U.S.C. § 794.

9

Affirmative Action and Police Selection

Managing Legal Boundaries and Psychometric Limits

Larry K. Gaines

Pamela J. Schram

INTRODUCTION

Over the past three decades, few issues have dominated the attention of police personnel practices and administration to the extent that affirmative action has. Few people have neutral feelings or opinions regarding the topic. On the one hand, its opponents see affirmative action as benefiting the undeserving or as catering to groups already provided too many benefits and accommodations (Stein, 1999). Proponents, on the other hand, see racism continuing in our country and therefore see a need for "fresh and fearless" new programming (Martinez, 1999). At the heart of the controversy is the question of what affirmative action is attempting to accomplish.

Most likely, affirmative action began as a legal mandate to eliminate or reduce discrimination by ensuring that everyone had an equal opportunity to seek and obtain employment. Over time, however, affirmative action came to be defined by many courts and segments within our society as aimed at achieving equal outcomes. That is, discrimination was said to have occurred when selection outcomes do not approximate the racial and ethnic makeup of the community or the applicant pool.

Nalbandian (1989) notes that, at some point, affirmative action came to be synonymous with distributive justice or social equity. For example, the state of California essentially eliminated affirmative action programming with the passage of a statewide proposition. The University of California, especially its two flagship institutions at

Berkeley and Los Angeles, has witnessed decreases in the number of minority applicants admitted to the universities. This is the result of the elimination of racial quotas. Affirmative action proponents charge discrimination, while opponents note that minorities have an equal opportunity for admission, but are not being selected because fewer of them possess the higher high school grade point averages and scores on college entrance exams relative to the students who are admitted.

Policing has not been immune from affirmative action. For example, the Albany, Georgia, Police Department was placed under a court order decree for more than twenty years which dictated that it hire and promote equivalent numbers of officers until its ranks approximated the racial composition of the city (Gaines, Southerland, & Angell, 1991). Similar court orders and consent decrees mandating racial quotas were enacted in agencies throughout the country. Glastris (1994) charged that such an order affecting the Chicago Police Department resulted in its hiring large numbers of unqualified minorities. Similarly, Mahtesian (1996) attributed police corruption and police abuse of power problems in several jurisdictions to substandard hiring practices as the result of court- or self-imposed quota systems. On the other hand, Felkenes (1991) found that hiring quotas for the Los Angeles Police Department did not affect the quality of recruits.

This chapter provides a historical discussion of affirmative action, including laws and court decisions, and it attempts to place the various mandates in perspective. The chapter will also provide a discussion of the current state of affairs for affirmative action and how it affects contemporary police selection practices.

TITLE VII OF THE 1964 CIVIL RIGHTS ACT

If individuals are to earn a living and maintain a meaningful and productive existence, employment opportunities must be made available on an equal basis to everyone regardless of race, sex, or religion. The enactment of the Civil Rights Act of 1964 constituted an acknowledgment by Congress of unlawful discrimination in the American workplace. Title VII of the act was intended to prohibit discriminatory practices by employers in employment decisions by removing artificial, arbitrary, and unnecessary barriers to employment opportunities for protected classes of individuals.

Title VII of the 1964 Civil Rights Act defined discrimination as the act of drawing distinctions from which to make selection and other personnel decisions based on considerations of race, color, sex, national origin, or religion. Section 703a of Title VII states that it is unlawful to:

1. fail, refuse to hire, discharge any individual, or otherwise discriminate against any individual with respect to his compensation, terms, conditions, or privileges of employment because of the individual's race, color, religion, sex, or national origin; or
2. limit, segregate, or classify employees or applicants for employment in any way that would deprive, or tend to deprive any individual of employment opportunities or otherwise adversely affect his stature as an employee because of such individual's race, color, religion, sex, or national origin.

The legislation contained two conditions that affected police personnel systems. First, it prohibited discrimination (disparate treatment) against individuals because of their race, color, sex, national origin, or religion. Second, the legislation was interpreted to mean that employers could not discriminate against classes or groups of people that fell under the protection of the act (disparate impact) (Gaines & Kappeler, 1990). To illustrate the differences here, there have been a number of cases in which police administrators discriminated against individuals; for example, a police chief refusing to hire a female applicant because he believed that females should not become police officers. Most discrimination cases, however, have resulted from agencies discriminating against groups or classes of people. Here, for example, is where the courts have found females or minorities underrepresented in an agency and subsequently ordered it to hire or promote additional minorities or females by imposing a quota. When the courts found that agencies discriminated against groups or classes, they generally struck down some or all of its hiring practices. For example, height requirements have been eliminated because they had adverse impact on females (Gaines, Falkenberg, & Gambino, 1996), and written tests, such as intelligence tests, have been found to be inappropriate because they discriminated against certain minority groups (Gaines, Costello, & Crabtree, 1989). Discrimination litigation has been used extensively over the years to challenge entry-level written tests, polygraph examinations, background investigations, drug testing or screening, physical agility tests, and minimum educational requirements.

Title VII was not universally applied until 1971, when the United States Supreme Court rendered its decision in *Griggs v. Duke Power Co.* In this case, the Court established new standards by which to judge the existence of discrimination in agencies. First, the Court ruled that it did not matter whether the discrimination was intentional or unintentional; all discrimination had to be eliminated. Second, the Court ruled that once a plaintiff established the existence of discrimination, the burden of proof fell upon the defendant agency to prove that its selection procedures were a business necessity or valid. That is, there could be differences in hiring rates if it could be proven that hiring practices were related to job performance. This finding forced police and many other organizations to research and validate their selection practices. The *Griggs* decision made it much easier for applicants who were discriminated against to file a Title VII action against a police department.

Later, in *Albemarle Paper Co. v. Moody* (1975), the Court expanded the effects of *Griggs* by requiring employers to prove that entry-level tests were job-related and to show that other, less discriminatory means of selection were not available. This requirement mandated that organizations explore all avenues of selection; and when a valid test was used which had adverse impact upon a protected class, it must be shown that no other valid test was available that would not have adversely impacted the protected class. In *Connecticut v. Teal* (1982) the Court expanded testing requirements even further by ruling that the outcomes of testing procedures may not be sufficient to dispel discrimination. If adverse impact exists on individual components of selection, even though there was no overall adverse impact, the testing procedure could be invalidated. *Teal,* perhaps, represents the pinnacle of court scrutiny of selection procedures.

AFFIRMATIVE ACTION AND QUOTA SYSTEMS

In fashioning remedies for violations of Title VII, Congress provided the courts with broad latitude. Section 708(g) provides that if a court finds that an employer has intentionally engaged in or is intentionally engaging in an unlawful employment practice, it may enjoin the employer from engaging in the unlawful practice and order any affirmative action that may be appropriate, which may include, but is not limited to, reinstatement or hiring of the protected individual, with or without back-pay, or any other equitable relief as the court may deem appropriate.

Title VII does not mandate the adoption of racial quotas or gender preferences for protected groups or individuals, although in the past the U.S. Supreme Court has permitted the use of such measures as remedies against employers for Title VII violations (42 U.S.C.A. Section 2000c-2(J)(1976)). Section 703(j) provides that

> nothing contained in Title VII shall be interpreted to require any employer, employment agency, labor organization, or joint labor-management committee to grant preferential treatment to any individual or group because of race, color, religion, sex, or national origin of such individual or group on account of an imbalance that may exist with respect to the total number or percentage of persons of any race, color, religion, sex, or national origin employed by any employer, referred or classified for employment by any employment agency or labor organization, admitted to membership or classified by any labor organization, or admitted to or employed in any apprenticeship or other training program, in comparison with the total number or percentage of persons of such race, color, religion, sex, or national origin in any community, state, section, or other area, or in the available work force in any community, state, section, or other area.

Congress, in passing the act, included Section 703(j) to assure congressional opponents to Title VII that quotas and preferences solely for the purposes of correcting imbalances in the workplace would not be required. Despite Congress's intent, Section 703(j) does not prohibit the use of quotas and preferences when such use is deemed necessary by the courts to remedy persistent or egregious discrimination.

In addition to the use of preferences and quotas as a remedy, the U.S. Supreme Court reaffirmed its position that public and private employers may consider such factors as race and sex when making employment decisions under certain circumstances. Specifically, an employer could provide preference with regard to the sex of the applicant or employee, and racial quotas may be utilized in situations where the employer is attempting to remedy the detrimental effects of past discriminatory practices.

In *United States v. Paradise* (1987), the Supreme Court upheld the requirement that 50 percent of the state trooper promotions in the Alabama Department of Public Safety be awarded to qualified black candidates. The Court clarified that this requirement was justified by a compelling governmental interest in remedying the past discrimination that permeated entry-level hiring practices and promotional processes within this organization. The *Paradise* case is representative of decisions from throughout the country that mandated hiring and promotion quotas in policing.

In the landmark case of *United Steelworkers of America v. Weber* (1979), the Court upheld the use of private, voluntary, race-conscious affirmative action plans by employers and provided vague guidelines for establishing permissible affirmative action plans. The Court did not establish rigid rules or clear guidelines, but did state that the affirmative action plan was permissible because (1) it did not unnecessarily trammel the interest of white employees, (2) it did not require the discharge of white employees and their replacement with new black employees, (3) it did not create an absolute bar to the advancement of white employees, and (4) it was only a temporary measure.

The Court in *Johnson v. Transportation Agency, Santa Clara County, California* (1987) held that this county transportation agency did not violate Title VII by considering a female employee's sex as one factor in her promotion over a male employee with a higher test score. The Court held that the agency's decision was not violative of Title VII because it was made pursuant to an affirmative action plan directing that sex or race be considered for the purpose of remedying the underrepresented, protected classes in traditionally segregated job categories. Additionally, the Court held that the agency's decision did not unnecessarily trammel the rights of male employees or create an absolute bar to their promotional advancement. The *Weber* and *Johnson* cases also are representative of case law that was being applied in the public service sector. For example, in *Talbert v. City of Richmond* (1981), the court allowed the city of Richmond to pass over a majority candidate with a higher score to promote a black police captain.

ASSAULTS ON AFFIRMATIVE ACTION

The primary methods for establishing discrimination are disparate treatment and disparate impact. Disparate treatment involves cases where individuals are discriminated against because of their membership in a protected class; for example, if fire or police departments refuse to hire females because the chief executive feels that women cannot adequately perform as firefighters or police officers. Disparate impact, on the other hand, is where classes of individuals are discriminated against. The primary modes of determining disparate impact are disparate rejection rates and population comparisons. With regard to disparate rejection rates, the courts examine how well females and minority applicants succeeded in passing the various selection tests and requirements. Their selection rates are compared to those for majority candidates, and if the rate is not at least 80 percent of the majority passing rate (what has come to be known as the four-fifths rule), then the courts generally determine that discrimination exists. For example, the court in *Vanguard Justice Society v. Hughes* (1979) found that the Baltimore Police Department's 5-foot 7-inch height requirement excluded 95 percent of the female population, while only 32 percent of the male population was excluded as a result of the standard. This standard obviously rejected females at a rate exceeding the 80 percent rule. Population comparisons have also been frequently used, especially in jurisdictions containing large minority populations. In these cases, the courts examine the percentage of minorities in the jurisdiction vis-à-vis the percentage of minorities on the police agency. If there are extreme differences, the courts determine that discrimination is taking place.

The Reagan administration and the first Bush administration attempted to reduce the impact of equal employment opportunity in the workplace. Swanson (1983) notes that President Reagan and the Justice Department, believing that the Court had erred in the *Weber* decision, were opposed to any discrimination remedy which depended on quotas or any other numerical formulae that resulted in race- or sex-conscious selection. As a result, Reagan made appointments to the U.S. Supreme Court that moved the Court to a more conservative view of equal employment opportunity issues.

In 1989, in *Wards Cove Packing Co., Inc. v. Antonio,* the Court made a major change to the allocation of the burden of proof in *Griggs*-type disparate-impact cases. The Court held that a plaintiff must first produce evidence of membership in a protected group that suffers a substantial disparate impact from a specific identifiable facially neutral employment practice or policy. Next, the employer must produce evidence of a substantial business justification for the employment practice or policy. Finally, the plaintiff must produce persuasive evidence either that the justification provided by the employer is insubstantial or that a less disparate means exists to serve equally well from a cost and efficiency perspective. Blumrosen's (1989, pp. 176–177) summary of the effects of *Wards Cove* are found in the accompanying box.

Box 9.1

1. It is more difficult to establish disparate impact. Plaintiff must now show more detailed statistics than in the past to demonstrate that there is a qualified minority or female workforce available. Establishing that the employer has a higher proportion of minorities and/or women in low-level jobs than in high-level jobs (even when both levels have unskilled workers) will no longer suffice. Furthermore, the test for disparate impact in the Uniform Guidelines on Employee Selection Procedure (UGESP), a comparison of the selection rates of whites and males with those of minorities and women, received a less-than-enthusiastic endorsement by four of the justices last year; see *Watson v. Fort Worth Bank and Trust Co.*, 108S Ct. 2777 (1989).
2. The plaintiff must establish the disparate impact of each selection procedure that is challenged and may not rely on the cumulative effect of multiple procedures.
3. The standard of "business necessity" has been replaced with a more relaxed standard, that of a "not insubstantial business reason."
4. The burden of persuasion on this defense has been shifted from the employer to the plaintiff.
5. The plaintiff's burden of showing an alternative which equally serves the employer's interest in production has become more important. Under pre-*Antonio* law, it was difficult for the employer to demonstrate business necessity. Therefore, the issue of alternatives rarely was reached. Under the new law, employers will be able to demonstrate business reasons with increased ease, and the issue will then become whether there are less discriminatory alternatives, a matter often of great difficulty for plaintiffs.

The Court noted that the burden of persuasion remained with the plaintiff at all times, and only the burden of production shifted to the employer. Liberal discovery under the Federal Rules of Civil Procedure was emphasized as a method for the plaintiff to collect sufficient evidence to demonstrate that the justification was more likely than not insubstantial or gratuitous. The Court noted that great deference should be provided to the employer because less disparate alternatives might not be truly equal in terms of cost and efficiency. Essentially, business necessity outweighed affirmative action goals.

Regarding a statistical showing of disparate impact, the Court reaffirmed the need to identify a qualified labor pool from which the employer acquires applicants. A disparity due to the absence of qualified applicants is not actionable unless the employer deterred such applicants from applying for employment.

The Supreme Court addressed the disparate treatment theory in *Price Waterhouse v. Hopkins* (1989). In this case, the Court held that the burden of persuasion shifts from the plaintiff to the employer when the plaintiff demonstrates that gender was a substantial factor in the employer's decision. Sexual stereotyping, including sexist statements, could constitute sufficient evidence to shift the burden of persuasion when the plaintiff demonstrates that the key decision-makers were involved in such conduct and infected the process. However, *Hopkins* essentially makes it easier for employers to adversely affect inadequate workers, even when the decision is influenced by discriminatory factors (Blumrosen, 1989).

The employer has a mixed-motive defense if it can be proven that sufficient business reasons existed, independent of the illicit factor or statement, for the adverse treatment of the plaintiff. Subjective evidence, if credible, may be sufficient to meet the burden of proving that the same decision would more than likely have been made despite the gender factor.

Finally, in *Taylor v. James River Corporation* the court issued a summary judgment in favor of the "validity generalization" argument (Sharf, 1990). Essentially, the court held that James River Corporation need not introduce evidence that tests had predictive validity and that validity generalization was satisfactory. Validity generalization is the process whereby an employer validates the selection procedures for one job, and uses the validation data to infer validity for the selection procedures for a similar job. Of course, problems can arise regarding how similar two or more different jobs are. This case clearly conforms to the principle that was laid out in *Wards Cove* (see also Potter, 1989), and it calls into question the standards laid out in *Albermarle*.

THE PROCEDURAL ASPECTS OF TITLE VII

Two other 1989 cases addressed the procedural side of Title VII. In *Lorance v. AT&T Technologies, Inc.* (1989), the Supreme Court reaffirmed that continuing violations had occurred but refused to apply the continuing violation theory to a change in a seniority system when the consequences only affected employees at a later time. The Court in this case recognized the importance of employer seniority systems and refused to negate them as a result of a Title VII challenge. This is particularly cogent for public safety agencies that make a number of human resource decisions based on seniority.

In *Martin v. Wilks* (1989), non-minority employees confronted with a consent decree involving affirmative action were permitted to challenge the operation of the decree even though they had not been parties to the underlying lawsuit. Absent mandatory joinder or intervention by such employees under the Federal Rules of Civil Procedure, a consent decree cannot be binding upon them. Essentially, *Martin* has a devastating effect on consent decrees in that a non-affected employee can contest them at a future date.

Another related case decided by the Court in 1989 was the Section 1983 action in *Will v. Michigan Department of State Police*. In this case, the Court eliminated Section 1983 suits as an avenue of redress by holding, in deference to the Eleventh Amendment immunity of states, that states and their officials acting in their official capacities are not "persons" who could violate Section 1983. Thus, civil rights claims can only be pursued against state officials acting in their individual capacity or against regional, county, or local governmental entities and officials acting in either official or individual capacities. The Court did, however, permit state officials to be sued in their official capacity for injunctive relief.

In summary, *Wards Cove* and the series of other cases discussed above substantially altered *Griggs,* disparate impact theory, and the procedures associated with Title VII litigation. Plaintiffs in affirmative action cases now had to go beyond showing that a disparate impact existed to show that disparate treatment occurred. That is, the courts were less likely to consider the fact that adverse impact existed, but were more interested in individuals showing that they were wrongfully treated in the selection process. Even with the existence of liberal federal discovery rules, it is difficult to show disparate treatment except in the most severe cases. This situation could eventually have resulted in a substantial reduction in the number of minorities in higher-level jobs in the workplace (Blumrosen, 1989; Henn & Pell, 1990; Varca & Pattison, 1993).

Wards Cove was poised to significantly affect selection procedures, especially in government and policing. Prior to *Wards Cove*, police departments had developed fairly elaborate selection procedures with a substantial amount of effort aimed at reducing adverse impact on minorities and females. The primary motivation behind these efforts was the numerous Title VII cases that police agencies across the country had litigated and often lost. *Wards Cove* basically removed the primary tool that the courts had used to find against the agencies. That is, in a majority of cases, the courts used population studies to establish adverse impact. Courts commonly examined the racial makeup of an agency and the community it served. When the ratios were fairly disparate, the courts often intervened. *Wards Cove* essentially eliminated this mode of review.

THE 1991 CIVIL RIGHTS ACT

After several years of controversy, President Bush signed a new Civil Rights Act into law in 1991. The controversy surrounding this bill pertained to the court decisions that had followed passage of the Civil Rights Act of 1964. Congress, controlled by Democrats, wanted to return civil rights laws and procedures to the *Griggs* standard. Bush, on the other hand, attempted to maintain the trend in *Wards Cove* whereby employers would not be subjected to court- or self-imposed quota systems. Congress maintained its social equality perspective, while Bush believed that quotas, whether court-imposed or self-imposed, forced employers to hire inferior employees that detracted from business efficiency. He also felt that they discriminated against white candidates, and that all forms of discrimination should be abolished.

The Civil Rights Act of 1991 forbids the use of any statistical adjustments or norming of scores based on gender or race. Prior to this act, employers used a variety of methods to adjust scores to avoid having adverse impact on protected classes. Police departments would employ dual lists for minorities and white candidates and add points to minorities' scores (see Gaines, Costello, & Crabtree, 1989). Such manipulations served as informal quota systems, and allowed agencies to avoid adverse impact and litigation. The intent of the 1991 act was to prevent employers from establishing and using such informal quota systems. The framers of the 1991 act wanted to ensure that everyone had an equal opportunity when applying for employment.

A second component of the 1991 act reestablished disparate impact as a method of determining whether discrimination by an employer existed. The 1991 act voided a substantial part of the *Wards Cove* series of cases. In doing so, it reconstituted disparate impact as a method of determining adverse impact, and moved decision-making back to the *Griggs* standard. Plaintiffs were again free to use population comparisons when attempting to show discriminatory patterns.

The 1991 act also reinstituted the business necessity standard that called for employers to show a more significant justification when a job standard or test had adverse impact on a protected class (Pynes, 1994). The *Wards Cove* cases had liberalized the standards used by employer defendants in discrimination cases. The defense standard under the *Wards Cove* cases was business justification. This was a less stringent standard than business necessity, which had become the standard as a result of *Griggs*.

At first glance, the Civil Rights Act of 1991 would seem inconsequential to police agencies. That is not the case, however. The following sections will describe how the Civil Rights Act of 1991 affected two specific aspects of the police selection process: physical agility testing and the use of written tests. The discussion of written tests, for the most part, also applies to the written tests used in promotion testing.

AFFIRMATIVE ACTION AND PHYSICAL AGILITY TESTING

The notion of police work being physical has led to a variety of tests and standards to ensure that police applicants could successfully complete the tasks required by the job. Historically, police departments developed height and weight standards. As stated above, by the 1970s and 1980s, these height and weight standards came under increasing criticism and litigation because of their disparate impact on women and minorities. Departments eventually abandoned height and weight standards in favor of some form of physical agility testing. The1980s witnessed an attack on physical agility testing as a result of adverse impact, and departments adopted health-based testing. This remained the primary mode of physical agility testing through the early 1990s. At that point, it was determined that the Civil Rights Act of 1991, which forbade gender-based norming of test results, precluded the use of health-based testing (Schofield, 1993). The following sections describe the evolution of physical agility testing in policing, beginning with the height and weight standards that were its first forms.

Height Standards as a Police Screening Device

Early height and weight standards for police officers were introduced in an effort to reduce the number of inferior political appointments of police officers (Fogelson, 1977). Around the beginning of the twentieth century, politicians typically appointed police officers without regard for their mental or physical qualifications. A number of medical and physical requirements were introduced in an effort to reduce political influence on the hiring process. For example, Richardson (1974, p. 63) provides an example of the kinds of problems which such requirements were intended to ameliorate: "One man in New York who had been rejected twice for syphilis passed on the third try, and candidates sometimes grew miraculously to reach the minimum height."

Later, height standards were seen as a necessity for ensuring that police officers were capable of performing the job adequately. Early police experts believed that police officers had to be tall, brutish males able to handle a wide range of physically challenging situations. Wilson (1963, p. 139) writes, " The patrolman is frequently called upon to display both strength and agility. . . . The larger [police officer] is better able to observe in a crowd, and his size tends to instill a respect not felt toward the smaller person." Leonard (1951) found that the majority of police agencies had minimum height requirements ranging from 5 feet 5 inches to 6 feet 6 inches; and a 1956 survey by the International Association of Chiefs of Police found that 85 percent of the police departments responding had a height requirement of five feet 8 inches or higher (O'Connor, 1962). A 1972 survey found that 97 percent of police departments had a height requirement for males, and 54 percent had height requirements for female applicants (Eisenberg, Kent, & Wall, 1973). Eisenberg and his colleagues attributed the lower number of agencies screening females to the fact that some departments did not employ female officers. Regardless, height requirements remained the mainstay of police physical agility testing into the 1970s.

The decade of the 1970s witnessed an open assault on police height requirements. Large numbers of police agencies openly discriminated against female applicants; and in many departments, when women were hired, they were relegated to non-operational jobs, such as working the complaints desk (Bloch & Anderson, 1974; Eisenberg, Kent, & Wall, 1973; Martin, 1989). Consequently, a number of Title VII lawsuits were filed. For example, the court in *Vanguard Justice Society v. Hughes* (1979) concluded that the Baltimore Police Department's minimum height requirement of 5 feet 7 inches excluded 95 percent of the female population but only 32 percent of the male population. The court found this disparate treatment to be prima facie evidence of gender-based discrimination.

Some agencies attempted to justify the height requirement on the grounds that it served to protect police officers from injury. The courts refused to accept arguments that women could not do the job and would be placed in danger. In *Mieth v. Dothard* (1976), a female applicant alleged that the Alabama State Police's physical stature standards constituted gender discrimination. The trial court rejected the argument that the exclusion of women was "for their protection and the protection of the public." In the absence of any evidence to the contrary, the court found the defendant's argument unsound and said, "women do not need protectors . . . [and] there is no evidence in the record that a woman cannot perform the duties of a patrol officer" (p. 1169).

Physical Agility Testing

Physical agility testing was an outgrowth of the courts' rejection of height standards (Gaines, Falkenberg, & Gambino, 1993). As the courts rejected minimum height requirements, police departments wanted to maintain a physical or tactical edge by ensuring that officers possessed the physical prowess to perform critical physical components of the job (Gaines, Falkenberg, & Gambino, 1993). Many began to introduce physical agility testing for this purpose. A wide range of physical activities was incorporated in the tests of various agencies (Gaines, Falkenberg, & Gambino, 1993). Initially, this took two directions: athletic examinations and performance-based physical agility tests (Gaines, Falkenberg, & Gambino, 1993).

The athletic tests incorporated such events as sit-ups, pull-ups, pushups, balance tests, and running. For example, in 1972, the Toledo, Ohio, Police Department's physical agility test included fifteen pushups, twenty-five sit-ups, a standing broad jump, and a 25-

second obstacle course [*Harless v. Duck* (1980)]. The athletic examinations were not organized around tasks or job sampling, but it was believed that applicants who were successful on such tests would be able to perform the job. Performance-based tests attempted to incorporate actual physical tasks that were performed by police officers. The New York City Police Department at one point used three events: (1) run stairs and restrain, (2) dummy drag, and (3) wall climb and obstacle course (Jordan & Schwartz, 1986). The California Commission on Peace Officer Standards and Testing developed a similar but more extensive test: (1) a body drag and lift using a 165-pound dummy, (2) a 6-foot fence climb and run, (3) a chain-link fence climb and run, (4) an agility run, (5) body lift and carry using a lifelike dummy, and (6) a 550-yard run (Berner & Kohls, 1982).

The physical agility tests resulted in gender discrimination problems and litigation. Females tended to fail in larger numbers and higher percentages relative to their male counterparts (Felkenes, 1991). A substantial problem with these tests was they were inadequately linked to the job. In *Officers for Justice v. Civil Service of San Francisco* (1975), the court ruled that the department's validation process for the physical agility test was inadequate. Specifically, the court criticized the department for inadequate sampling, low questionnaire response rate, and confusion regarding the questionnaire's items. The department's physical agility test resulted in only two of 166 eligible female applicants passing, as compared to 573 of the 906 eligible male applicants.

In *Blake v. City of Los Angeles* (1979), the court held the department's physical agility test to be discriminatory. The test consisted of five different events: scaling a wall and running, hanging from a chin bar, weight drag, dragging a dead weight, a tremor test consisting of holding a stylus steady, and running. The department's validation process consisted of correlating the physical agility scores with foot pursuit, field shooting, and emergency rescue simulations. The court found the validation process invalid for several reasons. First, the validation excluded persons who had failed the physical agility test, and as such revealed little in terms of who would be successful and who would not. Second, the department had selected thousands of male officers between 1968 and 1973 without benefit of a physical agility test. This earlier practice called into question the need for a physical agility test. Third, testimony supported the plaintiff's contention that other large city departments had successfully hired officers without benefit of a physical agility test. Finally, the validation study produced only modest correlations that called into question whether the test was a business necessity.

A second critical issue relative to physical agility tests is how cutoff scores are determined. The courts have demanded that cutoff scores must be related to job performance. For example, when an agency uses scores to rank-order candidates, higher-ranked candidates should perform better than lower-ranked candidates [see *Thomas v. City of Evanston* (1985)]. Even if rank-ordering is not used, the agency must provide evidence of a principled decision in establishing cutoff scores. Cutoff scores tend to be arbitrary and not linked to job performance (Gaines, Falkenberg, & Gambino, 1996). For example, Arvey, Nutting, and Landon (1992) and Hughes, Ratliff, Purswell, and Hadwiger (1989) provide elaborate discussions on how to validate physical agility tests, but they provide no data on how to establish cutoff scores. The heart of the problem is the cutoff score, since it determines who passes and who fails. If there is no reasonable scientific method for establishing cutoff scores, then police agencies are apt to encounter discrimination litigation.

Health-Based Physical Agility Screening

Police agencies moved to a health-based physical screening protocol as a result of the substantial litigation associated with physical agility testing (Schofield, 1993). The Aerobics Institute in Dallas became the leader in the field, and agencies from across the country had officers trained in health-based physical agility screening. Essentially, agencies adopted screening protocols that were similar to those used in the military. Several standards were established, including age and gender norms. That is, older applicants and female applicants had passing cutoff scores that were lower than those for younger males. A thirty-year-old female applicant's passing scores were determined by how well others in her age and gender group performed. Generally, the cutoff was set at the fiftieth percentile. This meant that applicants had to perform as well as 50 percent of the other applicants in their age and gender group. This procedure essentially eliminated adverse impact or discrimination against female applicants. The Aerobics Institute provided norms based on thousands of police physical agility screening tests across the country.

The protocols used in health-based screening usually consisted of five activities. First, cardiovascular capacity was measured using a 1½-mile run, step test, or treadmill. Second, upper-body strength was measured using pushups or a bench press. Third, abdominal strength was measured using sit-ups. Fourth, body-fat composition was measured using calipers or by weighing the applicant in a tank of water. Finally, flexibility was measured by how far an applicant could reach beyond his or her toes. These five measures provided a fairly comprehensive physical examination of police applicants.

Since the testing procedure used gender-based norms, the tests were not discriminatory. In one case, *United States v. Wichita Falls* (1988), the court ruled that the Wichita Falls Police Department had not discriminated against a female applicant who failed the screening protocol. The court ruled that the gender-based norms sufficiently reduced any gender biases in the physical agility screening process. The court also recognized that police officers had to perform a variety of physical tasks, and that police agencies have a business necessity to screen applicants for physical fitness.

The 1991 Civil Rights Act and Physical Agility Screening

As discussed above, the 1991 Civil Rights Act forbids the use of racial or gender norming in employee selection. Most agencies throughout the country abandoned the health-based screening protocols as a result of the 1991 act and reinstituted physical agility testing. Of course, the new physical agility tests face the same problems as those that were used before health-based screening.

In 1995, however, the Eighth Circuit of the United States Court of Appeals rendered a decision in *Peanick v. Reno* that allowed the continued use of health-based testing. The defendants in the case successfully argued that gender-based norms did not violate the Civil Rights Act of 1991. The court ruled that even though the cutoffs for males and females were different, the norms were used to establish that males and females were at the same level in terms of physical health. Even though different passing scores were used, they essentially measured males and females at the same health level. Although the case only applied to one U.S. circuit, *Peanick* essentially cleared the way for departments to reconsider using health-based screening. Further, it appears that health-based screening remains the most reasonable way of measuring applicants' ability to perform police tasks and responsibilities.

AFFIRMATIVE ACTION AND POLICE WRITTEN SELECTION TESTS

Historically, written tests have played an important role in the police selection process. O. W. Wilson (1963), in his early book on police administration, discussed the importance of selecting police officers who have adequate intelligence to perform the job. Wilson recognized the complexity of the job and reasoned that police officers needed to possess the intelligence to make good decisions as they enforced the law and provided services to citizens. He advised that police selectees should be of above average intelligence, and that departments should consider only applicants with an IQ of 112. Intelligence tests proved to be unacceptable when research showed that they were culturally and racially biased (Davey, 1984; Gruber, 1986; Nay, 1989). This prompted agencies to discard the use of intelligence tests and move to tests that attempted to measure candidates' aptitude for police work.

A majority of police agencies were using some form of written test in the selection process by the 1970s. Eisenberg, Kent, and Wall (1973) found that 97 percent of the agencies responding to their national survey used some kind of written examination to screen police applicants. A wide variety of tests were being used: tests produced by the International Personnel Management Association, locally developed tests, reading tests, the Otis Test Series, the Army General Classification Test, and tests developed by local universities. Some of these tests, such as those marketed by the International Personnel Management Association, attempted to test aptitude for police work by designing the tests around actual police job samples. For example, the National Police Officer Selection Test uses four scales: arithmetic, reading comprehension, grammar, and incident report writing (see Henry & Rafilson, 1997), while the tests marketed by the International Association of Personnel Managers tests ability to learn and apply information, ability to remember details, verbal ability, ability to accurately complete forms, spatial ability, and ability to use judgment and logic (see Gaines & Falkenberg, 1998). Most of these tests depend on content validity as the validation process and have the appearance of identifying fit candidates for police service.

Minority Performance on Written Tests

One area that has received a great deal of attention concerning racial discrimination is minority performance on written tests. There are two factors that contribute to this problem: scoring problems and sampling problems.

Minority Scoring   Minorities quite often score lower on police written selection tests than their majority counterparts. Research consistently indicates that minorities score at least one standard deviation below majority test takers on cognitive police selection tests (Sproule, 1984; Gaines, Costello, & Crabtree, 1989; Kenney & Watson, 1990). For example, Gaines and his colleagues examined three years of test outcomes from a medium-sized police department that used the standardized tests marketed by the International Personnel Managers Association. They found that minorities consistently scored at least one standard deviation below non-minority candidates. More specifically, in *Nash v. Consolidated City of Jacksonville, Duval County, FL* (1988), twenty-seven of ninety-seven questions had adverse impact on black applicants.

It is unclear why minorities, on the average, perform at a lower level than majority candidates. Regoli and Jerome (1975) attribute such disparities to test cultural biases. They made this assessment after examining the selection procedures in Miami, Berkeley, and Philadelphia. They concluded (pp. 411–412):

> Because of an educational handicap, blacks are barred from entering the police occupation by written entrance examinations. But the written entrance examinations are geared to the middle class white experience; thus, they discriminate against minority group members. Consequently, entrance examinations should be redesigned, testing a person's capabilities and potential for police work and not their understanding of descriptive phrases used by the dominant class. By misinterpreting the focus of written entrance examinations, blacks are at a serious disadvantage. If this handicap and its effects are not recognized prior to designing the tests, black applicants will continue to receive lower scores on them than their white counterparts. Educational inequalities between blacks and whites are becoming narrower, and simultaneously more blacks are being employed by urban police agencies. But nevertheless, blacks are still underrepresented on all urban law enforcement agencies.

The last several decades have witnessed considerable effort to improve police selection testing. There have been numerous validation studies, and it would seem that the cultural biases to which Regoli and Jerome refer have at least been substantially diminished (Poland, 1978; Rosenfeld & Thornton, 1979; Schmidt, Mack, & Hunter, 1984). The problem remains, however, that minority candidates pass at a much lower rate than majority candidates. The answer to this problem likely lies in education and socioeconomic opportunity (Gottfredson, 1997). Differences across races or classes of people in terms of education and socioeconomic opportunity will continue to equate to differences among the races when cognitive skills are compared.

Sampling Problems   Another factor in this complex problem is the rate at which minorities apply for the police service. Hochstedler and Conley (1986), upon examining police selection nationally, concluded that minorities are less likely to apply for entry into police service. That is, minorities are less likely to choose policing as a vocation. Along these lines, Gaines, Kappeler, and Vaughn (1999) discuss a variety of reasons why minorities are not attracted to policing. These include the view that police work is an undesirable job, the heavy recruiting of qualified minorities for better-paying jobs in business and industry, and the feeling that being a police officer will adversely affect their standing in their community or neighborhood.

Furthermore, there are no descriptive data describing what kinds of minorities apply for police service. There is some question whether minority applicants for police service are representative of the minority population, or whether they come from some subgrouping. It may be that selection tests have less adverse impact on the minority population as a whole than on the sample of minorities who apply for police officer jobs. This issue must be addressed before any determination about why minorities are not adequately represented in policing can be made.

Cognitive Skills Testing in Perspective

As noted above, there is an historical precedent in police selection to use tests that examine candidates' cognitive skills. There is increasing evidence that such testing substantially affects organizational effectiveness, regardless of profession or vocation (Schultz, 1984). Typically, a single bad hiring decision is thought to have minimal impact on the organization. It is shuffled into the organizational mix and has little impact on the organization's ability to fulfill its mission or achieve its goals. As mentioned above, however, bad selection decisions in combination can have a substantial negative impact on an organization, especially a police organization. For example, there is evidence indicating that police agencies which do not do an adequate job of selecting officers run the risk of corruption problems (Glastris, 1994; Mahtesian, 1996; Sechrest & Burns, 1992). It stands to reason that if inferior or inadequate selection testing can produce this result, departments are likely to also experience less obvious problems when high-quality police candidates are not selected.

Although many candidate attributes can contribute to poor selection decisions, deficient cognitive skills are of importance in policing. The discretionary nature of policing and the advent of community policing, which necessitates that officers make even more important decisions on a daily basis, equates to a need for officers with substantial cognitive ability. Schmidt (1988) advises that the failure to use cognitive testing in employee selection is likely to result in substantial economic loss to the organization. Hunter (1986, p. 342) has identified several positive outcomes associated with the use of cognitive screening: (1) general cognitive ability predicts performance ratings in all lines of work, though validity is higher for complex jobs than simple jobs, (2) general cognitive ability predicts training success at a uniformly high level for all jobs, (3) data on job knowledge show that cognitive ability determines how much and how quickly a person learns, and (4) cognitive ability predicts the ability to react in innovative ways to situations where knowledge does not specify exactly what to do. In one study, Hunter (1979) predicted that the Philadelphia Police Department lost $12 million a year by not employing better applicants.

The need for employee candidates that possess superior cognitive skills or at least the cognitive skills to successfully perform the job is underscored by Schmidt and Hunter's assertions. It calls into question a system whereby police organizations focus on equal outcomes and employ selection systems in which racial and cultural parity overwhelm ability. It also points to the need to better refine selection testing to ensure that fit police candidates are employed.

Interpreting Cognitive Test Scores: The Devil Is in the Detail   Most police agencies use a written test as the first screening device after the initial application. This is because the written test is one of the least expensive screening instruments and generally screens out the largest number of applicants. It therefore plays a critical role in the selection process because it can reduce a burgeoning applicant pool at the lowest cost (Gaines, Kappeler, & Vaughn, 1999).

From a psychometric standpoint, the written test poses several problems. First, as noted above, police selection tests consistently have adverse effects on minorities. Candidates who are minorities tend to score lower than majority candidates. Although some minorities have high levels of cognitive skills, the minority population is skewed lower than the majority population (Gottfredson, 1997). Since there are generally fewer minority candidates in a department's applicant pool, the fact that a smaller proportion of the minority applicants pass the exam, and when they do pass are usually clustered at or near the bottom of the eligibility list, significantly minimizes the probability of minorities being selected. That is, even if everything was equal, minorities would continue to be underrepresented.

Second, there is a validity question about many police written tests. As noted above, most of the written tests depend on content validation to establish their validity. There are very few criterion-related validity studies. This means that departments must take these tests at face value, and there is sparse evidence that they effectively identify qualified police candidates. Although the literature is replete with validation studies, and there are numerous court decisions focusing on the question of validity, there are no definite standards of sufficient validity and reliability. As a result, reliability and validity coefficients should be considered in light of other factors, such as the range of test scores and the selection system used in conjunction with the test [see *Cuesta v. State of New York Office of Court Administration* (1987)]. For example, if scores are compressed (as a result of a large number of test takers or reduced range of scores), higher validity and reliability coefficients are required. It is this interaction of validity and reliability coefficients with the range of test scores and how test results are used that may lead to the exclusion of minority applicants in selection processes.

The data tend to indicate that test score compression is rather common in police testing. For example, in *Guardian Association of the New York City Police Department, Inc. v. Civil Service Commission of the City of New York et al.* (1980), half of the 36,797 applicants on an entry test scored 91 or higher on the city's 100-item test, and 2,000 applicants had scores in the range of 94 to 97. Although New York City may be atypical, most jurisdictions will experience some degree of test score compression.

Third, there exists no good method for determining passing cutoff scores. Gaines and Falkenberg (1998) reviewed the selection test validity literature and found very little discussion on how to determine who has passed a police entry test. For example, an examination of the test marketed by the International Personnel Managers' Association reveals an extensive discussion of the content validation process, but no guidance is given on how to establish cutoff scores. If cutoff scores are not psychometrically based, then they become arbitrary, and open to litigation. Many agencies use a cutoff score of 70 percent or determine the number of passing applicants by the number of positions that will be filled as a result of the current test administration. These are not sound decisions, and they cannot be justified using the *Griggs* standard. The problem lies in the fact that such cutoff scores are not related to performance, negating any content or predictive validity.

In one interesting development, a court ruled that the Nassau County, New York, police written test was discriminatory, and the department fell under a consent decree. Gottfredson (1996) reported that the U.S. Justice Department worked with the police department to develop a test that was racially neutral. The methodology consisted of administering a number of test items to white and African-American test subjects and selecting those items for the test that were racially neutral. Gottfredson called the scheme "racial gerrymandering." She pointed out that the results most likely could not be validated using any validity procedure, and even though the test may indeed not have had an adverse impact on any protected class, no one could discern what it was really measuring.

The state of affairs regarding police written selection tests remains perplexing. As noted above, most of these tests have adverse impact on minorities. Furthermore, because of the 1991 Civil Rights Act, police agencies are able to norm scores or otherwise adjust scores to avoid adverse impact. Since few agencies have expended the resources to perform validation studies, many remain in peril from Title VII litigation. Agencies should initiate validation studies. These might enable them to make better selection decisions and avoid future Title VII litigation.

CONCLUSION

Title VII of the 1964 Civil Rights Act has had a profound impact on employment selection, particularly police selection. After almost four decades under the act, it is questionable as to how far we have progressed in police selection. The two areas where affirmative action has had the most impact are physical agility screening and written selection tests. After decades of effort, although we have made substantial progress in identifying qualified police applicants, there remains considerable work in these areas. Fortunately, litigation in the area of police selection has decreased, but unfortunately, so has the interest in developing more reliable and valid selection instrumentation.

REFERENCES

ARVEY, R. D., NUTTING, S. M., & LANDON, T. E. 1992. Validation strategies for physical ability testing in police and fire settings. *Public Personnel Management, 21*(3), 301–312.

BERNER, J., & KOHLS, J. 1982. *Patrol officer physical performance testing manual.* Sacramento, CA: California Commission on Police Officer Standards and Training.

BLOCH, P. B., & ANDERSON, D. 1974. *Policewomen on patrol: Final report.* Washington, DC: Police Foundation.

BLUMROSEN, A. W. 1989. The 1989 Supreme Court rulings concerning employment discrimination and affirmative action: A minefield for employers and a gold mine for their lawyers. *Employee Relations Law Journal, 15*(2), 175–186.

DAVEY, B. W. 1984. Personnel testing and the search for alternatives. *Public Personnel Management, 13*(4), 361–374.

EISENBERG, T., KENT, D. A., & WALL, C. R. 1973. *Police personnel practices in state and local governments.* Washington, DC: International Association of Chiefs of Police and the Police Foundation.

FELKENES, G. 1991. Affirmative action in the Los Angeles Police Department. *Criminal Justice Research Bulletin, 6*(4), 1–9.

FOGELSON, R. 1977. *Big-City police.* Cambridge, MA: Harvard University Press.

GAINES, L. K., & FALKENBERG, S. 1997. An evaluation of the written selection test: Effectiveness and alternatives. *Journal of Criminal Justice, 26*(3), 175–183.

GAINES, L. K., & KAPPELER, V. 1990. What works in police selection? In G. Cordner & D. Hale (Eds.), *What works in policing?* Cincinnati: Anderson.

GAINES, L. K., COSTELLO, P., & CRABTREE, A. 1989. Police selection testing: Balancing legal requirements and employer needs. *American Journal of Police, 8*(1), 137–152.

GAINES, L. K., FALKENBERG, S., & GAMBINO, J. 1996. Police physical agility testing: An historical and legal analysis. In D. Kenney & G. Cordner (Eds.), *Managing police personnel* (pp. 25–41). Cincinnati: Anderson.

GAINES, L. K., KAPPELER, V., & VAUGHN, J. B. 1999. *Policing in America.* Cincinnati: Anderson.

GAINES, L. K., SOUTHERLAND, M. D., & ANGELL, J. E. 1991. *Police administration.* New York: McGraw-Hill.

GLASTRIS, P. 1994. The thin white line: City struggles to mix standardized testing and racial balance. *U.S. News and World Reports, 117*(7), 53–54.

GOTTFREDSON, L. S. 1996. Racially gerrymandering the content of police tests to satisfy the U.S. Justice Department. *Psychology, Public Policy, and Law, 2*(3/4), 418–446.

GOTTFREDSON, L. S. 1997. Editorial: Mainstream science on intelligence: An editorial with 52 signatories, history, and bibliography. *Intelligence, 24*(1), 13–24.

GRUBER, G. 1986. The police applicant test: A predictive validity study. *Journal of Police Science and Administration, 14*(2), 121–129

HENN, E. M., & PELL, S. W. 1990. *Wards Cove Packing Co., Inc. v. Antonio:* The changing rules of civil rights. *Education Law Reporter, 61,* 11–16.

HENRY, M. S., & RAFILSON, F. M. 1997. The temporal stability of the National Police Officer Selection Test. *Psychological Reports, 81,* 1257–1265.

HOCHSTEDLER, E., & CONLEY, J. A. 1986. Explaining underrepresentation of black officers in city police agencies. *Journal of Criminal Justice, 14,* 319–328.

HUGHES, M. A., RATLIFF, R. A., PURSWELL, J. L., & HADWIGER, J. 1989. A content validation methodology for job related physical performance tests. *Public Personnel Management, 18*(4), 487–504.

HUNTER, J. 1979. An analysis of validity, differential validity, test fairness, and utility for the Philadelphia police officers selection. Report to the Philadelphia Federal District Court (*Alvarez v. City of Philadelphia*). Princeton, NJ: Educational Testing Services.

HUNTER, J. 1986. Cognitive ability, cognitive aptitude, job knowledge, and job performance. *Journal of Vocational Behavior, 29,* 340–362.

JORDAN, D., & SCHWARTZ, S. 1986. NYC's physical performance testing program. *Police Chief Magazine, 53*(6), 29–30.

KENNEY, D. J., & WATSON, S. 1990. Intelligence and the selection of police recruits. *American Journal of Police, 9*(4), 39–64.

LEONARD, V. 1951. *Police organization and management.* Brooklyn, NY: Foundation Press.

MAHTESIAN, C. 1996. The big blue hiring spree. *Governing* (January), 28–31.

MARTIN, S. E. 1989. Female officers on the move? A status report on women in policing. In R. Dunham & G. Alpert (Eds.), *Critical issues in policing: Contemporary readings* (pp. 313–322). Prospect Heights, IL: Waveland Press.

MARTINEZ, E. 1999. Beyond black/white: The racism of our time. In A. Aguirre & D. Baker, (Eds.), *Notable selections in race and ethnicity* (pp.77–86). New York: Duskin/McGraw-Hill.

NALBANDIAN, J. 1989. The U.S. Supreme Court's "consensus" on affirmative action. *Public Administration Review* (Jan.–Feb.), 38–45.

NAY, W. E. 1989. A review of the full range of abilities and characteristics in police selection tests. Paper presented at the annual meeting of the Academy of Criminal Justice Sciences, Washington, DC.

O'CONNOR, G. 1962. *Survey of selection methods.* Washington, DC: International Association of Chiefs of Police.

POLAND, J. M. 1978. Police selection methods and the prediction of police performance. *Journal of Police Science and Administration, 6*(4), 374–393.

POTTER, E. E. 1989. Supreme Court's *Wards Cove Packing* decision redefines the adverse impact theory under Title VII. *Industrial-Organizational Psychologist, 27*(1), 25–31.

PYNES, J. E. 1994. Police officer selection procedures: Speculation on the future. *American Journal of Police, 13*(2), 103–112.

REGOLI, R. M., & JEROME, D. E. 1975. The recruitment and promotion of a minority group into an established institution: The police. *Journal of Police Science and Administration, 3*(4), 410–416.

ROSENFELD, M., & THORNTON, R. F. 1979. *The development and validation of a police selection examination for the city of Philadelphia.* Princeton, NJ: Educational Testing Service.

RICHARDSON, J. F. 1974. *Urban police in the United States.* Port Washington, NY: Kennikat Press.

SCHMIDT, F. 1988. The problem of group differences in ability test scores in employment selection. *Journal of Vocational Behavior, 33*, 72–292.

SCHMIDT, F., MACK, M. J., & HUNTER, J. E. 1984. Selection utility in the occupation of U.S. Park Ranger for three modes of test use. *Journal of Applied Psychology, 69*(3), 490–497.

SCHOFIELD, D. 1993. Hiring standards ensuring fitness for duty. *FBI Law Enforcement Bulletin, 62*(11), 27–32.

SCHULTZ, C. 1984. Saving millions through judicious selection. *Public Personnel Management Journal, 13*(4), 409–415.

SECHREST, D., & BURNS, P. 1992. Police corruption: The Miami case. *Criminal Justice and Behavior, 19*(3), 294–313.

SHARF, J. C. 1990. Post *Wards Cove Packing Co. v. Antonio* burden of proof, round 1: Federal district court grants summary judgment in favor of VG argument. *Industrial-Organizational Psychologist, 27*(2), 65–67.

SPROULE, C. F. 1984. Should personnel selection tests be used on a pass-fail, grouping, or ranking basis? *Public Personnel Management Journal, 13*(4), 375–394.

STEIN, N. 1999 Affirmative action and the persistence of racism. In A. Aguirre & D. Baker (Eds.), *Notable selections in race and ethnicity* (pp.87–104). New York: Duskin/McGraw-Hill.

SWANSON, S. C. 1983. Affirmative action goals: Acknowledging the employer's interest. *Personnel Journal* (March), 216–220.

VARCA, P. E., & PATTISON, P. 1993. Evidentiary standards in employment discrimination: A view toward the future. *Personnel Psychology, 46*, 239–258.

WILSON, O.W. 1963. Police administration (2nd ed.). New York: McGraw-Hill.

Cases Cited

- *Albermarle Paper Co. v. Moody,* 422 U.S. 405 (1975).
- *Blake v. City of Los Angeles,* 595 F.2d. 1367 (9th Cir. 1979).
- *Connecticut v. Teal,* 457 U.S. 440 (1987).
- *Cuesta v. The State of New York Office of Court Administration,* 657 F. Supp. 1084 (S.D.N.Y. 1987).
- *Griggs v. Duke Power Co.,* 401 U.S. 424 (1971).
- *Guardian Association of the New York City Police Department, Inc. v. Civil Service Commission of the City of New York et al.,* 630 F.2d 79 (1980), cert. denied, 452 U.S. 940 (1981).
- *Harless v. Duck,* 619 F.2d 611 (1980).
- *Johnson v. Transportation Agency, Santa Clara County, California,* 480 U.S. 616 (1987).
- *Lorance v. AT&T Technologies, Inc.,* 490 U.S. 900 (1989).
- *Martin v. Wilks,* 490 U.S. 755 (1989).
- *Mieth v. Dollard,* 418 F. Supp. 1169 (1976).
- *Nash v. Consolidated City of Jacksonville, Duval County,* FL, 837 F.2d 1534 (1988).

- *Officers for Justice v. Civil Service Commission of the City and County of San Francisco,* 395 F. Supp. 378 (N.D. Cal. 1975).
- *Peanick v. Morris,* 96 F.3d 316 (1996).
- *Price Waterhouse v. Hopkins,* 485 U.S. 933 (1989).
- *Talbert v. City of Richmond,* 454 U.S. 1145 (1981).
- *Taylor v. James River Corporation,* 51 Fair Empl. Prac. 893 (1989).
- *Thomas v. City of Evanston,* 610 F. Supp. 612 (D.C. Ill. 1985).
- *United States v. Paradise,* 480 U.S. 149 (1987).
- *United States v. Wichita Falls,* 704 F. Supp. 709 (N.D. Tex. 1988).
- *United Steelworkers of America v. Weber,* 443 U.S. 193 (1979).
- *Vanguard Justice Society v. Hughes,* 471 F. Supp. 670 (D. Md. 1979).
- *Wards Cove Packing Co., Inc. v. Antonio,* 490 U.S 642 (1989).
- *Watson v. Fort Worth Bank and Trust,* 487 U.S. 977 (1988).
- *Will v. Michigan Department of State Police,* 491 U.S. 58 (1989).

10

The Age Discrimination in Employment Act (ADEA) and Police Agencies

Joseph E. Pascarella

❖

INTRODUCTION

The Federal Age Discrimination in Employment Act (ADEA) and police agencies endure a tenuous relationship that must be continually refined when considering the individual civil rights of police applicants and incumbent police officers, the safety of the public, and the current political and judicial climate. Application of the ADEA has become dependent on factors beyond the issue of age discrimination and policing standards. Consequently, the ADEA's relationship with police agencies is continually being restructured to remain compliant with existing legislation and case law.

Court interpretation of the ADEA, like the fractured history of the ADEA itself, is often ambiguous, overlapping, and incongruous to prior case precedents. Application has generally been imprecise, obsolete, or misunderstood. This chapter will present a brief overview of the policy issues and contextual legal framework relevant to the application and implementation of such policies as maximum hiring ages and mandatory retirement ages in policing, and it will discuss the relevant legal issues raised while litigating the legality of age restrictions in policing. The chapter will also provide an empirical analysis to investigate the factors that may predict the chances that a particular court decision will uphold a maximum hiring age or mandatory age policy or render it invalid or illegal.

THE ADEA, POLICY ISSUES, AND POLICING

Police agencies have traditionally restricted employment opportunities for police officers to applicants who are within certain age parameters. Generally, persons must be at least twenty years old or older (commonly referred to as minimum appointment ages) to be appointed police officers. The reasoning behind minimum appointment ages derives from the basic operational characteristics of policing. Police officers have the responsibilities of possessing and using a firearm, and the power to restrict a person's liberty (ranging from temporary detention to the use of deadly physical force) based upon levels of proof as low as probable cause of involvement in criminality. These responsibilities and powers demand that an officer have achieved an acceptable degree of maturity reached only by attainment of age and expectation of maturity commensurate with age. These conceptions, generally agreed upon by police officials and administrators, political officials, and the public, have led to policy decisions to mandate minimum appointment ages; and these policies have remained virtually unchallenged. The maximum age at which a person may be appointed (maximum hiring age) and the age at which an incumbent officer must involuntarily retire (mandatory retirement age), however, are also based upon intersubjective concepts; but the policies regarding these issues are not generally agreed upon or easily applied in practice.

The occupational specifications of police officers are physically, mentally, and emotionally challenging; and younger, physically fit persons may be more adaptable to this type of work. As such, police agencies have been legally allowed to discriminate against older persons with relative impunity throughout the history of policing in the United States.

Police officers must always be mentally and physically prepared. They are constantly involved in rapidly evolving and unpredictable situations. Police officers are also idle for long periods of time, then suddenly thrust without warning into physically and mentally exerting situations. This idleness then sudden exertion places an additional onus on police officers to remain physically fit. Police officers are often required to run, jump, climb, and wrestle to protect not only themselves but the public. There is a legitimate public interest in maintaining a police force that is physically fit; hence, the courts have been willing to grant greater latitude to police agencies in allowing age discrimination.

The nexus between aging and deteriorating physical fitness is a difficult axiom, given the individual variance of aging, nutritional habits and physical-fitness training regimens. However, with age everyone is subject to an inevitable and natural deterioration. Police officers endure natural changes with age, but demographically violent criminals do not. Most of the people in this nation who commit violent crimes are between the ages of sixteen and twenty-four, a figure that has remained relatively stable since the 1960s (Uniform Crime Reports, 1995). This presents perennial mismatches between young persons with a propensity for physical violence and aging police officers. Even a perception of physical superiority by a citizen may have a psychological effect on police officers during police-citizen encounters, and escalate the encounter toward violence.

The civil rights revolution of the 1960s granted some protections to older Americans as well as racial minorities and women. The ADEA, initially enacted in 1967, was intended to protect a class of person that had been dropped from the final version of the Civil Rights Act of 1964 (Finklestein, 1989). The ADEA was explicitly designed to protect workers from age discrimination. United States Senator Jacob Javitz originally introduced legislation into Congress in 1951 (ADEA, 1967; ADEA, 1977). Senator Javitz's efforts resulted in the passage of the ADEA in 1967. Perhaps because of haste and political jockeying, the incompleteness and ambiguity of the original act has resulted in inconsistent and often confusing interpretations since its original passage in 1967. The Age Discrimination in Employment Act was originally meant explicitly for the private workforce. It was subsequently amended and modified several times. In 1974, the ADEA was applied to employees of state and local governments. In 1978, the maximum age protected under the ADEA was extended from sixty-five years old to seventy years old.

The ADEA sought to protect workers from discrimination based on age. Although the legislative intent was to prohibit all age discrimination, special deference was given to mandatory retirement ages. The ADEA presumes that all age restriction policies applicable to persons within the forty- to seventy-year-old range (e.g., a mandatory retirement age of fifty-five) are de facto discriminatory, and the employer has the burden of proving that the age restriction is not discriminatory. To overcome this presumption, local government entities (and hence police agencies) must prove that age is a bona fide occupational qualification (BFOQ) that is "reasonably necessary to the normal operation of the 'particular business,'" meaning that a person's age is relevant to the job functions (ADEA, 1967). The "particular business" relating to policing is ensuring public safety. The BFOQ defense entails an admission that age is an important factor in determining employment but that the discrimination can be justified. Since younger police officers may be more effective, age may be a relevant factor and therefore a BFOQ. According to the Seventh Circuit Court of Appeals in *EEOC v. City of Janesville* (1980), the "particular business" meant the entire police department. For example, a desk sergeant who does primarily clerical work is in the same particular business as a patrol officer who is responding to calls for service and apprehending violent felons. Two years later, the court ruled in *EEOC v. City of Minneapolis* (1982) that a police captain performing primarily administrative duties should not be involuntarily retired at age fifty-five.

The United States Secretary of Labor was originally granted the authority to administer and enforce the provisions of the ADEA. In 1979, the administration and enforcement powers of the ADEA were transferred to the Equal Employment Opportunity Commission (ADEA, 1978; Soehnel, 1986).

The remedies of ADEA violations provide for the recovery of back pay and other appropriate equitable relief. Injunctive relief can range from a court order to hire the individual person litigating or the entire group of persons challenging the policies or subject to the policies to ordering the specific age restriction policy invalid.

The ADEA currently contains a public safety exemption, meaning that specific public safety occupations, such as police officer and firefighter, are exempt from its provisions. The necessity of this exemption is constantly debated between those who believe that younger officers are necessary for ensuring public safety and those who feel that individual rights should supersede perceptions of diminished public safety from the presence of older officers. The original ADEA did not contain a public safety exemption, nor did the 1974 amendment to the ADEA. The exemption was inserted as one of the 1986 amendments. Congress explicitly stated, however, that the exemption was only for a seven-year period (until December 31, 1993), during which time research was to be conducted to determine (1) whether physical and mental fitness tests were valid measures of the abilities of competent police officers, (2) which tests most effectively measured ability, and (3) what, if any, recommendations were in order (ADEA, 1986).

A research group at Pennsylvania State University was selected to conduct a study under the above mandates (Landy et al., 1992). The Landy Study consisted of a meta-analysis of over 5,000 studies related to aging and public safety, and analysis of data related to age, mortality rates, and retirement policies (Landy et al., 1992). The study's primary conclusion was that chronological age was not an adequate predictor of job performance in the public safety profession. The Landy Study, according to some public safety lobbying organizations, did not meet the objectives mandated by Congress (Whitehead & Bullon, 1993). The exemption expired on December 31, 1993 because of congressional inaction.

Theoretically, there were no age restrictions in policing once the exemption expired on December 31, 1993. Many states determined that their existing laws might be unconstitutional and many voluntarily invalidated statutes concerning maximum hiring and retirement ages. An intensive lobbying effort by police officials continued during this period. A new public safety exemption to the ADEA was signed into law on September 30, 1996 by President Clinton (H.R. 849; ADEA, 1996). Congress then mandated another study to be conducted by the National Institute for Occupational Safety and Health (NIOSH) within three years to determine alternative ways of measuring competence other than age, and within four years to determine the most accurate ways to determine competency for public safety officers other than age (ADEA, 1996). No study has yet been published by NIOSH, nor has Congress modified the ADEA. The public safety exemption as inserted in 1996 is still applicable.

Case law since the original passage of the ADEA regarding its application to police agencies has not been unified, although federal and state courts are in general agreement on the necessity of a standard when assessing bona fide occupational qualifications related to public safety. The two cases defining public safety standards and BFOQs do not involve police officers or police agencies. The first case, *Usery v. Taminani Trail Tours Incorporated* (1976), adopted a two-pronged standard for age as a BFOQ. First, the qualification must be reasonably necessary to the employer's business, and second, there must be a factual basis, predicated on empirical data, for the employer to believe that almost everyone over a specific age will be prevented from performing the job safely or efficiently due to age alone. In addition, individual fitness assessments of employees by employers must be either impractical or impossible. The Supreme Court formally adopted this standard in *Western Air Lines Incorporated v. Criswell*, a 1985 case that struck down the Federal Aviation Administration's (FAA) policy to involuntarily retire commercial pilots at age sixty. The Supreme Court ruled that the employer must establish a connection between age and ability to perform specific duties related to public safety. Although *Usery* and *Criswell* did not involve police officers or police agencies, both cases attempted to establish a public safety standard.

The ADEA is also currently enmeshed in the perennial federalism debate. The question here pertains to the extent of the federal government's authority to regulate the administrative affairs of state and local governments' administrative affairs. More succinctly, does the federal government have the power to interfere in a state or local police agency's decision to mandate age restriction policies? States have challenged the application of the ADEA to state and local governments under various constitutional claims.

One such claim is that the ADEA violates the Tenth Amendment protection against the federal government impeding the basic operational functions of local governments. The Tenth Amendment provides that those powers not delegated to the federal government by the United States Constitution or prohibited to the states are reserved to the states or to the people. Generally, the Tenth Amendment defers to state and local governments on internal matters, such as local government, education, and regulation. The Supreme Court ruled in *EEOC v. Wyoming* (1983) that the ADEA did not violate the Tenth Amendment and that game wardens in Wyoming could be protected by the ADEA when the state of Wyoming enforced a mandatory retirement age of fifty-five. Two years later, in a case that challenged the legality of a county's mandatory retirement age of sixty-five for all county employees, the Court of Appeals for the Seventh Circuit ruled in *EEOC v. County of Calumet* (1985) that Congress may forbid employment discrimination by interfering with a state's rights of sovereignty granted by the Tenth Amendment. Alternatively, the Commonwealth Court of Pennsylvania ruled in *City of Philadelphia v. Pennsylvania Human Relations Commission* (1996) that the provisions of the ADEA supersede local and state law when invoking the public safety exemption on an overage police applicant.

The most recent case involved in the United State Supreme Court's redefinition of federalism and congressional authority to regulate state government affairs is *Kimel v. Florida Board of Regents* (2000). *Kimel* did not involve police applicants or incumbent officers, but it has ramifications for state and local police agencies. The Supreme Court ruled in *Kimel* that Congress cannot, through passage of the ADEA, take away a state's right of immunity against lawsuits granted by the Eleventh Amendment of the United States Constitution; and furthermore, the power to remove this right exceeds congressional authority under Section 5 of the Fourteenth Amendment. The Supreme Court did mention in *Kimel* that age discrimination complaints filed by individuals may be addressed by the specific state of occurrence. According to the *Kimel* ruling, state and local police agencies are bound by their individual state's age discrimination laws when establishing age restriction policies.

The perplexing history of judicial interpretation of the application of the ADEA to state and local police agencies since its original enactment often confounds those charged with formulating police agency personnel policy. Maintaining compliance with the ADEA is a dynamic process in which a police agency's policy must be continually updated to reflect the current law. Changes in court interpretation of the ADEA affect personnel policy decisions. The empirical analysis in the next section endeavors to provide a predictive model of court interpretation of the ADEA as it applies to police agencies to provide guidelines for police administrators and policy officials.

METHODOLOGY

The outcome of an age discrimination lawsuit involving a police agency may be dependent on who initiates the lawsuit, where the case is initially filed (jurisdiction) or disposed, and what specific policy issue is disputed. The analysis in this section explores the factors that predict the outcome of a court's decision and thus that may determine a police agency's success in having the court rule in favor of upholding age restriction policies.

Research Design and Operational Definitions

A search was conducted using the Westlaw and Lexis legal research databases. The cases sought for this analysis consisted of legal challenges to laws and/or policies of age restriction or physical fitness testing. Although a small percentage of the cases refer to age restrictions applied to "protective service" workers, this analysis will focus on police officers. Although other protective service workers, such as firefighters, emergency service personnel, medical technicians, correction officers, and airplane pilots share a common interest in public safety, public order entails job demands unique to police officers. For example, the insularity of the police profession (often described in degrees of intensity ranging from ambivalence ["police subculture"] to malevolence ["the Blue Wall of Silence"]) is a job-related factor unique to policing. Another factor unique to policing is the stress arising from a combination of psychological and physiological stress. For example, a firefighter is usually stationed physically at the fire station when an alarm to respond to a fire is sounded. As the firefighter puts on a uniform and protective gear, the mental preparation begins for the arduous and potentially life-threatening task ahead. Police officers are not always afforded the luxury of mental preparation before a stressful event.

For the purposes of this analysis, police officers are primarily municipal and local police officers, county police officers, county sheriffs (assigned mostly as patrol officers, not correctional officers), and state police officers. The analysis also includes any person with peace officer status whose primary responsibilities consist of maintaining public order, investigating complaints and criminal activity, and detecting and apprehending suspects.

Maximum hiring age restrictions are operationally defined as the maximum age before one becomes ineligible for appointment as an entry-level police officer as mandated by a specific law, local ordinance, or agency policy. Mandatory retirement is operationally defined as the maximum age at which a police officer is allowed to work before involuntary retirement. The term "age restriction" will denote either a maximum hiring age or a mandatory retirement age policy, and will mean a policy or law mandating a maximum hiring age, mandatory retirement age, or both. Physical fitness testing was used as a variable in the analysis because the courts generally favor individual assessments (such as fitness testing) as opposed to general age restrictions. Physical fitness testing is operationally defined as a cardiovascular endurance and/or a muscular strength test given to police applicants or incumbent members of a police agency as a condition of initial or continuing employment.

The court in which the policy was analyzed and ruled upon was determined to be the court of final adjudication. For example, if a case was initiated in a state court that rendered a decision subsequently reversed by a federal district court, then denied certiorari by the United States Court of Appeals, the court of final adjudication would be the federal district court.

A total of eighty cases fit the criteria of the above parameters. The earliest case, *Metcalf v. McAdoo,* was litigated in 1905 and concerned a Brooklyn, New York, police sergeant (a Civil War veteran) who was terminated for exceeding the mandatory retirement age and being unfit for duty due to obesity. The New York State Appellate Division ruled that, although he was unfit to perform the duties of patrolman, he could perform the job of desk sergeant, regardless of his age or physical condition. *Metcalf* merits attention because it was written eighty-five years before the Americans with Disabilities Act (ADA) but included the concepts of essential job functions and reasonable accommodation concept central to the pretense of the ADA. The next case, *Sheets v. Portsmouth* in 1944, was an Ohio State Supreme Court case that dealt with the police chief contesting the legality of an ordinance mandating a retirement age of sixty-five for police officers. The Ohio State Supreme Court upheld the policy. Most of the litigation, however, begins in the 1970s. Not surprisingly, more than 95 percent of the cases in the analysis were argued after passage of the 1974 amendments to the ADEA.

The cases were analyzed, scored, and coded based on six variables relating to (1) policy issues involved, (2) provisions of the law violated, (3) initiation of civil rights organizations, such as the EEOC, (4) court of final adjudication, (5) region of country where the case originated, and (6) the year the case originated. A logistic regression model was then constructed to determine which variables were significant and substantial in predicting whether or not the law or policy would ultimately be ruled legal or illegal. Logistic regression was chosen because the dependent, the court decision, variable is dichotomous, (coded as a 1 or a 0). A logistic regression using a dichotomous dependent variable can indicate how much the log (log-likelihood ratio) of the dependent variable odds change when the independent variables change by one unit (Bohrnstedt & Knoke, 1994). For example, when the predictor (independent) variables increase by one unit, the log odds (percentage change) can be estimated in the dependent variable. The logistic regression can predict the percentage of the decision of the case explained given a set of variables in the coding scheme. For example, if the case's jurisdiction has moved from the United States Court of Appeals to the United States Supreme Court, the percentage change of the likelihood that the law will be deemed illegal or upheld can be predicted with a certain degree of statistical significance.

Variables and Coding Scheme

As can be seen in the appendix, a total of seven variables were used in the analysis—one dependent variable, and six independent variables. As stated previously, the dependent variable, the decision of the court (*COURT*), is a dichotomous variable and was coded as 1 if the court supported an age restriction policy or 0 if the court invalidated the policy or law or deferred ruling to another body to decide.

The specific policy issue (*HIRE/RETIRE*) was constructed into a coding scheme for the analysis. It can be argued that there is general agreement that police officers must, in general, be physically fit, that there should be a mandatory retirement age, and that there should be a maximum retirement age. The strength of beliefs are dependent on the specific policy issue. People feel strongly about physical fitness standards, but there is not a strong consensus about age, and the variables were coded accordingly based on these conceptions. Cases argued exclusively on the issue of maximum hiring age received a score of 1, cases challenging the policy of mandatory retirement age received a score of 2, cases that challenged the policy of physical fitness standards received a score of 3, and cases that consisted of a combination of physical standards and an age restriction received a score of 4. According to this coding scheme, the tested relationship is attempting to determine whether physical fitness testing is more likely to be upheld than the other categories.

Court cases are generally challenged on one of two issues: a question of law or a question of fact. When a question of fact is at issue, a particular event or a person's involvement in that event is at issue. When a question of law is the issue, the legality, applicability, and legitimacy of a particular law, not the event, are at the foundation of the challenge. In virtually every case in this analysis, a question of law was at issue; therefore, the particular law in question (*LAW*) was included as an independent variable. Federal laws are generally more powerful than state or local laws, and thus more likely to be held as legal in court. Also, when comparing federal laws, a challenge under the ADEA may be more successful than a challenge under the equal protection clause of the Fourteenth Amendment. The scores on this variable ranged from 0 to 5. There were three cases that were local laws, and those cases received a score of 0. Cases argued under existing state laws received a score of 1. Cases that were argued under other federal laws such as the ADA or the Fair Labor Standards Act (FLSA) received a score of 2. There was one case argued under the provisions of the Eleventh Amendment, and that case received a score of 3. Cases argued under issues relating to an equal protection analysis received a score of 4. Finally, cases argued under issues relating to the ADEA received a score of 5. This coding scheme was constructed to establish a confrontation between the federal government's laws regarding age discrimination and policies relating to age restrictions.

Involvement by the Equal Employment Opportunity Commission was seen as a viable a priori independent variable in this analysis because of the number of challenges initiated by the EEOC. The EEOC is charged with enforcing provisions of the Age Discrimination in Employment Act; therefore, challenges initiated by the EEOC may have a better chance of declaring an age restriction policy illegal. The independent variable EEOC was coded as a 0 for cases initiated by individual plaintiffs without any assistance from an outside organization. Cases were coded as 1 if the plaintiff initiating the challenge was aided by an individual-rights-based organization such as the American Civil Liberties Union (ACLU), and a 2 if the plaintiff was aided by the EEOC. This coding scheme was based on the assumption that specific groups with power, such as the EEOC, may be more likely than individuals to be successful because they have more power to alter a particular agency's policies and because they have the financial, technical, and intellectual resources to challenge government agencies.

The court of final adjudication (*COURT*) was also hypothesized to be related to support of age restrictions. The higher the court, starting with local courts and proceeding to the United States Supreme Court, the higher the score in the coding scheme. Local courts were coded as 0. Lower state courts were coded as 1, while the highest state court was coded as 2. Federal district courts were coded as 3, while the United States Courts of Appeals were coded as 4. The United States Supreme Court was coded as a 5. This variable was coded in this manner to determine whether the court ruling on the age policy restriction was related to the court of final adjudication. More specifically, the coding scheme was constructed to determine whether the United States Supreme Court or higher federal courts were more likely than state or local courts to validate or invalidate age restrictions.

The particular region of the United States (*USREGION*) was also used as an independent variable. It may be argued that conservatives are generally more supportive of policy issues advocated by police officials and administrators and less likely to favor policies that extend individual rights at the expense of perceived compromises of public safety. Conservative regions of the country were coded according to data obtained by the General Social Survey (1993) conducted by the National Opinion Research Center and the United States Census Bureau (United States Department of Commerce, 1990). It was determined that the Southern, Mountain, and Midwest regions of the United States are generally more conservative than the Pacific region and the Northeast region. Court cases emanating from liberal regions received a score of 0 while court cases emanating from conservative regions received a score of 1. There were six cases that were initiated by federal law enforcement officers; these cases received a score of 0.5. This coding scheme was designed to determine the percentage increase (or decrease) in the chances of a court upholding an age restriction policy if the case is argued in a conservative or liberal region of the country.

The year (*YEAR*) in which the case was argued was also used as an independent variable in the analysis. Cases that were heard before passage and application of the ADEA or during one of the exemption periods (1986–1993, 1996–present) were coded as 0. Cases that were heard in years in which age restriction policies mandated by the ADEA were in effect were coded as 1. This coding scheme was designed to determine whether exemption from the ADEA had any effect on the ruling.

RESULTS

The relevant cases were analyzed and coded according to the coding scheme for each individual variable. The purpose of including the variables and coding was to determine what effect certain factors have on upholding or overturning age restriction policies.

Descriptive Statistics and Cross-Tabulations

Eighty cases were identified and included in the analysis. Seventy percent of the decisions upheld the legality of a maximum hiring age, mandatory retirement age, or physical fitness testing, while 30 percent of the cases ruled that either an age restriction or a physical fitness policy was invalid. Two of the eighty cases were argued before the United States Supreme Court, *Massachusetts Board of Retirement et al. v. Murgia,* decided in 1976, and *Equal Employment Opportunity Commission (EEOC) v. Wyoming et al.,* which was decided in 1983. The Supreme Court held in *Murgia* that a Massachusetts state statute mandating mandatory retirement for state police officers at age fifty did not violate the equal protection clause of the Fourteenth Amendment. Although there was no specific ADEA claim in *Murgia,* the case was included in the analysis because of its precedence and importance regarding policing and mandatory retirement ages. As noted previously, the court ruled in *EEOC v. Wyoming* (1983) that the ADEA was a valid exercise of congressional power.

Federal district courts ($N = 31$, 39 percent of the total) were the most frequent court of final adjudication. Lower state courts ($N = 21$, 26 percent of the total) were the second-most-frequent court of final adjudication, followed by United States courts of appeals ($N = 15$, 19 percent of the total), higher state courts ($N = 10$, 12.5 percent of the total), and the United States Supreme Court ($N = 2$, 2.5 percent of the total). One case's court of final adjudication was a local court.

Both the maximum hiring age and mandatory retirement policies as the primary policy challenges consisted of twenty-nine (36 percent of the total) legal challenges. Legal challenges of physical fitness standards consisted of eighteen cases (23 percent of the total), while a combination of policies within one challenge consisted of four cases, or 15 percent of the total.

Twenty-three of twenty-nine cases (79 percent of the maximum hiring age cases) that challenged the legality of a policy of a maximum hiring age upheld the policy. The courts upheld the legality of a mandatory retirement age in nineteen of the twenty-nine cases, for a total of 66 percent of the mandatory retirement cases. The courts upheld policies of physical fitness standards in fourteen out of eighteen cases, or 78 percent. This low percentage is counterintuitive; in the cases where the policy was outlawed, the agency often failed to establish that the particular fitness test was a bona fide occupational qualification. For example, in the most recent case, *Lanning v Southeastern Pennsylvania Transportation Authority (SEPTA)* (1999), the court debated whether physical fitness tests should be gym-based, such as running a timed half-mile and lifting weights, or criterion-based, which meant testing job tasks such as pulling dummies and climbing over walls. The plaintiffs argued that the gym-based criteria had a disparate impact on women. The Unite States Court of Appeals (Third Circuit) remanded the case back to the United States District Court for the Third Circuit, stating that a gym-based criterion is valid as long as it represents the minimum qualification of the business necessity standard for the BFOQ.

United States district courts ruled on thirty-one cases involving age restrictions or fitness policies, and upheld the policies nineteen times, or 61.3 percent of the time. The highest state court ruled on ten cases, upholding existing policy or law eight times, or 80 percent of the time. Lower state courts ruled on twenty-one cases, ruling in favor of the policies eighteen times, or 85.7 percent of the time. There was one case that was argued in a local court, and that court upheld the policy.

The Equal Employment Opportunity Commission was involved in twenty of the eighty challenges, or 25 percent of the time. Although the EEOC was only successful in nine cases, or 45 percent of the time, the chances were greater than initiating a legal challenge without any assistance. There were fifty-seven cases in which the plaintiff initiated the challenge without the assistance of an individual-rights-based organization, and only eleven (19.3 percent) of those cases were successful in invalidating an age restriction law or policy. There were three cases (one American Civil Liberties Union–assisted and two state human rights commission–assisted) in which another individual-rights-based organization assisted, and they were successful in invalidating the law or policy once, or 33 percent of the time.

When the specific policy was at issue, maximum hiring ages were most successful and a combination of policies was least successful. Maximum hiring ages were upheld in twenty-three out of twenty-nine cases, or 79.3 percent of the time. There were four cases in which a combination of policies were at issue; and in all four, the court invalidated the policy or the law.

When a specific law was at issue, cases arguing that the policy or law violated the ADEA were, as expected, the most successful. There were forty-five cases argued under the provisions of the ADEA, and plaintiffs were successful in having the policy or law overturned twenty-one times, or 46.7 percent of the time. There were three cases in which another federal law, such as the Fair Labor Standards Act (FSLA), was at issue; and in all three, the courts upheld the policy or law. Nineteen cases were argued under violations of the equal protection clause of the Fourteenth Amendment or a federal civil rights act, and only one plaintiff was successful. The plaintiff who argued that age restriction policies were in violation of the commerce clause was unsuccessful. State laws mandating age restriction policies or laws were upheld in seven of the nine cases, or 77.8 percent of the time; and policies encoded in local laws were upheld in all three of the challenges.

There were thirty-nine cases originating in designated liberal regions of the country and thirty-five cases from conservative regions. The cases emanating from the designated liberal regions upheld age restriction policies in twenty-nine of the cases, or 74.4 percent of the time. The cases emanating from conservative areas upheld age restriction policies in twenty-two cases, or 62.9 percent of the time. This finding was somewhat counterintuitive and may be because the majority of the large urban areas are located in the Northeast and the Pacific region, which were designated as liberal regions. Large, urban police departments' age restriction policies tend to garner a significant amount of support from constituents, and subsequently from politicians. Five of the six Federal law enforcement policies of age restrictions were upheld.

There were thirty-one cases argued during the time periods in which police agencies were exempt from the ADEA, or before the 1967 signing of the ADEA into law. The age restriction or physical fitness policies were upheld twenty-three times, or 74.2 percent during this time. There were forty-nine cases, or 67.3 percent, argued when police agencies were required to comply with provisions of the ADEA and the policies were upheld.

Bivariate Analysis

A bivariate analysis was conducted to determine the relationship of the independent variables on the dependent variable and to observe any misleading relationships between independent variables that would create an interaction effect that might undermine the logistic regression, and ultimately the internal validity of the research design. A bivariate correlation matrix revealed that there were no strong correlations (the strongest significant correlation was *LAW* and *COURT*, $r = .42$) between any of the independent variables. This finding obviates any potential interaction effects within the logistic regression. Each independent variable was then tested separately to determine the effect on the dependent variable. The value was then computed into a log-likelihood ratio equation to determine the increase or decrease in percent change on the dependent variable when the independent variable increased by one unit. For example, the bivariate, logistic regression analysis when testing the effect of *COURT* on *DECISION* is as follows:

$$\textit{DECISION} \qquad\qquad \textit{COURT}$$
$$\text{(Log-likelihood } (.69)(1 - .69) = -.57 \text{ (beta coefficient value)}$$
$$\text{Transformation } (.69)(.31)(-.57) = -.36 = 36\% \text{ decrease}$$

The variance (.69) is based on the value that 69 percent of the cases upheld the age restriction policies, .31 is the inverse probability of the dependent variable value of (.69), and $-.57$ was the bivariate beta coefficient for *COURT* when placed in a logistic regression. It can be concluded from the bivariate analysis that if the case was argued in the next-higher court, there is a 36 percent decrease in the odds that the age restriction policy would be upheld. This finding was significant beyond the .05 level.

The independent variable *EEOC* had the strongest relationship, as hypothesized, when analyzing the descriptive statistics. The beta coefficient value was − .83, and based on the above calculations, would result in a 62 percent chance of decreasing for every unit increase in the independent variable. For example, a case that was initiated by an organization had a 62 percent greater likelihood of overturning an age restriction policy than a case initiated by a lone plaintiff. If the case was initiated by the EEOC itself, the likelihood of overturning the age restriction policy increased another 62 percent. This variable was significant at the .001 level.

The independent variable *LAW* displayed a 32 percent decrease in the chances of the court upholding the existing policy and the specific policy issue. This means that when a challenge to an age restriction policy claims a violation of the ADEA, it is more likely to be declared illegal than a challenge to an age restriction policy contained in a local or state law.

HIRE/RETIRE displayed a 29 percent decrease in the chances of the policy being upheld for every one unit increase in the independent variable; both were significant beyond the .05 level. According to this finding, a maximum hiring age policy is more likely than a mandatory retirement age policy to be upheld, and a combination of policies with physical fitness standards was the least likely to be upheld.

The independent variable *YEAR* displayed a slight positive increase, and *USREGION* a slight decrease, meaning that the year the case was commenced would increase the chances of upholding an age restriction policy, and cases originating in liberal areas of the country were more likely to uphold an age restriction policy than cases originating in conservative areas of the country. *YEAR* and *USREGION* were not significant, and therefore few inferences may be drawn from the results regarding these two variables.

Multivariate Analysis

The first logistic regression tested all the variables in the equation, regardless of the variable's significance or interaction effect. The overall model fit was fairly good, with a goodness of fit value of 81.65, in excess of the critical value of 19.49 needed to reject the null hypothesis. When the null hypothesis is rejected, it is a given that a least one of the independent variables has a nonzero value. The model also yielded an overall pseudo-R value of .34, meaning that 34 percent of the variance in the dependent variable is explained by the independent variables. This can be interpreted by stating that about one-third of the reason the courts ruled the way they did was because of these six independent variables. The beta coefficient variables are as follows:

$$DECISION = CONSTANT + HIRE/RETIRE + LAW + EEOC + YEAR$$
$$+ COURT + USREGION$$

$$Y = 4.7 + (−.78) + (−.53) + (−.70) + (.92) + (.009) + (−.06)$$

$$(p = .0011) \ (p = .045) \ (p = .06) \ (p = .03) \ (p = .64) \ (p = .97) \ (p = .91)$$

When given a set of hypothetical independent variables, the log-likelihood ratio can be transformed, then subsequently predicted. For example, a hypothetical case in which a court case consisted of a challenge to a maximum hiring age (*HIRE/RETIRE* = 1), under provisions of the ADEA (*LAW* = 5), without the aid of the EEOC (*EEOC* = 0), in a year in which the public safety exemption was active (*YEAR* = 1), argued in the highest state court (*COURT* = 2) in a conservative region of the country (*USREGION* = 1) would yield the following beta coefficient values in the logistic regression equation:

$$Y = 4.7 + [(1)(-.78)] + [(5)(-.53)] + [(0)(-.53)] + [(1)(.92)] + [(2)(.009)] + [(1)(-.06)] = 2.20$$
$$Y = 2.20 = (e)(9.03)/1 + (e)\ 9.03 = .90 = 90\%$$

Given this set of hypothetical independent variables, there would be a 90 percent chance that the court would uphold the existing policy of a maximum hiring age. If a mandatory retirement age policy (*HIRE/RETIRE* = 2) was at issue under the equal protection clause of the Fourteenth Amendment (*LAW* = 4), with the assistance of the EEOC (*EEOC* = 2) in a year (*YEAR* = 0) in which there was not a public safety exemption to the ADEA and was argued in the United States Court of Appeals (*COURT* = 4) in a designated liberal region of the country (*USREGION* = 0), the equation would yield the following beta coefficient values:

$$Y = 4.7 + [(2)(-.78)] + [(4)(-.53)] + [(2)(-.53)] + [(1)(.92)] + [(4)(.009)] + [(0)\ (-.06)] = .83$$
$$Y = .83 = (e)(2.29)/1 + (e)\ 2.29 = .7 = 70\%$$

Given the above set of hypothetical values, there is a 70 percent chance that the court will uphold the existing mandatory retirement age policies, compared to 90 percent in the previous example.

The next step was to remove variables not deemed to contribute to the model. The parameters were set at the .01 level, meaning that any independent variable that was not significant at the .01 level was removed from the equation. The variables that were significant at the .01 level or better and remained were *EEOC*, *HIRE/RETIRE*, and *LAW*. *USREGION*, *COURT*, and *YEAR* were removed from the final model. The goodness of fit value once again exceeded the critical value, rejecting the null hypothesis that all independent variables are zero (0). The pseudo-R value of .34 in this model did not improve from the previous model. Once again, this can be interpreted by stating that approximately one-third of the variance in the court's decision is the result of the policy issue, the law, and the involvement of the Equal Employment Opportunity Commission. The beta coefficients for this model are as follows:

$$DECISION = CONSTANT + HIRE/RETIRE + LAW + EEOC$$
$$Y = 4.7 + (-.64) + (-.51) + (-.58)$$

Hypothetically, a challenge of a maximum hiring age (*HIRE/RETIRE*) under the provisions of the ADEA (*LAW* = 5) without the assistance of the EEOC (*EEOC* = 0) would result in the following values:

$$Y = 4.7 + (1)(-.64) + (5)(-.51) + (0)(-.58) = 1.51$$
$$Y = (e)(4.52)/1 + (e)(4.52) = .8188 = 82\%$$

Given the above set of variables, the logistic regression equation predicts that there is an 82 percent chance that the court would uphold the age restriction policy. This logistic regression equation is substantial and significant.

The analysis used a variable coding scheme with six independent variables and the construction of logistic regression to determine whether a court's decision can be predicted given a set of independent variables. The findings suggest that the policy issue, EEOC involvement, and provisions of the law challenged are valid predictors of the decisions of the courts. The EEOC was a very strong lone predictor variable. Cases in which the EEOC was involved had a higher chance of invalidating the age restriction and policy, perhaps because the EEOC is an experienced "repeat player" in policy litigation (Galanter, 1974). The EEOC may also be successful not only because it has superior legal skills and financial resources but also because it only litigates the most egregious cases of age discrimination. Police officers and potential candidates generally do not have unlimited financial resources, as they are drawn from the working and middle socioeconomic classes. A long and protracted legal struggle challenging a large organization or municipality may be an unrealistic quest for a lone individual or a small class.

When the specific policy issue is a maximum hiring age, it is more likely to be upheld than to be declared illegal by the courts, consistent with public perceptions that vigor and fitness are clearly associated with youth. At the other end of the age issue, a trend is developing in the courts. Justices are more likely to uphold a mandatory retirement law if there are physical fitness standards in agencies with mandatory retirement policies. Although there were too few cases to report any significant conclusions, a legitimate hypothesis can be formulated based upon the data used in this analysis regarding future trends.

DISCUSSION

The Age Discrimination in Employment Act is a potentially powerful law regarding the control of age restriction policies in state and local agencies. Although the Supreme Court's recent *Kimel* decision exempted local and state police agencies from the provisions of the ADEA, police agencies do not have impunity against complaints of age discrimination. The *Kimel* decision did not relieve state and local police agencies of justifying age restriction policies. They must still adhere to state statutes (and in some jurisdictions to local laws as well) regarding age discrimination. Based upon the prior history of the ADEA, the *Kimel* decision probably has only temporarily relieved police agencies of the burdens of the ADEA. A different political and/or judicial climate may develop, and then the Supreme Court may overturn *Kimel*, or Congress may remove the public safety exemption from the ADEA. Police agencies have to comply with existing laws regardless of the dynamics of the ADEA and contemporary case law. Police agencies should, in the interim, develop uniform guidelines for physical fitness tests as a business necessity, such as annual fitness exams, wherever practical. All fitness tests should be analogous to the unique operational functions of the particular agency. Fitness tests may provide the most judgment-proof methods to resolve the age discrimination issue and balance the delicate policy concerns of public safety and individual rights. When costs seem prohibitive, especially to large agencies with numerous employees, the only way to ensure a physically fit police agency is to impose age restrictions and err on the side of public safety. When compelled to impose age restriction policies, policy-makers must constantly remain vigilant to the applicability of the ADEA and other age discrimination laws.

APPENDIX: VARIABLE CODING

Dependent Variable

DECISION
Upheld age restriction policy or law = 1
Invalidated age restriction policy or law = 0

Independent Variables

LAW
ADEA = 5
Equal protection/civil rights = 4
Commerce clause = 3
Other federal law = 2
State law = 1

COURT
Supreme Court = 5
Court of appeals = 4
District court = 3
Highest state court = 2
State court = 1
Local court = 0

HIRE/RETIRE
Maximum hiring age = 1
Mandatory retirement age = 2
Physical standards = 3
Combination = 4

EEOC
No initiation = 0
Rights-based organization = 1
EEOC-initiated = 2

USREGION
Conservative = 1
Liberal = 0
Federal = .5

YEAR
ADEA exemption = 1
No ADEA exemption = 0

REFERENCES

AGE DISCRIMINATION IN EMPLOYMENT ACT of 1967, 1974, 1977, 1986, and 1996, 29 U.S.C.A. 623.

BOHRNSTEDT, G., & KNOKE, D. 1994. *Statistics for social data analysis* (3rd ed.). Itasca, IL: Peacock.

FINKLESTEIN, M. 1989. Minimum physical standards-safeguarding the rights of protective service workers under the Age Discrimination in Employment Act. *Fordham Law Review, 57,* 1053–1078.

H.R. 849: Public safety exemption to the Age Discrimination in Employment Act (ADEA). 104th Con. 1st Sess. 1995 (testimony of Harris W. Fawell).

H.R. 5383: The committee on human resources, to which was referred the Bill To Amend The Age Discrimination In Employment Act. 95th Con.1st Sess. 1977 (testimony of Jacob Javitz).

LANDY, F. J., BLAND, R. E., BUSKIRK, E. R., DALY, R. E., DeBUSK, R. F., DONOVAN, E. J., FARR, J. L., FELLER, I., FLEISHMAND, E. A., GEBHART, D. L., HODGSON, J. L., KENNY, W. L.,

NESSELROADE, J. R., PRYOR, D. B., RAVEN, P. B., WARNER SCHRIE, K., SOTHMAN, M. S., TAYLOR, M. C., VANCE, R. J., & ZARIT, S. H. 1992. *Alternatives to chronological age in determining standards of suitability for public safety jobs.* University Park: Pennsylvania State University.

SOEHNEL, S. 1986. Actions under Age Discrimination in Employment Act: Challenging hiring or retirement practices in law enforcement employment. *American Law Reports, 79,* 373–440.

Uniform Crime Reports. 1995. Washington, DC: United States Department of Justice, Federal Bureau of Investigation.

UNITED STATES DEPARTMENT OF COMMERCE. 1990. *1990 Census of Population and Housing.* Washington, DC.

WHITEHEAD, A., & BOLLON, V. 1993. *Age discrimination in employment act: Exemptions for public safety employees.* United Firefighters Association.

Cases Cited

- *City of Philadelphia v. Pennsylvania Human Relations Commission,* 684 A.2d 204 (1996).
- *EEOC v. City of Janesville,* 630 F. 2d 1254 (7th Cir. 1980).
- *EEOC v. City of Minneapolis,* 537 F. Supp. 750, 756 (D. Minn. 1982).
- *EEOC v. County of Calumet (Wisconsin),* 686 F.2d 1249.
- *EEOC v. State of Wyoming,* 460 U.S. 226 (1983).
- *Kimel et al. v. Florida Board of Regents et al.,* 120 S.Ct. 631 (2000).
- *Lanning v. S.E.P.T.A.,* W.L. 53517821 (E.D. Pa. 1997).
- *Massachusetts v. Murgia,* 427 U.S. 307 (1976).
- *Metcalf v. McAdoo,* 184 N.Y. 286 (N.Y. 1906).
- *Sheets v. City of Portsmouth,* 148 Ohio St. 302 (Ohio 1944).
- *Usery v. Tamiani Trails, Inc.,* 531 F. 2d 224, (5th Cir. 1976).
- *Western Airlines v. Criswell,* 472 U.S. 400 (1985).

11

Policing and the Law

More Than Just a Question of Arrest

Mark L. Dantzker

Since the creation of the oldest surviving written set of laws, the Code of Hammurabi, societies have continued the practice of creating means to control citizen behavior. These controls have fallen under the guise of civil or criminal laws. Both types of law require someone to enforce them. Generally, it is the police who are called upon to be society's law enforcers, thus placing the police in an interesting position.

> The relationship between the police and the law is unique in that the existence, powers, duties, and behavior of the police stem directly from or are a result of the law. The application of the law to policing is provided through statutes created according to the constitutions of the United States and of the states themselves. (Dantzker, 2000, p. 160)

The discussion of the police and the law typically falls into one of two categories, general enforcement by the police and violation of the law by the police. The general enforcement discussions tend to focus on the types of crimes (felonies and misdemeanors) and the associated rules for police enforcement. Violation discussions generally revolve around police misconduct, brutality, and corruption. This text takes a somewhat different path of discussion by examining a variety of relationships between the police and the law. Particularly, it focuses on several ways of using the law to enforce specific types of criminal activities, the position of the courts, and how certain laws affect the police operationally and regarding policy. Regardless of the overall emphasis of the discussion, none can take place until the fundamentals of the law and the police have been established, which Walker does in the opening chapter.

In Chapter 1, Walker focuses on the movement by the courts and lawmakers to incorporate the Bill of Rights to the states and to make it applicable to police agencies. He takes the reader through a look at the constitutional applications to policing as reinforced by the courts. He begins with one of the most fundamental elements of police enforcement of the law, probable cause.

Probable cause represents a continuous area of examination by the courts. Walker demonstrates this with a variety of applicable cases, including *Brinegar* (1949), *Draper* (1959), *Aguilar* (1964), *Spinelli* (1969), *Gates* (1983), and *Sokolow* (1989). Each of these cases attempts to clarify and, in some cases, narrow the definition and application of probable cause. The knowledge of how the courts interpret probable cause is important to the police officer because the basis of every arrest made rests upon probable cause. In conjunction with the arrest is the use of evidence obtained during the arrest, another area to which the courts have paid particular attention. Walker's discussion of the exclusionary rule through such cases as *Weeks* (1914), *Mapp* (1961), *Wong Sun* (1963), and *Williams* (1984) assists in establishing the weight placed on police officers to make sure that the evidence is obtained in a constitutionally acceptable manner.

Walker continues his foray into the constitutional aspects of policing and the law through examination of cases relevant to the amendments most related to policing: the Fourth, Fifth, and Sixth. Starting with the Fourth Amendment, which protects persons from unreasonable searches and seizures, Walker provides relevant court cases for the major areas under the purview of this Amendment. Regarding searches in general, there are *Greenwood* (1988), *Ramirez* (1988), *Garrison* (1987), *Wilson* (1995), and *Richards* (1997). For consent searches, cases such as *Matlock* (1974) and *Rodriguez* (1990) are discussed. With respect to plain view searches, *Ciraola* (1986) and *Hicks* (1987) are emphasized. Vehicle search cases included *Carroll* (1925), *Chambers* (1969), *Carter* (1981), and *Knowles* (1998). The area of stop and frisk, often a contentious one, includes such cases as *Terry* (1968), *Hensley* (1985), and *Dickerson* (1993). Finally, for searches after an arrest, Walker examines *Chimel* (1969) and *Robinson* (1973). He concludes the Fourth Amendment discussion with arrest cases such as *Dunaway* (1979), *Chesternut* (1988), and *Bostick* (1991).

For the Fifth Amendment, Walker highlights the issue of *Miranda* and self-incrimination, identifying several cases that either support or weaken the principles behind *Miranda* (1964), such as *Quarles* (1984). A similar approach is taken for the Sixth Amendment with the discussion of such cases as *Gideon* (1963), *Escobedo* (1964), and *Henry* (1980). Overall, Walker provides a fundamental understanding to policing and the law through his identification and discussion of pertinent court cases that reinforce the constitutional limitations of police activity while trying to enforce the law.

Perhaps one of the most closely scrutinized arenas of policing and law enforcement in the country today is the war on drugs. It has expanded into a multi-billion-dollar industry. Despite the concern about the continuing increase in drug problems, the police have not been given unrestricted authority to address this problem. In actuality, some argue, the police fight against drug crime is continuously hampered by the courts. With Walker having laid the foundation of constitutional applicability to policing using Supreme Court cases, the legal issues surrounding the war on drugs were discussed in Chapter 2. In this chapter, Hemmens focused on Supreme Court cases that dealt with the review of investigatory practices of police in their war on drugs and the impact these cases have had on police efforts. In particular, Hemmens focused on knock and announce and traffic stops.

Hemmens begins his exploration with an examination of the history of the Supreme Court and the police through such cases as *Barron* (1833), *Weeks* (1914), *Wolf* (1949), *Elkins* (1960), *Mapp* (1961), *Camara* (1967), and *Terry* (1968), followed by a brief discussion of the war on drugs. He suggests that there has been a somewhat cavalier approach by the courts and society, with little sympathy for those arrested on drug-related charges. This attitude led to the adoption of zero tolerance policies. Furthermore, the Supreme Court endorsed such police methods as sobriety checkpoints, drug courier profiles, and random drug testing of adults and children. The result has been that the police have pushed the envelope of the Fourth Amendment. With this in mind, Hemmens focuses on two areas for which Court scrutiny has increased, the investigatory practices of knock and announce and traffic stops.

With respect to knock and announce, Hemmens includes a variety of cases, such as *Miller* (1958), *Wong Sun* (1963), *Ker* (1964), *Wilson* (1995), *Richards* (1997), and *Ramirez* (1998). Ultimately, he demonstrates that the courts have given the police some leeway in the use of knock and announce particularly if exigent circumstances exist, such as the possibility of officers being injured or evidence destroyed because of the warning given.

Regarding traffic stops, Hemmens notes that increases in traffic have required police to increase traffic stops, which has led the courts to define the constitutional parameters of these stops. He states that the police must identify a traffic violation or reasonable suspicion of criminal activity to stop a vehicle. From there he discusses such cases as *Robinette* (1996), *Whren* (1996), *Wilson* (1997), and *Houghton* (1999), in which the courts looked at issues of consent, dealing with passengers, pretextual stops, and contraband.

In concluding, Hemmens suggests that the courts have continued to support certain police activities regarding drug-related crime that may still have Fourth Amendment implications. However, while chastising the court for its decisions, he does acknowledge that not all decisions favor the police (e.g., *Knowles*), but there still is a need for closer court scrutiny of police investigatory actions.

Following Hemmens, in Chapter 3 Golden and VanHouten look specifically at the use of police checkpoints or roadblocks to detect and interdict the use of drugs. They begin by establishing the rights and reasons given by the courts for the police to stop a vehicle and be able to search it. This is followed by a discussion of how the courts are taking a new and closer look at checkpoints and roadblocks. The discussion begins with a review of the most recent court decisions regarding the use of checkpoints and roadblocks, the *Edmond* (1999) case, which addressed the use of a checkpoint by police officers seeking evidence of any type of criminal activity. The court held that this type of roadblock violated the seizure provisions of the Fourth Amendment because it did not fit previously established exceptions that included illegal immigrants, sobriety, and license and registration checks.

Golden and VanHouten then identified several cases for each of the three areas of acceptance for the use of checkpoints and roadblocks. They conclude by noting that the Supreme Court has put police officers on notice regarding the use of checkpoints/roadblocks: (1) they are prohibited for general crime control, and (2) the purpose of the checkpoint must not be a pretext for generalized intrusion.

During the past fifteen to twenty years, there has been an increase in the number of lawsuits filed against police officers and agencies. Although there are a number of reasons that could lead to a police officer being sued, many of these cases result from the decision to make an arrest. This has raised the question of whether uniformed police officers are less likely to perform their duty if they have a perception or fear of being sued; a question that Stevens examines in Chapter 4.

Stevens begins his exploration of this question with a background discussion on civil liability issues. He acknowledges that most lawsuits against the police are the result of violations of the Fourth, Fifth, Sixth, and/or Eighth Amendments as protected through 42 U.S.C. Section 1983. Furthermore, Stevens suggests that a major concern for police officers with respect to these types of lawsuits is the lack of support by the public, agency, or the city.

To address this question, Stevens conducted a survey of 658 police officers from twenty-one police agencies. His results indicated that the threat of becoming a defendant in a civil liability suit does interfere with officers' decisions to conduct probable cause arrests. Officers were, however, more likely to arrest persons who were not a strong candidate to file a suit, such as those arrested for driving while intoxicated, politically powerless immigrants, and domestic violence participants. His results have both negative and positive implications. Under the threat of potential lawsuits, officers are more aware of the law but are making fewer arrests (even though the arrests may be necessary). Obviously, if the potential for lawsuits against police officers rises, the impact it could have on arrest possibilities is substantial, and something that police agencies may need to address.

As noted in Chapter 2, with the amount of drugs being smuggled into this country increasing, police response has had to change. In Chapter 2 Hemmens discussed how the Supreme Court was addressing police investigatory techniques in the war against drugs; and in Chapter 3, Golden and VanHouten examined the use of checkpoints and roadblocks. In Chapter 5, Golden and Walker review another investigatory technique that has come under question: the use of canines for searching and seizure.

Golden and Walker focus on the legal implications of the use of police dogs in the detection of narcotics, concentrating specifically on the area of search and seizure. They look at four areas in particular: packages in transit, places and people, public transportation, and automobiles. For each area, they provide relevant court cases that specifically focus on the use of the canine under each circumstance. They conclude that any government intrusion using a narcotics-detection dog must meet a test of reasonableness, often defined as the public smell doctrine. Furthermore, they note that the police should take care to use narcotics-detection dogs in a manner consistent with established constitutional safeguards, particularly in the area of privacy. Finally, they acknowledge that there does appear to be a tremendous amount of latitude given the police with respect to canine sniffs.

One of the fastest-growing areas for criminality is the computer. Its use as a tool to commit crime, as well as to investigate crime, is just now coming into its own. Taylor and Morgan, in Chapter 6, address some major issues surrounding policing and the use of computers, in particular, the Internet. They begin with a discussion of the growth in the use of computers and the Internet, and how society seems to be heading toward becoming a virtual society. With this growth, there will be abuses and a need for the police. Unfortunately, current conditions in most police agencies make investigation of computers and the Internet difficult. As a result, Taylor and Morgan address four major areas of policing the Internet, beginning with cybercrimes.

To understand the nature of cybercrime, Taylor and Morgan identify three main areas of knowledge or understanding: computers as targets, computers as tools, and computers as access. Exploring these areas, they discuss the various types of crimes that can be committed, including one of the more frustrating and debilitating for computers: viruses. They also discuss the role of the media and the need for Internet legislation. They also discuss constitutional issues such as pure speech and privacy, offering several cases in support of such activities despite the fact that they can include hate speech, bomb-making instructions, and pornography. In essence, Taylor and Morgan suggest that a plethora of potential crimes is possible through the Internet.

The second area they offer revolves around the issue of surveillance. While the courts have supported the more traditional means of electronic surveillance, wiretapping, no such support through law or court cases has been established for computers. The need for police to be able to gain access to electronic transmissions is growing, and, as they note, the ability of the police to do their jobs regarding computer crimes will require legislative and court support.

A third area of exploration by Taylor and Morgan was the international nature of the Internet. As they note, because of its widespread use throughout the world, the difference in local laws, and the lack of international laws, there is not much the police can do about cross-national criminality. In their discussion, they identify and elaborate on seven obstacles to policing the Internet from an international perspective.

The last major area they examine is practical limitations. In particular, they focus on the training problem. A majority of police officers have minimal knowledge about computers and their use in general terms, and even less knowledge of how to investigate computer crimes. This will require special training; and police agencies must recognize that their personnel need this knowledge and have to deliver it to them economically.

Taylor and Morgan close by looking at the role of the police in policing the Internet. It is their position that this will be a growing area for police intervention; but, as with traditional policing, a delicate balance must be maintained between society's needs and individual rights. In closing, they suggest that the "police must develop an attitude of attempting to understand the current legal requirements and ramifications of computer crime investigations, and they must begin to look beyond their current jurisdiction in understanding those laws." Wynne (2001, p. 24) would concur with Taylor and Morgan's stance that "police officers must learn to quickly adapt to changes in the law and in technology if they are to continue policing the Internet"; and he suggests that police officers must learn to use technology to "beat the criminals at their own 'computer games.'"

It is rather common that each year a new set of laws take effect. Whether completely new or a revision of an old law, the change must be addressed by those who enforce the law, mainly police officers. How police agencies adapt to change is the subject of Chapter 7, in which Buerger identifies four types of change in the legal environment that require adaptation by police agencies. These are:

1. A radical redefining of substantive criminal law or a shift in political climate that places new emphasis on a previously ignored area.
2. Sweeping procedural law changes.
3. Lesser and incremental procedural changes.
4. Impact of civil judgments.

Buerger suggests that the police reaction to these changes is either tactical or strategic and may be positive or negative. He notes that talk about police response to changes in law require specifying which aspect of policing is being discussed: an abstract occupational entity, a specific organization, the order-takers or order-givers within the organization, or the broad commonality referred to as the police subculture. He argues that the formal organization often responds to changes in the law either by issuing new operational directives or altering old ones to reflect the new legal standard. Unfortunately, he notes, it is what happens on the street that is at issue. Buerger identifies four types of police response: avoidance and monkey-wrenching, which he suggests are illegitimate and negative responses, and distinguishing and lobbying, which are legitimate and positive responses.

At the heart of this chapter, Buerger focuses on the due process revolution, response to domestic violence, radical redefinition of substantive criminal law, and enhanced personal liability. With respect to the due process revolution, Buerger reports that while the perceptions are often of an adverse affect on policing, reality has found little negative impact. For domestic violence, he claims that the closest we have seen to a new strategic course in police operations is the response to new legal mandates for handling domestic violence cases, even if they did come about more as a result of lawsuits than the true need for change. In this case, police agencies have responded with mandatory arrest policies. As for the radical redefinition of substantive criminal law, it primarily has led to an armistice in the war on drugs. Finally, the enhanced personal liability that is often the result of lawsuits has raised the awareness of police officers about how they go about doing their jobs, even if it is detrimental (as suggested by Stevens in Chapter 5).

In closing, Buerger suggests that "those who would foster change in police activities through changes in the law would be well advised to regard formal changes in policy as merely the first step, not as evidence of a job well done." As he notes, the implementation of formal changes cannot be piecemeal or haphazardly. It requires "a combination of continuous review, training that provides not only a statement of the law but also a moral framework justifying or validating the change, reinforcement of positive responses, and vigilance against monkey-wrenching and foot-dragging." Ultimately, he suggests, change often occurs too slowly, and police organizations have to be better at implementing change based on changes in the law in a more proficient, faster pace for the good of the community and the agency.

One of the most fundamental rights that all citizens have is the right to privacy. Although the Constitution is meant to protect that freedom, there has been some question as to whether this freedom is different for police officers. Bloss, in Chapter 8, addresses this issue as he examines privacy as it applies to policing. In particular, he addresses workplace searches, drug testing, communicable disease testing, and sexual conduct.

Bloss begins with an examination of the emergence of constitutional privacy standards as established through the courts. He notes how the expectation of privacy standard was established in *Katz* (1967), but that in *Ortega* (1987) the courts established what is know as the competing interest test. This test is applied to four areas as they relate to police officers: workplace searches, drug testing, communicable disease testing, and sexual conduct.

Beginning with searches in the police workplace, Bloss points out that warrantless searches are permissible in the presence of suspected work-related misconduct involving departmental property or work areas. Searches can be of offices, lockers, desks, brief-cases, or issued vehicles. For example, if an officer is suspected of removing items from the police property room, a warrantless search is permissible of any of the above areas to which the officer has access.

One of the more recent concerns, drug testing, has become more common in polic-ing. As Bloss advises, neither the Fourth Amendment warrant requirement nor probable cause and its reasonable suspicion exception is necessary to compel police employees to submit to suspicionless workplace drug testing. This practice was upheld by the courts in the *Von Raab* (1989) decision, which established a bright-line rule allowing suspicionless drug testing of police employees.

For decades, this country has gone through periods of concern regarding communi-cable diseases. In more recent years, this concern has revolved around HIV, particularly in the police environment. While policing has taken steps to help protect officers from con-tracting the virus during the course of executing their duties, there has recently been a concern over hiring persons as police officers who are HIV carriers. Yet, as Bloss indi-cates, due to federal legislation such as the Rehabilitation Act of 1973 (as amended in 1988) and the Americans with Disabilities Act (1990), police agencies cannot disqualify a person with HIV from being a police officer if that person is otherwise qualified or able to perform essential functions of the job.

The last topic Bloss discussed was employer regulation of police employee sexual conduct. He notes that, unless the behavior has a direct bearing on the effectiveness of the organization, then employee sexual conduct cannot be regulated. The ability to regulate must be supported by the demonstration of a nexus between the behavior and on-job per-formance or adverse affect on agency operation, morale, or reputation. In closing, Bloss suggests that the courts have permitted increased police-employer regulation of employ-ees in the specific privacy related areas identified in Chapter 8.

Perhaps one of the hottest employment topics in the past few years has been the ap-plication of affirmative action in selection processes, especially in policing. In Chapter 9, Gaines and Schram take a closer look at affirmative action and police selection. Their major focus is on the history of affirmative action, which began with Title VII of the 1964 Civil Rights Act and how it affects contemporary police selection practices. From here, they introduce a series of court cases that have furthered the application of affirmative action.

This discussion begins with *Griggs* (1971), in which the court established new stan-dards to judge the existence of discrimination. This was followed by *Moody* (1975), which expanded *Griggs* by requiring that entry-level tests be job-related. In the 1982 *Teal* case, the courts further expanded testing outcomes; and in the 1987 *Paradise* case, the courts supported the use of preferences and quotas as a remedy against past discrimina-tion practices. Gaines and Schram also offer *Weber* (1979) and *Johnson* (1987) as sup-porting cases.

By the mid- to late 1980s, the assault against affirmative action had begun. Gaines and Schram argue that the two primary methods for establishing discrimination are dis-parate treatment (individual basis) and disparate impact (group or class). Before 1989, employers bore the burden of proving that they were not discriminating. In the 1989 *Anto-nio* decision, the burden of proof moved to the plaintiff to first produce evidence of mem-bership in a protected group suffering from disparate impact. Later the same year, the

Hopkins decision was handed down, shifting the burden back to the employer, but only as it related to gender. Gaines and Schram continue their discussion with cases that address other procedural issues of Title VII. Ultimately, regarding disparate impact, Gaines and Schram conclude that plaintiffs in affirmative action cases must go beyond just showing that disparate impact exists to show that disparate treatment occurred.

Additional discussion by Gaines and Schram includes the 1991 Civil Rights Act and how it forbade the use of any statistical adjustments or norming of scores based on gender or race. It also reestablished disparate impact as a method of determining whether discrimination existed. They also look at affirmative action and physical agility testing and written selection tests.

Regarding physical agility testing, Gaines and Schram start with height standards. By the 1970s, the court had forced agencies to eliminate this standard, which led to physical agility testing. The courts would eventually examine this practice and determine that the agility tests must be job-related. As Gaines and Schram note, this change led to a movement to health-based agility screening. As a result of the 1991 Civil Rights Act, however, they indicate that police departments began abandoning the health-based agility tests, returning to physical agility testing. Today, the courts hold fast to the requirement that the tests must be work-related.

With respect to police written selection tests, Gaines and Schram discuss the use of and history behind this type of testing. Since the main emphasis behind the use of such tests is to determine cognitive skills, an important aspect of police work, its use has been supported by the courts. Despite the overall support, there still exists concerns over minority pass rates and that tests not be racially biased. Concluding their discussion, Gaines and Schram acknowledge that Title VII of the 1964 Civil Rights Act and all its antecedents have had a profound affect on police selection, particularly with respect to the issue of physical agility and written selection testing.

How old an individual should be to enter into policing, and the age for retirement was the primary focus of Chapter 10. In this chapter, Pascarella looks at policy issues and contextual legal framework relevant to the application and implementation of such policies as maximum hiring ages and mandatory retirement ages in policing.

Pascarella begins by suggesting that while there appears to be a consensus on minimum age requirements in policing, no consensus exists on maximum hiring age and mandatory retiring age. To support his discussion, he brings into play the Age Discrimination in Employment Act (ADEA), which was designed to protect American workers from age discrimination.

Pascarella points out that age has been accepted as a "bona fide occupational qualification." However, he is quick to note that the ADEA currently contains a public safety exemption; that is, such occupations as police officer and firefighter are exempt from its provisions. Despite the provision, he indicates that the courts may have taken another view of age discrimination in policing. To examine this possibility, Pascarella conducted a study in an attempt to provide a predictive model of court interpretation of the ADEA as it applies to police agencies. This study was also conducted to provide guidelines for police administrators and policy officials.

To reach his goal, Pascarella conducted an analysis of eighty court cases related to age issues. The variables he studied included the policy issues involved, provision of the law violated, initiation by civil rights organizations, court of final adjudication, region of the country where the case originated, and year of origination. His results indicated that 69 percent of the decisions upheld the legality of maximum hiring age, mandatory retirement age, and physical fitness testing. He concludes that policing needs to be aware of the ADEA and to be able to demonstrate how age is relevant to the tasks at hand.

LEGAL CHALLENGES FACING THE POLICE IN THE FUTURE

Based on the information in the preceding chapters, it is evident that there is more to policing and the law than just enforcement. Of particular interest is how much control court decisions have on police enforcement of the law. The outcomes of court cases, especially those handed down from the U.S. Supreme Court, play an important role in police activities. As such, it is apparent that policing will need to pay close attention to what the Court may say because even accepted practices can be scrutinized by the courts, and sometimes the police win and sometimes they do not, as illustrated in the following cases.

Probable Cause

A long-standing element of police procedure is probable cause. There are issues, however, that continue to be debated concerning probable cause, including when probable cause exists, whether a warrant is required if there is time to obtain one, and whether police can keep a subject from entering a home unaccompanied. This combination of issues was addressed in *Illinois v. McArthur* (2001).

The facts of the case are that police officers, based on probable cause, believed that McArthur had marijuana hidden in his home. While obtaining a warrant, officers prevented McArthur from entering his home unaccompanied by an officer for about two hours. Upon getting the warrant and entering the home, officers found drug paraphernalia and marijuana and arrested McArthur. At his trial, McArthur moved to suppress the evidence on the grounds that it was the fruit of an unlawful police seizure, namely, the refusal to let him enter his home unaccompanied. The Supreme Court held that, given the nature of the intrusion and the law enforcement interest at stake, the brief seizure of the premises was permissible under the Fourth Amendment.

Anonymous Tip

Today's policing efforts have been assisted significantly by such programs as Crime Stoppers that allow people to anonymously call the police and leave information about a crime. While this information may be legitimate, an anonymous tip, in and of itself, is not enough to affect an arrest, as demonstrated in the case of *Florida v. J. L.* (2000).

In this case, an anonymous caller reported to the police that a young black male standing at a certain bus stop was carrying a gun. The only other description was that he was wearing a plaid shirt. Officers responding to the tip went to the bus stop where they observed three black males, one of whom was wearing a plaid shirt. With the exception of the tip, the officers had no reason to suspect any of the three of illegal conduct. No firearm or any unusual movements were observed by the officers, yet one of them frisked the male wearing the plaid shirt (J. L.), finding a gun in his pocket. J. L. was charged with carrying a concealed firearm. At trial, J. L. moved to suppress the gun as the fruit of an unlawful search, which the court granted. On appeal, the Supreme Court held that an anonymous tip without more to justify a police officer's stop and frisk of someone is a violation of Fourth Amendment protections.

Reasonable Suspicion

Although an arrest must be based on probable cause, an investigatory stop that may lead to an arrest can be based on reasonable suspicion. What represents reasonable suspicion often requires interpretation by the courts. For example, does flight from an approaching police vehicle provide reasonable suspicion to justify a stop by police officers? This was the question in *Illinois v. Wardlow* (2000).

When a caravan of police vehicles as observed converging on an area of Chicago known for heavy narcotics trafficking, Wardlow began to flee the area on foot. Two Chicago police officers caught up with him on the street, and one of them conducted a protective pat-down search for weapons because, based on the officer's experience, there were usually weapons in the vicinity of narcotics transactions. Discovering a handgun, the officers arrested Wardlow.

The Supreme Court held that the officers' actions did not violate the Fourth Amendment because this case, which involved a brief encounter between a citizen and a police officer on a public street, was governed by *Terry,* where an officer who has a reasonable, articulable suspicion that criminal activity is afoot may conduct a brief, investigatory stop. The Court noted that, although reasonable suspicion is a less demanding standard than probable cause, there must be at least a minimal level of objective justification for the stop. An individual's presence in a high-crime area, standing alone, is not enough to support a reasonable, particularized suspicion of criminal activity. However, it did advise that a location's characteristics are relevant in determining whether the circumstances are sufficiently suspicious to warrant further investigation. Since the area did provide circumstances for the officer to have reasonable suspicion of criminal activity, when combined with Wardlow's unprovoked flight, there was enough to arouse the officers' suspicion and justify the stop and frisk.

Conclusion

As demonstrated by the preceding cases, the Court's examination of recognized rights continues. In some instances, the results favor the police, and in others the individual. This practice by the courts will continue as long as we have police officers and there exists the potential for violation of an individual's rights. Further, as shown elsewhere in this text, police officers may also find themselves subjected to the legal system when their rights are violated. In conclusion, there is more to policing and the law than simply trying to enforce it. In fact, policing and the law are more than what merely happens on the street but what takes place in the courtroom as well. The future of policing will continue to require an awareness and understanding of both arenas.

REFERENCES

DANTZKER, M. L. 2000. *Understanding today's police* (2nd ed.). Upper Saddle River, NJ: Prentice Hall.

WYNNE, M. 2001. Use of technology to beat criminals at their own computer games. *Police, 25* (5), 24–27.

Cases Cited

- *Florida v. J. L.* (98–1993) (Decided March 28, 2000).
- *Illinois v. McArthur* (99–1132) (Decided 2/20/2001).
- *Illinois v. Wardlow* (98–1036) (Decided January 12, 2000).

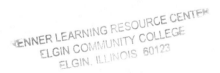